The Politics of Personalised Medi(

Pharmacogenetics, the use of genetic testing to prescribe and develop drugs, has been hailed as a revolutionary development for the pharmaceutical industry and modern medicine. Supporters of 'personalised medicine' claim the result will be safer, cheaper, more effective drugs, and their arguments are beginning to influence policy debates. Based on interviews with clinicians, researchers, regulators and company representatives, this book explores the impact of pharmacogenetics on clinical practice, following two cases of personalised medicine as they make their way from the laboratory to the clinic. It highlights the significant differences between the views of supporters of pharmacogenetics in industry and those who use the technology at the clinical 'coalface'. Theoretically, this work builds on the developing area of the sociology of socio-technical expectations, highlighting the way in which promoters of new technologies build expectations around it, through citation and the creation of technological visions.

ADAM HEDGECOE is Lecturer at the Department of Sociology, University of Sussex.

Cambridge Studies in Society and the Life Sciences

This interdisciplinary series focuses on the social shaping, social meaning and social implications of recent developments in the life sciences, biomedicine and biotechnology. Original research and innovative theoretical work will be placed within a global, multicultural context.

Other books in the series include:

Narrating the New Predictive Genetics: Ethics, Ethnography and Science by Monica Konrad

The Human Genome Diversity Project: An Ethnography of Scientific Practice by Amade M'Charek

The Politics of Personalised Medicine
Pharmacogenetics in the Clinic

ADAM HEDGECOE
University of Sussex

CAMBRIDGE
UNIVERSITY PRESS

PUBLISHED BY THE PRESS SYNDICATE OF THE UNIVERSITY OF CAMBRIDGE
The Pitt Building, Trumpington Street, Cambridge, United Kingdom

CAMBRIDGE UNIVERSITY PRESS
The Edinburgh Building, Cambridge, CB2 2RU, UK
40 West 20th Street, New York, NY 10011–4211, USA
477 Williamstown Road, Port Melbourne, VIC 3207, Australia
Ruiz de Alarcón 13, 28014 Madrid, Spain
Dock House, The Waterfront, Cape Town 8001, South Africa

http://www.cambridge.org

© Adam Hedgecoe 2004

First published 2004

Printed in the United Kingdom at the University Press, Cambridge

Typeface Times 10/13 pt.   *System* LaTeX 2_ε [TB]

A catalog record for this book is available from the British Library

Library of Congress Cataloging in Publication data
Hedgecoe, Adam.
The politics of personalised medicine : pharmacogenetics in the clinic / Adam Hedgecoe
p.   cm. – (Cambridge studies in society and the life sciences)
Includes bibliographical references and index.
ISBN 0 521 84177 1 (hardback) – ISBN 0 521 60265 3 (paperback)
1. Pharmacogenetics – Social aspects.   I. Title.   II. Series.
RM301.3.G45H435   2004
615.5′8 – dc22   2004047383

ISBN 0 521 84177 1 hardback
ISBN 0 521 60265 3 paperback

Contents

Figures

vi

Acknowledgements

I would like to thank the Wellcome Trust for funding this research with a three-year postdoctoral research fellowship, and the staff, past and present, of the Trust's Biomedical Ethics Section, who have helped coordinate research in this area, organise meetings and focus attention on this topic. I especially want to thank my grants officer at the Trust, Caroline David.

Secondly I owe an enormous debt of thanks to all the people I interviewed for this research, without whom, clearly, this book would have been impossible. Very busy people set aside time to talk to me even when they were unsure as to the value of their contribution. I hope this book reassures them.

Thanks to the staff at the Department of Science and Technology Studies at University College London (where I began this project) and at the Department of Sociology, the University of Sussex (where I finished it) for providing supportive and congenial working environments. I would particularly like to thank Jon Turney and Brian Balmer at UCL, and Luke Martell and John Abraham at Sussex.

A number of people have read and commented on parts of this book. Thanks to Mike Parker, Allen Roses, Oonagh Corrigan, Margaret Lock and especially Jon Turney and Richard Ashcroft. Over the past three years I have gained much from talking through my ideas with others working in this area, particularly Paul Martin and Oonagh Corrigan, discussions with whom have forced me to raise my game and think hard about my results. Thanks to Nik Rose for editorial guidance and to Sarah Caro and Alison Powell at Cambridge University Press for guiding this book through the publication process.

Finally, I wish to thank my parents, and Sheridan for her unfailing support, humour and the image on the front cover. And Davis for waiting until after I finished this manuscript to be born.

1

Personalised medicine – a revolution in healthcare

There are few words so widely disseminated and belonging so naturally
to modern political vocabulary as the term 'revolution'.

Reinhart Koselleck (1985:159)

It was a most peculiar newspaper headline. On 8 December 2003 the British
broadsheet newspaper the *Independent* announced: 'Glaxo chief: Our drugs do
not work on most patients' (Connor 2003a). The subsequent report covered a
conference at which Allen Roses, vice-president of genetics at the pharmaceutical giant GlaxoSmithKline, admitted the 'open secret within the drugs industry
that most of its products are ineffective in most patients' (Connor 2003a). Yet
rather than this being a cause of outrage and falling share prices, for Roses
and others like him in the industry such an admission is the first step on the
road to a revolution in the way drugs are developed and, in the long run, how
healthcare is provided. For Allen Roses 'is a pioneer of a new culture within
the drugs business based on using genes to test for who can benefit from a drug'
(Connor 2003a). And it is this use of genetic testing to develop and prescribe
drugs, pharmacogenetics, that will drive the coming revolution. As Roses states,
'Pharmacogenetics has the promise of removing much of the uncertainty' that
surrounds current drug use (Connor 2003a).

Industry's intense interest in pharmacogenetics and genomic technologies
as a whole is relatively recent, dating from around 1997, but it has stimulated
considerable investment on the part of pharmaceutical companies. As a report
from the investment bank Lehman Brothers (co-researched by the management
consultants McKinsey & Co.) notes, 'The excitement over genomics has been
far-reaching. The pharmaceutical industry has poured hundreds of millions of
dollars into genomics technologies, and investors have poured billions into
financing the new industry that has evolved from these technologies' (Lehman
Brothers 2001: 8). Although definite figures are hard to come by, one estimate

suggests that somewhere between 10 and 20 per cent of big pharmaceutical company R&D budgets are now directed towards genomics (Pricewaterhouse Coopers 1998: 9). This puts total annual investment in genomic R&D at between 4 and 8 billion dollars, a figure supported by Lehman Brothers, who suggest that overall investment in 2005 will be 'at about $6 billion' (Lehman Brothers 2001: 81).[1] In terms of individual firms, Roche, one of the industry leaders in pharmacogenetics, claims to be investing about 5 per cent of its total R&D budget in these techniques (Branca 2002). For a company to even join the pack in this new way of developing drugs, 'annual spending on this technology to a certain point (approximately $100 million) appears necessary' (Lehman Brothers 2001: 7). In this context, Allen Roses's admission of the weakness of the modern pharmaceutical industry and its products looks less like an error of judgement and more like a call to arms. The failures and inefficiencies of modern drugs are an opportunity for those companies willing to take the risk, invest in new technology and revolutionise the way in which drugs are developed.

Such excitement on the part of industry has not gone unnoticed. Of course newspapers have covered the development of pharmacogenetics, the move towards personalised medicine; it made the cover of *TIME* magazine, after all (15 January 2001). But academic scientists and medics have also become enamoured. Normally serious researchers can be found spinning futuristic scenarios about the way healthcare will be delivered in the pages of equally serious academic journals. Such vignettes are usually set ten or twenty years into the future, involve the reader going to see a doctor who either samples their DNA there and then or reads their genome off a medical identity card that will have superseded written medical records (see e.g. Phillips *et al.* 2001; Akhtar 2002). Inevitably, politicians and health policy makers have become caught up in this whirl of expectation; the possible benefits of these new technologies are too good to ignore. Responses have varied from the low-key – the US government's funding of a Pharmacogenetics Research Network and Database information resource through the National Institutes of Health – to the high-profile – the British Genetics White Paper of June 2003, which set aside £4 million for research into pharmacogenetics (Department of Health 2003).

Yet however much money is going into research and however excited people in industry and elsewhere become over the promises of personalised medicine, the bright pharmacogenetic future lies tantalisingly out of reach. The aim of this book is to explore the kinds of expectations that have been created around these new technologies, to concepts such as 'pharmacogenetics' and 'personalised medicine', and to show how this technology works its way out in practice.

---

[1] This $6 billion by 2005 figure is supported by a more recent report from the market research firm Frost and Sullivan (GenomeWeb 2001).

Politics

As its title suggests, this book adopts a broadly political approach to the topic of pharmacogenetics. Such a position covers issues such as healthcare rationing, the economic effects of expensive drugs and the relation between pharmaceutical companies, regulators and researchers. But following Bruno Latour's (in)famous rephrasing of von Clausewitz – that science 'is Politics by Other Means' (Latour 1988: 229) – this book also explores the politics of the way in which scientific ideas progress, develop, fail and get rejected. At this level, the participants involved are not political parties, electorates and parliaments, but researchers, clinicians, genes and drugs. At the core of this position is the idea that 'The political need not only be associated with the control of political institutions, the activities of the state or the fermentation of social movements. Instead I take the political to refer to the ways in which artefacts, activities, or practices become objects of contestation' (Barry 2001: 5–6). Theoretically then, this book comes out of broad research traditions within Science and Technology Studies, starting with the constructivist sociologies and histories of science of the late 1970s and early 1980s, moving through approaches variously described as the Social Construction of Technology (SCOT), the Social Shaping of Technology (SST) and Actor Network Theory (ANT).[2]

At this point, it must be confessed that this book does not address the most political (however one defines it) aspect of pharmacogenetics: race and ethnicity. In the growing ethical and social literature in this area, there is acute concern that genetically based differences in reactions to certain drugs might be mapped onto ethnic categories and serve as a basis for the biologising of race. For example, in a recent collection edited by Mark Rothstein, four out of fifteen chapters looking at the social and ethical impact of pharmacogenetics focused on ethnic or group-based differences (Rothstein 2003). Even Craig Venter, the 'arch-privateer' of the Human Genome Project (Rose 2003), 'hope[s] your goal in life isn't just to find genetic variation to identify ethnic groups. That would get us all in trouble pretty quickly' (Venter 2000: 17). This book does not address these issues because they simply did not arise in the two case studies that formed the core of my research. The analysis of pharmacogenetics offered in this book is rooted in the empirical setting of the two drugs I focus on. In neither one were ethnic differences relevant to variations in response to the drugs. There is a book to be written on the racial politics of personalised medicine, but this is not it.

---

[2] For a broad introduction to these approaches, see Bijker, Hughes & Pinch 1987, Bijker and Law 1992, MacKenzie & Wajcman 1999. For a recent review focused on medical technology, see Timmermans & Berg 2003.

Terminology

The word *pharmacogenetics* is derived from 'pharmacology' and 'genetics', and has traditionally been defined as: 'genetically determined variability in drug response' (Wolf, Smith & Smith 2000: 987). For over forty years the term remained uncontroversial, with little dispute over what people meant when they spoke of a pharmacogenetic reaction to a drug. In 1997 a new word appeared in the literature, 'pharmacogenomics', the meaning of which was less clear than in the case of pharmacogenetics, with competing definitions of the term vying for recognition.[3] Recently there has been a move towards a consensus on the differences between the two terms, coming into line behind the idea that pharmacogenetics is about testing individuals for drug response,[4] whereas pharmacogenomics is used more broadly to describe the 'the concept of using whole-genome information to predict drug action' (Roden & George 2001: 37). As Roche's Klaus Lindpaintner puts it, pharmacogenetics is about 'one drug, many genomes' while pharmacogenomics, with a focus on how the same genome may vary its expression in the face of a variety of different products, concerns 'many drugs, one genome' (Lindpaintner 2003: 317–18).

Surrounding discussions of pharmacogenetics and pharmacogenomics are less technical, perhaps more publicly acceptable terms; 'tailor-made treatments', and, of course, personalised medicine (Cockett, Dracopoli & Sigal 2000; Mancinelli, Cronin & Sadée 2000; March 2000; Murphy 2000; Ginsburg & McCarthy 2001; Liggett 2001). Because of disagreement and doubts over the exact meaning of the word *pharmacogenomics*, in this book I tend to talk about pharmacogenetics, with 'personalised medicine' as something of a catch-all, covering a range of approaches currently being developed. Stripped of any obvious terminological link to potentially off-putting words such as 'genetics', personalised medicine might seem a perfect example of pharmaceutical industry marketing speak.[5] Perhaps because it seems less like jargon, or because it does not obviously invoke ethical issues, personalised medicine has been enthusiastically adopted in newspaper coverage of these new technologies.[6]

---

[3] For a fuller analysis of these debates, see Hedgecoe 2003.

[4] 'how to characterize a person with respect to disease susceptibility, severe adverse events . . . or whether the medicine is effective for treatment or prevention of disease' (Roses 2002b: 1472).

[5] The need to make clear in the public mind the difference between pharmacogenetics and traditional, disease genetics is a consistent feature of the debates around this technology. As the first half of this book will show, this distinction is not always that easy to make.

[6] Bonnor 1998; Connor 1999; Kolata 1999; McKie 1999; Pilling 1999a; Pilling 1999b; Pollack 1999a; Connor 2000; Griffith 2000; Pollack 2000; Independent 2000; Weiss 2000; Abate 2001a; Abate 2001b; Bowe & Pilling 2001; Griffith 2001; Highfield 2001; Kendall 2001; Lappin 2001; Moore 2001; O'Connell 2001; Feltham 2002; Highfield 2002; Jenkins 2002; Pollack 2002; Griffith 2003b.

A familiar caveat at this point is to note that personalised medicine in the form of pharmacogenetics is not personalised in the same way a car number plate can be personalised. Misleadingly, some authors make comparisons with

> Health clubs [that] offer personal trainers; TC^2 and Levis offer personalized body scanning and custom-made clothing: Gateway and Dell computers advertise the customization of a personal computer based on the user's needs. This adaptation of this strategy within the healthcare industry would be personal pills.
> *(Anderson, Fitzgerald & Manasco 1999: 266)*[7]

But it is perhaps more accurate to say that personalised medicine is about putting people into treatment groups; certainly these proposed groups will be smaller and more predictable than the current division of patients. But to regard them as personalised, in the sense of being shaped and structured around an individual's specific needs (as opposed to the needs of the group that she or he has been assigned to) is to have an idiosyncratic definition of what the word *personalised* means. If we consider the parallel concept of 'tailor-made medicine', then what is being proposed is more a case of buying a small, medium or large T-shirt from The Gap than being fitted for a Savile Row suit.[8]

Interviews

The empirical 'core' of this book is based on interviews with sixty-six people involved in either Alzheimer's disease, breast cancer or broader issues to do with drug regulation or development.[9] Interviewees' names were gathered from internet searches, a review of scientific articles and snowball sampling. The interviews were carried out between April 2001 and July 2003, and most were taped and transcribed and lasted between 20 and 80 minutes. Specialist interviewees were asked to classify themselves as either clinicians, researchers or clinician researchers, with most clinician researchers (in both case studies) classifying themselves as such due to involvement in clinical trials (rather than laboratory-based research, for example). In writing up this material, I have

---

[7] Such comparisons frequently occur in the literature: 'Customized products, from personal computers to cars, are becoming increasingly popular' (Bracco 2002: 166).
[8] Thanks to Steven Rose for this comparison.
[9] There were twenty-seven Alzheimer's specialists (4 clinicians, 15 clinician researchers and 8 researchers: three were US-based, the rest from the UK), four people from companies involved in developing Alzheimer drugs, and one AD policy person. One researcher, one clinician and one clinician researcher were US-based. For breast cancer there were twenty-five specialists (2 clinicians, 20 clinician researchers, 1 researcher, and 2 oncological pharmacists), two policy-based interviewees, one regulator, one person from a company and two people from breast cancer charities. There were also three regulators.

chosen to use a significant number of excerpts from these interviews, rather than paraphrasing or summarising the general themes that emerged. In practical terms, I hope this approach brings out the interviewees' voices: they say things far better than I could.

The stories that this book explores, stories from the clinical coalface (to use a term that cropped up in a number of my interviews), are not ones that get told in debates around personalised medicine. Strange as it may seem, clinicians who are beginning to use this technology, an apparently powerful group with important things to say about its use and impact, are almost totally excluded from discussions in this area. The ethical debates around pharmacogenetics have tended to focus on the issues raised by pharmacogenetic research: informed consent; the encryption of DNA and medical records; who has access to this data; do the results of such research get fed back to participants?[10] These are all vital topics that need to be explored if we are to regulate the development of pharmacogenetic products appropriately, but it is not enough to assume that a focus on pharmacogenetic research means that such technologies are not being used at the moment, or that the impact they might have on clinical practice is not at least as great as that on drug development. Two recent comprehensive reports, one by the US-based Consortium on Pharmacogenetics (Buchanan *et al.* 2002) and the other by the British Nuffield Council on Bioethics (Nuffield Council on Bioethics 2003), have gone a long way towards redressing the balance in terms of questioning the ethical issues surrounding the clinical use of pharmacogenetics. Yet even in these reports there are necessarily gaps in terms of the 'complexity of the empirical'. Coming from STS, it is natural to see the ethical issues raised by pharmacogenetics as socially constructed, in the same way that technical, scientific issues are. This is an obvious point, but not one that is necessarily highlighted in philosophically rooted bioethics literature. Thus just as my political approach sees scientific debates as inherently sociotechnical, so are ethical discussions socioethical. This book provides the means to make messy current consideration of the ethics of personalised medicine.

Themes and structure

As chapter 2 makes clear, pharmacogenetics is a heterogeneous technology. For some people it is about avoiding adverse drug reactions, for others it is about discovering the genetic basis to common diseases. Based on the experiences,

[10] For a review of the literature, see Møldrup 2001. For examples: Chadwick 1999; Issa 2000; Clarke, English, Harris & Wells 2001; March, Cheeseman and Doherty 2001; Thomas 2001; Robertson 2001; Rothstein & Griffin Epps 2001; Issa 2002; Vaszar, Rosen & Raffin 2002; Lipton 2003; Vaszar, Cho & Raffin 2003.

attitudes and beliefs of the clinicians and researchers interviewed, several themes arise and run through this book, which can best be presented as contrasting ideas, or dichotomies. The first is between the way those at the clinical coalface view particular examples of pharmacogenetics, and the kinds of expectations created around these examples in the broader pharmacogenetic literature. At its most crude, those industry scientists and academic geneticists and pharmacologists who cite the two case studies I use in this book, Alzheimer's disease and breast cancer, have a greatly simplified, almost unrecognisable, view of these examples, when compared to the technically complex, ethically messy, position taken by those who actually use the technology.

The second comparison I wish to highlight is between the view of pharmacogenetics as an ordinary, as opposed to a revolutionary, technology. The standard view of pharmacogenetics is that it will revolutionise the contexts within which it is applied. While this may well be the case for drug development, it seems to me that the clinical context is far more resistant to revolution than many commentators assume. When a pharmacogenetic drug arrives in the clinical setting, as in the case of Herceptin and the breast cancer clinic for example, then the drug and its test become incorporated into clinical practice, compared with other treatments and tied into networks of funding, testing and professional practice. The pharmacogenetic treatment becomes 'ordinary'. Rather than pharmacogenetics arriving and revolutionising the clinic, new treatments arrive and are redefined in terms of ordinary clinical practice.

The final dichotomy is between knowledge and resistance. A regular feature of discussions around the movement of new genetic technologies into the clinic is the need for clinician education. Educating clinicians, giving them knowledge about new technologies this argument goes, will increase acceptance of the new technology and lead to faster, wider uptake. Based on the research in this book, it seems quite clear that lack of knowledge is *not* the main cause of clinical resistance to pharmacogenetics. The reasons why clinicians are reluctant to adopt such apparently beneficial technologies vary from technical uncertainty through financial limitations to the usefulness of interventions and the morally risky nature of some pharmacogenetic tests. We need a more socially nuanced understanding of how technologies move into clinical practice.

This book is structured as follows. Chapter 2 gives details about the history and context of pharmacogenetics and personalised medicine, and sketches out the theoretical framework for my research; the sociology of expectation. Next, two case studies in pharmacogenetics are presented. Chapters 3, 4 and 5 discuss the relationship between Alzheimer's disease, a gene called APOE4 and the anti-Alzheimer's drug Tacrine. The story follows APOE4 from the discovery in the early 1990s that it is associated with increased risk for developing Alzheimer's and the professional debates that surrounded its use in the clinic (chapter 3), through its link to the reduced effectiveness of Tacrine and clinicians' attitudes towards this putative pharmacogenetic association (chapter 4), to the role of APOE testing in research and the attitude of industry towards APOE4 and the possibility that it may play some pharmacogenetic role in prescribing drugs (chapter 5). The second case study – chapters 6, 7 and 8 – concerns the breast cancer drug Herceptin, which is used to treat tumours with too much of a certain gene, called HER2. I follow the drug as the pharmaceutical company Roche tried to overcome clinical resistance and persuade UK clinicians to adopt both Herceptin and the HER2 test that accompanies it (chapter 6), through to more formal hurdles, as Herceptin was assessed by the UK's National Institute for Clinical Excellence in an attempt to make it eligible for NHS funding (chapter 7), until finally, we see how a pharmacogenetic drug works in the clinic, how it impacts on the doctor–patient relationship, and how, in this context, it needs to be seen as an ordinary technology (chapter 8). Chapter 9 ties these various themes together and shows how this research can be of use to regulators, policy-makers and the wider public in debating pharmacogenetics.

2

Pharmacogenetics, expectation and promissory science

In an age when people in developed societies expect individual treatment in all spheres of life, the provision of drugs often appears clumsy.

Andrew Marshall (1998)

A brief history of pharmacogenetics

The aim of this chapter is to briefly set out the debates about personalised medicine in the professional literature, outline theoretical ideas that might help us get to grips with these arguments, and introduce the two case studies used in this book. As a sociologist of science, one of the interesting things about coming to personalised medicine is the sheer range of people who are willing to write about it and tell you how they think it will develop. The profusion of reviews, editorials and opinion pieces in scientific and medical journals (what we might collectively call 'commentaries') that speculate about how medical practice and drug development might look in a few years' time provides a wonderful resource for sociological analysis. What follows is an attempt to unpack some of the claims being made about pharmacogenetics by academic scientists, company representatives and other commentators. Although it is not a comprehensive, quantitative review such as those found in the scientific literature, it does provide a detailed outline of the kinds of concerns that form the context within which pharmacogenetics will move into clinical practice.

Depending on one's source, pharmacogenetics was either founded by Pythagoras, with his observation of adverse reactions to fava beans in 510 BC (Nebert 1997; Ensom, Chang Patel 2001; Rusnak *et al.* 2001) or Freud, with his discovery in 1885 that different people have different pharmacological reactions to cocaine (Pfost, Boyce-Jacino & Grant 2000). The term *pharmacogenetics* itself was coined by Friedrich Vogel in 1959, following groundbreaking work

9

by Arno Motulsky two years earlier (see Weber 2001 for a detailed historical review).

At the core of pharmacogenetics is the idea that humans differ one from another in their reactions to drugs. Individuals may differ in the way in which they metabolise drugs, the way in which the drugs actually operate within their bodies, and the rates and extent to which products are removed. The results of these variations mean that some people metabolise a standard dose of a drug so fast that they do not gain any therapeutic benefit from it; others who are slow metabolisers run the risk of adverse drug reactions (ADRs) and have to be prescribed much lower doses of particular drugs.

Although in the early years of the discipline, important discoveries were made, such as Glucose-6-phosphate dehydrogenase (G6PD) deficiency in 1956 and the genetic variation in ethanol metabolism in 1964 (Kalow 1990), pharmacogenetics expanded slowly, with specific drug–gene relationships becoming clear as and when investigators came across them, rather than there being any active search for such links.

The emergence of molecular biology provided the means for improved investigation of the genetics of drug response, with the 'molecular turn' in pharmacogenetics dating from 1988, when Frank Gonzalez and his colleagues isolated several alleles of the human CYP2D6 gene, part of the P450 cytochrome complex of genes responsible for drug metabolism in the liver (Gonzalez *et al.* 1988). This study opened up the field to the 'new genetics'. The 1990s brought the Human Genome Project, and new technologies gave scientists a greater understanding of genetic variation and gave rise to an increased interest in pharmacogenetic studies.

Industry

Any discussion of the rise of personalised medicine has to set industry ('big pharma' as well as small biotech firms) at the centre of the story. Industry involvement dwarfs any investment from governments or charitable institutions. Company concerns shape the timing of our increased interest in this technology, the scientific debates that are taking place over the shape pharmacogenetics will take in the future and even the ethical discussions going on around personalised medicine (Hedgecoe & Martin 2003).

Traditionally, pharmaceutical companies have adopted a 'one size fits all' principle with regard to different people's reactions to drugs (Mancinelli, Cronin & Sadée 2000; Liggett 2001). Although acknowledging variations in dosage (because of age, sex and body size), the general approach has been the development of mass-market therapies based on the assumption that everyone responds in the same way. Despite pharmacogenetics' long history, at an industry level there has been a profound reluctance to admit the extent of genetic variation and its effect on drug response (Glaser 1998; Corrigan 2002). This may be due to the fact that until recently very little could be done, but another reason is the understandable unwillingness of industry to admit to the huge scale and very real risks posed by genetically based ADRs (Abraham 1995).

Yet as chapter 1 suggests, in a very short space of time commercial concerns have become fascinated by the potential of these new technologies, investing billions of dollars in largely unproven technologies. If we want to answer the questions 'Why pharmacogenomics? Why now?', we need to look at a number of factors (Housman & Ledley 1998). In historical terms, commentators identify pharmacogenetics as the most obvious application of the technologies and information generated by the Human Genome Project (Evans & Relling 1999; Mancinelli, Cronin & Sadée 2000; Persing & Cheek 2000; Chamberlain & Joubert 2001; Liggett 2001; Phillips *et al.* 2001; Shi, Bleavins & Iglesia 2001; Weber 2001; Roses 2002b; Weinshilboum 2003). Building on the success of the marriage, albeit shot-gun, of the public and private approaches to human genome sequencing, 1999 saw 'a remarkable collaboration' (March 2000: 16) between eleven companies and the medical charity the Wellcome Trust.[1] The result, the SNP Consortium, set out to locate the thousands of single nucleotide polymorphisms (SNPs – pronounced 'snips') in the human genome. SNPs are changes in single base pairs, the smallest unit of genetic information, that tend to differ between people. On average, there is an SNP every 1,000 bases, so in the human genome, with 3 billion bases, there are around 3 million SNPs, which act as excellent signposts for disease susceptibility and drug reaction. For authors interested in promoting personalised medicine, SNPs are one of the vital means by which to link groups of people to differences in drug reaction.[2] The formation of the SNP Consortium and its successful completion in autumn 2001 helped kick-start industry interest in pharmacogenetics (Lau & Sakul 2000; Mancinelli, Cronin & Sadée 2000; Pfost, Boyce-Jacino & Grant 2000; Ginsburg & McCarthy 2001; Jazwinska 2001; Akhtar 2002).

---

[1] The companies are: Amersham Biosciences, AstraZeneca PLC, Aventis, Bayer AG, Bristol-Meyers Squibb Company, F. Hoffmann-LaRoche, GlaxoSmithKline, IBM, Motorola, Novartis, Pfizer Inc, Searle. The work was carried out at four major academic centres: Stanford Human Genome Center, Washington University School of Medicine (St Louis), the Sanger Centre and the Whitehead Institute for Biomedical Research.

[2] Anderson, Fitzgerald & Manasco 1999; Moyses 1999; Cockett, Dracopoli & Sigal 2000; Kurth 2000; Meyer 2000; Roses 2000b; Liggett 2001; Roden & George 2002; Norton 2001; Schmitz, Aslanidis & Lackner 2001; Wieczorek & Tsongalis 2001; Hoban 2002; Chamberlain & Joubert 2001; Roses 2002a,b.

Next on the list of technological advances that many commentators think will push pharmacogenetics into the clinic are DNA arrays or 'gene chips' (Evans & Relling 1999; Wolf, Smith & Smith 2000; Chamberlain & Joubert 2001; Tsai & Hoyme 2002). These small, hand-held devices are being developed to allow the cheap, fast and large-scale screening of populations for genetic markers, which are correlated to either positive or negative reactions to specific drugs. Although still in their infancy, one such DNA array targeting the pharmacogenetically important cytochrome P450 complex is already commercially available (Sadée 1999) and in June 2003 Roche launched its own CYP450 chip-based mico-array, which 'enables understanding of how variations in certain human genes affect metabolism of a wide variety of commercially available drugs' (Roche 2003).

But beyond obvious technological explanations for the increased interest in possibilities offered by pharmacogenetics and pharmacogenomics, there are also external factors, both structural and psychological, behind the industry rush towards personalised medicine. Anthony Regalado suggests a psychological explanation, that the high cost of drug development means that industry executives are keen to adopt any technology that will reduce their R&D expenditure. If other companies are already using that technology (emphasised by a high-profile alliance, for example), then the pressure becomes even greater. The result is a 'follow-the-leader' effect, where large pharmaceutical companies, fuelled by the smaller genomics firms, which have high overheads and research costs and thus a pressing need to sell some sort of product, are forced to jump on the pharmacogenetic 'bandwagon' for fear of being left behind (Regalado 1999: 42–3). They also gain latecomer advantage, keeping their costs down by learning from the leader's mistakes (Freeman & Soefe 1997). Companies may be forced to join the bandwagon, even if they do not want to: 'Merck & Co., for example . . . is busy developing capabilities to reproduce pharmacogenetic analyses conducted by its competitors, if only to disprove any claims that a rival drug might be superior to its own' (Tollman *et al.* 2001: 36).

Much of the apparent drive towards personalised medicine comes from the need for reduced drug expenditure in the US healthcare system, driven by recent changes in the way healthcare is provided (Anderson, Fitzgerald & Manasco 1999; Murphy 2000; Tsai & Hoyme 2002). This centres on the growth of managed care organisations (MCOs) in the US healthcare sector, organisations that not only fund but also provide healthcare (i.e. hospitals and medical practices) (Brown 1998; Housman & Ledley 1998). Their defining feature is the drive to reduce healthcare costs and increase efficiency and thus they are usually seen in opposition to the pharmaceutical industry (Murray & Deardorff 1998). The tension between healthcare providers and drugs manufacturers produces an environment where a technology that promises to reduce drugs expenditure (through targeted prescription and the reduction of ADRs) while also reducing drug development costs will be looked on favourably.

If healthcare providers could look to pharmacogenetics to reduce their drug budgets, then pharmaceutical companies suggest that new technologies may provide a vital tool to reduce the costs of drug development (Hoban 2002). It is a truism among industry executives and commentators that the development of modern pharmaceuticals is an astronomically expensive business. The kinds of numbers offered up are that bringing a new drug to market costs somewhere in the region of $500 million (Housman & Ledley 1998; Lau & Sakul 2000; Mancinelli, Cronin & Sadée 2000; Jazwinska 2001; Norton 2001). Although the expense of drug development is taken as an accepted fact in debates around the need for pharmacogenetics, the actual numbers presented by industry are the subject of considerable dispute. The $500 million figure is usually taken to be derived from a 1991 study by the economist Joseph DiMasi, who also updated these figures to around $800 million in 2003 (DiMasi, Hansen, Grabowski & Lasagna, 1991; DiMasi, Hansen & Grabowski 2003). However, based on a study carried out by the US Congress Office of Technology Assessment, critics have pointed out that the $500 million figure 'includes significant expenses that are tax deductible' and that using DiMasi's own figures, the after-tax cash outlay on drug R&D (including failures) drops to $110 million (Young & Surrusco 2001: i; see also Relman & Angell 2002). Using the pharmaceutical industry's own R&D data and FDA approval rates, these authors recalculate the cost of bringing a new drug to market to be between $71 and $150 million.

Whatever the true cost of drug development, and DiMasi's critics do not go unchallenged (Frank 2003), little of this debate makes it into the literature surrounding personalised medicine. For supporters of pharmacogenetics, it is a given that drug development is expensive, financially risky and in need of a technological boost. Yet even if we are sceptical about these claims, what does seem less debatable is that however much it costs industry to produce a new drug, there are fewer and fewer new products making it onto the market. In a review of products licensed by the FDA and EMEA (the US and the EU licensing authorities) in 2002, Frantz and Smith note that with eighteen and thirteen new molecular entities approved by the regulators respectively, 'the number of new products reaching the market is still declining'. A longer view of approval trends 'clearly shows how the absence of new products emerging from the pipeline . . . is creating a feeling of unrest among industry management and analysts' (Franz & Smith 2003: 95–6; see also Reichert 2003). Since current drugs only work on about 500 possible sites in the body ('targets'), and recent developments in human genetics are meant to have opened up 3,000–10,000 other possible sites (Cockett, Dracopoli & Sigal 2000; Ginsburg & McCarthy 2001; Norton 2001), the possible benefits of pharmacogenetics for industry's parlous drug pipeline are clear to see. A number of different reviews suggest ways in which pharmacogenetic and pharmacogenomic technologies could be incorporated into the drug development process, with these approaches playing different roles at different stages of the clinical trial (Bailey, Bondar & Furness 1998; Cockett, Dracopoli & Sigal 2000; Murphy 2000; Ginsburg & McCarthy 2001; Chamberlain & Joubert 2001; Hoban 2002; Ferentz 2002).

The third group destined to benefit from personalised medicine, according to supporters of the technology, are members of the public. As already noted, traditionally, industry has been coy about acknowledging the extent of adverse reactions to pharmaceutical products, but pharmacogenetics presents a potential way of accepting that there is a need for improvement (without actually accepting responsibility) at the same time as making personalised medicine relevant to the broader public. The usual way of indicating such concerns in a review article or editorial is to cite one study in particular, Lazarou, Pomeranz and Corey's 1998 metareview of adverse drug reactions in hospitalised patients. What these authors found is the now mantra-like figure, that in 1994, 106,000 deaths were caused by ADRs, making drug reactions between the fourth and the sixth leading cause of death in the US (Lazarou, Pomeranz & Corey 1998: 1202). While academic scientists and medics mentioning that pharmaceutical products are so dangerous is not that surprising (Lau & Sakul 2000; Meyer 2000; Wolf, Smith & Smith 2000; Phillips *et al.* 2001; Roden & George 2002; Schmitz, Aslanidis & Lackner 2001; Akhtar 2002; Tsai & Hoyme 2002; Steimer & Potter 2002), it is interesting that industry-based supporters of pharmacogenetics seem quite willing to cite this study (e.g. Anderson, Fitzgerald & Manasco 1999; Mancinelli, Cronin & Sadée 2000; Murphy 2000; Pfost, Boyce-Jacino and Grant 2000; Ginsburg & McCarthy 2001; Spear, Heath-Chiozzi & Huff 2001). And although there has been some dispute over these figures, more recent work seems to support the seriousness of ADRs (Pirmohamed and Park 2001, 2003).

Industry's willingness to accept the scale of ADRs can be explained if we consider the interpretation of this study made by supporters of pharmacogenetics. When the risks of ADRs are stated, commentators implicitly accept that the solution for this serious public heath problem lies in the development of personalised medicine, that the underlying cause for these ADRs is necessarily genetic. Yet it is not at all clear that this is the case: certainly it is not clear that this study revealed a significant *genetic* basis for common ADRs. While the Lazarou study screened out ADRs resulting from medication errors, many factors impact on drug metabolism (e.g. age, gender and diet): to assume that pharmacogenetics is the solution to this problem (as outlined in this study at

least) is to tell only part of the story. Even a recent attempt to assess the contribution of genetic factors to ADRs notes: 'It is currently difficult to estimate
the attributable impact of genetic variability on ADRs' (Phillips *et al.* 2001:
2276). Few of the reviews, editorials and opinion pieces written to promote
personalised medicine are prepared to disentangle ADRs from an automatic
genetic cause, with Ruth March of AstraZeneca, who accepts that 'only a small
number of these [ADRs] will be from genetic cases', being a rare exception
(March 2000: 17).

Constructing a pharmacogenomic future

Thus there seem to be a number of features characteristic of the debates surrounding personalised medicine in need of explanation. Why, when so much
money is being invested in this technology, is there no widely agreed definition
of pharmacogenomics? Why is a term like personalised medicine used when it
is not clear that these approaches will lead to significant personalisation? Why
are so many industry-based authors so willing to cite studies implicating their
products in the death and harm of thousands of people a year?

The simplest explanation for the discourse surrounding pharmacogenetics
would be to dismiss it as a typical example of 'hype', the kind of exaggerated
claims that critics and supporters of these technologies often worry about. The
concern is that hype, which is 'purely emotional and promotional, makes sweeping claims, and lacks evidence', misrepresents the potential value and timeframe of new technologies (Guice 1999: 85). In scientific debates, hype is often
contrasted with 'hope' (e.g. Pang & Weatherall 2002; Shapiro 2003; Brown
2003), or with some alternative underlying reality (e.g. Diederich 2002), yet a
growing body of literature in science and technology studies questions whether
these distinctions are at all helpful. From this perspective – often referred to as
the sociology of technological expectations – rather than dismissing speculative statements, we need to see them as performing an important function in the
development of new technologies.

First, there is the practical problem of separating hype from legitimate claims
about technological development. As Guice points out, drawing a sharp distinction between hype and genuine scientific promotion is fruitless. Scientific
promotion always carries some appeal to emotion, and hype, although low on
content, does serve to relate developments in a particular field to a social context
(Guice 1999: 85). Beyond this practical issue is a concern with the performative
function speculative statements about new technologies fulfil; put simply, what
does 'hype' do? If we re-envisage hype as a form of rhetoric, then we can see the

kinds of optimistic statements made by supporters of pharmacogenetics – the kinds of statements that make these new technologies relevant to many different interest groups, that solve several different problems at once – as a normal part of bringing a new technology into being. Those involved in developing new technologies need to persuade people to use their products; they need to persuade regulators to approve their products; they need to persuade competitors not to challenge their products; and they preferably need to do all these things before the product is even available.

Thus hype, or more helpfully, speculative statements about particular technological developments, 'create . . . a "space" in which promises can be floated: generally to whoever is willing to listen, and specifically directed towards sponsors of R&D who have an interest in promising areas of science' (Van Lente & Rip 1998: 222). There is, so far, no agreed definition of *pharmacogenomics* because the word is redefined each time a particular author wants to persuade their readers that the technology is developing in a particular direction (Hedgecoe 2003). *Personalised medicine* is used because, as already noted, it obscures the connection to possibly worrisome issues raised by the word *genetics*, and serves as a jargon-free way of enlisting the interest of those without a scientific or medical background. And industry-based authors are willing to suggest that ADRs are a significant public health risk because this enrols the general public into supporting pharmacogenetics; it makes these new technological developments relevant to the average patient. The success of this approach in enrolling support for pharmacogenetics can clearly be seen if one looks at the response to Allen Roses of GlaxoSmithKline and his statement about the poor efficacy of most drugs, introduced at the beginning of chapter 1. While the newspaper report and further discussion in the paper were critical of industry's previous unwillingness to be quite so open about its products' limitations, these stories report pharmacogenetics in very favourable terms, with a leader column concluding that while 'Drugs multinationals are not usually acclaimed for their public-spiritedness . . . for his directness and honesty about the promise of pharmacogenomics, Dr Roses deserves our praise' (Independent 2003). By confessing to the weakness of current drugs development, and providing a solution, Roses has successfully enrolled at least one supporter into his expectation about how pharmacogenetics will develop.

The need for those developing technologies to pre-emptively shape the social and economic context for their products clearly fits neatly with John Law's view of technologists as 'heterogeneous engineers', people who have to manage and shape not just physical objects, but other people, ideas and social systems (Law 1987). But rather than generating support for something already developed, the sociology of technological expectation focuses on the building of alliances behind something that does not yet exist, except, perhaps, as a concept, like 'personalised medicine'. In his study of the gene therapy industry, Paul Martin notes how firms try to construct markets for products while they are still designing technologies, shaping both the use and the development of their product prior to its appearance (Martin 1995). Michael Fortun has explored the role of 'forward-looking statements' in biotechnology firms' financial documents (Fortun 2001). In these terms, we can see pharmacogenetics (in the clinic at least) as a 'promissory science', a discipline that exists more in the speculations and promises of its supporters than in terms of scientific results and marketable products.

Before exploring some of the ways in which commentators create and shape our expectations about pharmacogenetics, it must be made clear that by claiming that scientists, technologists, companies and supporters are using rhetoric to speculate about a promissory science, I am not claiming that they are doing anything particularly unusual. The growing literature in this area confirms just how normal the creation of such expectations are in the development of new technologies (see Brown, Rappert & Webster 2000 for a recent collection). Nor am I suggesting that these people are being dishonest, disingenuous or otherwise misleading the public. It is precisely to get away from the unhelpful name-calling implied by the term *hype* that I have chosen to adopt ideas from the sociology of expectation. Rather than petulantly dismissing what supporters of a technology say to promote it as not corresponding to some external reality, it is far more interesting to look at how such statements help construct the future context for said technology and our ideas about it. As at least one scientific commentator suggests, current debates around the use of these genomic technologies in drug development are characterised by 'Expectation, promise, innovation, optimism' (Hoban 2002: 429). It is not unreasonable to expect sociologists to explore the context and use of such interesting words.

How to create expectations

One of the most important ways in which expectations about personalised medicine are being constructed is through the deployment of technological *visions*. These are internally consistent discursive constructions that 'act as both a means of enrolling support and resources into the emerging socio-technical network and as a guide to the physical design of artefacts' (Martin 1999: 520). We could follow John Guice and phrase such techniques in terms of self-fulfilling prophecies: 'by supposing something to exist, one makes it exist in collective imagination . . . one lends support to a particular view of the issue and defines it as an issue in the first place' (Guice 1999: 84). While there are a number of different ways of classifying the visions present in debates around pharmacogenetics, the most obvious contrast is between those who see personalised medicine as focused on the avoidance of ADRs, and those who see it as providing a deeper understanding of the genetic basis for common disease. Such visions are more than just statements in the scientific literature. They are shaping both academic and industrial research and can be seen in the business plans of most biotechnology firms and big pharmaceutical companies interested in this area (Hedgecoe & Martin 2003).

Another tool for the construction of expectations is the use of a particular genre of science writing, the review article. Greg Myers has written extensively about the role of review articles in the construction of scientific disciplines, where a review 'shapes the literature of a field into a story in order to enlist the support of readers to continue that story' (Myers 1991: 45). It is the construction of knowledge in reviews that allows certain experimental reports to be seen as 'key' articles and even the idea of a specific event as the 'discovery' of a particular fact depends upon review articles to organise the claims and techniques in a particular direction (Myers 1990b; Sinding 1996). In the case of personalised medicine, review articles and other commentaries also allow authors to construct *the future*. This is why between 1997 and 2000 more review articles using the term *pharmacogenomics* were published than papers presenting original research (Hedgecoe 2003). If one is constructing a promissory science, a review article allows an author to pull together a range of different areas and to construct an argument, not just about how things were (whether a particular event was a discovery) and how they are (what counts as the boundaries of a particular discipline), but also how they will be (the nature of the clinical encounter in ten years' time). Scientific reviews, editorials and opinions pieces give supporters of personalised medicine a discursive space within which to speculate about particular technologies and to create expectations about how pharmacogenetics may impact on healthcare provision and practice in the future; about the shape of personalised medicine.

Clearly the most obvious way to construct expectations about pharmacogenetics is to prove it works by citing successful examples of this technology in action. And it is this method of enrolling supporters for personalised medicine that provides the two case studies that are the focus for the rest of this book. Reading through the various review articles on pharmacogenetics and pharmacogenomics published over the past few years, the same examples crop up again and again. At the head of the queue are the cytochrome P450s, a family of enzymes intimately involved in drug metabolism in the liver (often the enzyme/gene called CYP2D6).[3] There are examples from chemotherapy, usually mutations in the thiopurine methyltranserase (TPMT) gene that are associated with effects on tolerance and dose intensity of 6-mercaptopurine (6-MP), which is used in the treatment of childhood acute lymphoblastic leukaemia.[4] Sometimes there is the example of asthma and the ALOX5 gene (Lau & Sakul 2000; March 2000; Jazwinska 2001; Lindpaintner *et al.* 2001; Schmitz, Aslanidis & Lackner 2001; Spear, Heath-Chiozzi & Huff 2001; Johnson & Evans 2002; Evans & McLeod 2003), or the anti-schizophrenia drug Clozapine (Sadée 1999; March 2000; Vesell 2000; Johnson & Evans 2002; Evans & McLeod 2003), or different alleles of the CETP gene and varying response to Prevastatin.[5] In the more recent reviews, GlaxoSmithKline's anti-HIV/AIDS drug Abacavir often makes an appearance (Lindpaintner 2002; Roses 2002c). All these examples so consistently cited by supporters of pharmacogenetics are of common or expensive diseases, or of genes that interact with a large number of drugs, making them relevant to a wide range of doctors, healthcare funders, patients and companies. And two of the examples so regularly cited stand out, the one for the breadth of its citation, the other for its regular and widespread use in the clinic.

Case Studies in pharmacogenetics and the clinic

Alzheimer's disease

In 1995 a paper in the prestigious *Proceedings of the National Academies of Sciences* claimed that there was a link between carriers of a particular version of a gene (or allele) and reduced response to the anti-Alzheimer's drug Tacrine.

---

[3] Bailey, Bondar & Furness 1998; Anderson, Fitzgerald & Manasco 1999; Evans & Relling 1999; Moyses 1999; Sadée 1999; Kurth 2000; Lau & Sakul 2000; Maitland-van der Zee, de Boer & Leufkens 2000; Mancinelli, Cronin & Sadée 2000; March 2000; Meyer 2000; Murphy 2000; Persing & Cheek 2000; Rioux 2000; Vesell 2000; Wolf, Smith & Smith 2000; Chamberlain & Joubert 2001; Norton 2001; Shi, Bleavins & Iglesia 2001; Roden & George 2002; Schmitz, Aslanidis & Lackner 2001; Shi, Bleavins & Iglesia 2001; Spear, Heath-Chiozzi & Huff 2001; Weber 2001; Akhtar 2002; Ferentz 2002; Johnson & Evans 2002; Steimer & Potter 2002; Tsai & Hoyme 2002; Evans & McLeod 2003; Weinshilboum 2003.

[4] Bailey, Bondar & Furness 1998; Lau & Sakul 2000; March 2000; Meyer 2000; Rioux 2000; Wolf, Smith & Smith 2000; Ensom, Chang & Patel 2001; Roden & George 2002; Schmitz, Aslanidis & Lackner 2001; Spear, Heath-Chiozzi & Huff 2001; Weber 2001; Johnson & Evans 2002; Steimer & Potter 2002; Tsai & Hoyme 2002; Mancinelli, Cronin & Sadée 2000; Chamberlain & Joubert 2001; Evans & McLeod 2003; Weinshilboum 2003.

[5] Kleyn & Vesell 1998; Lindpaintner 1999; Moyses 1999; Maitland-van der Zee, de Boer & Leufkens 2000; March 2000; Rioux 2000; Roses 2000 a&b; Vesell 2000; Norton 2001; Schmitz, Aslanidis & Lackner 2001; Roden & George 2002; Shi, Bleavins & Iglesia 2001; Johnson & Evans 2002; Tsai & Hoyme 2002; Evans & McLeod 2003.

In this paper, from a team led by the Montreal-based researcher Judes Poirier, only 40 per cent of Alzheimer's patients carrying the APOE4 allele responded to the drug, as opposed to 80 per cent of those carrying the other versions of the gene, APOE2 or 3. In the intervening years, this paper has become the subject of considerable interest on the part of commentators discussing the possibilities offered by pharmacogenetics and pharmacogenomics. Picked up in Andrew Marshall's 1997 review for *Nature Biotechnology*, the APOE4–Tacrine link is described as 'the best current illustration of the power of pharmacogenomics' (Marshall 1997: 1249). Marshall discusses the Poirier result and similar work done on the drug S12024, pointing out that 'Pharmacogenomics is widely used in developing treatments for Alzheimer's disease' (p. 1250).

Since then the Poirier group's E4–Tacrine result has become 'one of the most widely cited pharmacogenomic studies' (Evans & Johnson 2001: 27).[6] For scientific commentators speculating about the possible role pharmacogenetics might play in future healthcare provision, it is an almost obligatory reference. It may be cited in a table with other examples of pharmacogenetics,[7] or as just a perfunctory citation with no real analysis (Latour 1987).[8] On other occasions there is comparison with other pharmacogenetic results in Alzheimer's disease (Lau & Sakul 2000:263) or a more in-depth discussion of how the Tacrine–APOE4 result fits into the genetics and treatment options of Alzheimer's disease as a whole.[9] Some reviews suggest that such genotyping is regularly used in the clinic (March 2000). This example has even moved into the world of policy documents (Barton 2000) and financial reports (Thomas & De Ribains 1998; Bogdanovic & Langlands 1999).

As chapters 4 and 5 will show, the attitude of Alzheimer's professionals towards this result is very different, with extreme scepticism tending to dominate their discussion of the link between APOE alleles and response to Tacrine and other drugs. But the authors of these commentaries do not come from an Alzheimer's specialist background. The majority of the authors of these reviews are either academic pharmacologists/pharmacists or work for industry (both big pharmaceutical companies and small biotechs). There are certainly no Alzheimer's specialists among these commentators. The one review written

[6] The ISI science citation index shows that the 1995 Poirier article has been cited over 265 times, over a hundred since the beginning of the year 2000. For a discussion of the role of such citation data, see Hedgecoe 2003.
[7] Kleyn & Vesell 1998; Chamberlain & Joubert 2001; Rusnak *et al.* 2001; Roden & George 2001; Akhtar 2002.
[8] Anderson, Fitzgerald & Manasco 1999; Evans & Relling 1999; Lindpaintner 1999; Kurth 2000; Persing & Cheek 2000; Vesell 2000; Ensom, Chang & Patel 2001; Norton 2001; Ingelman-Sundberg 2001; Steimer & Potter 2002.
[9] Emilien *et al.* 2000; Maitland, de Boer & Leufkens 2000; McLeod & Evans 2001.

by neurologists is lead-authored by a multiple sclerosis specialist (Maimone, Dominici & Grimaldi 2001).

The pharmacologists among these review authors are building expectation about how their discipline will become increasingly relevant over the coming decades. As pharmacogenetics moves into the clinic, it seems likely that pharmacologists and pharmacists will become more and more involved in advising clinicians on the appropriate use of drugs in the clinical setting. As one author puts it: 'The future impact of pharmacogenomics is likely to be in improved point-of-care health services . . . and in improvements in new drug development. Pharmacists and pharmaceutical scientists will likely be involved in both instances' (Akhtar 2002: 299). The same article describes pharmacists as 'key players in the dispensing of drugs based on an individual's gene profile' (p. 296). It seems quite reasonable that pharmacists and other academic pharmacological scientists would be involved in constructing expectations about the importance of their own role in the implementation of clinical pharmacogenomics.

Similarly, it should come as no surprise that industry-based authors are well represented in the reviews citing the APOE4–Tacrine result. These authors come from large firms such as the then Glaxo Wellcome (Anderson, Fitzgerald & Manasco 1999) or Roche (Chamberlain & Joubert 2001; Lindpaintner 1999), or from small genomics-based biotech firms such as Millennium Predictive Medicine (Kleyn & Vesell 1998), Phenogenex (Kurth 2000) or Genaissance (Oestreicher 2001). These companies' futures depend, to a significant extent, on the future of drug discovery lying in pharmacogenomics. Both Glaxo-Wellcome and Roche have spent the past few years restructuring themselves to take advantage of new genomic technologies (FT 1997; FT 2001). The importance of the success of pharmacogenomics to small genomic biotech firms hardly needs spelling out. In terms of the theoretical approach adopted in this chapter, the Tacrine–APOE4 link proposed by the Poirier group is an important resource for those commentators trying to shape the final form of the promissory science of pharmacogenetics. Alzheimer's disease, a increasingly common condition with serious resource implications, is an ideal example if one is constructing expectations around pharmacogenetics and the targeting of treatment of those patients who will benefit most.

Of course, close reading of these reviews reveals variations in the way in which the Tacrine–E4 hypothesis is cited. Perhaps the most interesting is the way in which despite some authors' uncertainty about the result, they continue to cite it as an example of pharmacogenetics. For example reviews co-authored by the pharmacologist William Evans move between straightforward endorsement of the link between APOE4 and Tacrine (Evans & Relling 1999: 490), via scepticism, both on the grounds of the biological basis of the result (McLeod &

Evans 2001: 108) and on practical clinical grounds (Evans & Johnson 2001: 27), back to certainty with a confident mention of APOE4 and Tacrine (Johnson & Evans 2002: 302) followed by uncertainty on the grounds of genetic complexity (Evans & McLeod 2003: 544). Despite Evans and his co-authors' inconstant views about the Tacrine–E4 hypothesis, they continue to cite it as an example of pharmacogenetics, if only to show how complex the clinical application of this technology might be. Of the commentaries that cite the 1995 Poirier paper, I found one that expressed scepticism (Bracco 2002) and only one that was openly critical of this result, that in essence reflects the views of clinicians and researchers working on Alzheimer's disease:

> the reported association of the apolipoprotein E polymorphism with the response to treatment with Tacrine [reference to Poirier *et al.* 1995] is a good example for a spurious genetic association. It is a good reminder of the general problems observed with association studies that are well known from many trials [ref.], and that fully apply also to pharmacogenomic investigations.
>
> *(Schmitz, Aslanidis & Lackner 2001: 47)*

There are obviously dangers in lumping a number of authors together and concluding that they all have the same view of a particular scientific fact. But that said, the authors who cite the Poirier result tend to be involved in the construction of expectations about pharmacogenomics, and need resources to do this. The Tacrine–E4 hypothesis is such a useful resource, to the extent that the link between APOE4 and non-response to Tacrine has taken on a life of its own. Commentators need no longer cite the original 1995 paper by Judes Poirier and his colleagues; it is enough to cite other reviews that do so.[10]

Breast cancer

My second case study concerns a drug that, for the newspapers at least, is at the leading edge of a new wave of drug development, the standard-bearer for a revolution in the way in which drugs are produced and prescribed. The arrival of Herceptin suggests that 'a new era could be dawning', with targeted cancer treatments superseding the clumsy, blunderbuss approach used today (Perlman 1999). Herceptin is variously described as: the 'first fruit of breakthrough discoveries involving the molecular workings of cancer' (Hall 1999); a 'gene-based designer drug' (Altman 2000); the 'front runner of this new pharmaceutical wave' (Cookson 1999); one of the few medicines 'that is indisputably a product

---

[10] Persing and Cheek (2000) cite two other reviews (Evans & Relling 1999 and Regalado 1999) rather than original research papers.

of genomics' (Pilling 2000); quite simply, 'one of the first drugs to be used in conjunction with a genetic test . . . known as pharmacogenetics' (Firn 2000).

For many in the press, interest in Herceptin is sparked not just because of its innovative nature, but also because of its financial value. In 2002 Herceptin was Roche's fifth biggest selling drug, with a value of £460 million (Guardian 2003). For Genentech, the biotech firm that originally developed the drug, Herceptin was even more important. Combined with its other cancer product, Rituxan, it drove the company's profits up by 21 per cent over the same period (Griffith 2003b). For the genomics industry, Herceptin is proof not just of the scientific principle underpinning personalised medicine, but also of the financial principles that have driven investment in the biotechnology sector and led pharmaceutical companies into their mergers and acquisitions of genomics firms. Herceptin proves that the expectations generated over pharmacogenetics and pharmacogenomics are not misplaced; you can make money from personalised medicine. Related to this, Herceptin is important because it treats cancer, and the 'total oncology market is expected to reach more than US \$32 billion in size by 2005'. As a result, 'for biotech firms, oncology projects dwarf all other R&D projects' (Booth, Glassman & Ma, 2003: 609). As an example of not just a financially successful personalised medicine but of one that treats *cancer*, Herceptin raises industry expectations over what might be possible in the near future.

In scientific commentaries on pharmacogenetics, the view of Herceptin is broadly similar to the position in the popular press. Perhaps Klaus Lindpaintner and colleagues overegg the pudding somewhat when they claim that Herceptin is 'the most frequently cited example' of pharmacogenetics (Lindpaintner *et al.* 2001: 76); as I have shown, that honour has already been claimed by the Tacrine – APOE4 link. Yet Herceptin's position in the clinic is a useful resource for pharmacogenetic commentators. For Akhtar, mentioning Herceptin is a way of challenging the idea that pharmacogenetics is 'purely futuristic' (Akhtar 2002: 298). Ginsburg and McCarthy cite Herceptin as 'an important precedent for regulatory approval of personalized medicine' (2001: 494), and the FDA's licensing of Herceptin is praised in a *Nature Biotechnology* editorial as 'Pharmacogenomics at work' (Anon. 1998). A number of authors suggest that if we want to know about the 'future regulation of pharmacogenomics', we ought to look at 'what the FDA has already done in this area', suggesting Herceptin as an example (Czaban 2001: 33; see also Anderson, Fitzgerald & Manasco 1999; Rioux 2000; Ginsburg & McCarthy 2001). And one of the regulators I spoke to agreed that 'for efficiency, we had the cases already which have been approved on genomic knowledge. One is Herceptin . . . and as regulators, we wanted to be sure that, as the predictive values are very high, there's no point to treat the ones that don't have the receptor' (Reg 3). At the same time, Herceptin's very success in getting licensed has highlighted the difficulties faced by other drugs trying to get through the process (Murphy 2000). For some authors, Herceptin is the first example of pharmacogenetics in the clinic (Johnson & Evans 2002: 302), the only case of a pharmacogenomic drug making it through clinical trials (Murphy 2000: 2).[11] For these commentators, Herceptin is 'proof of concept' (Hoban 2002) for newer cancer medication, medication that 'takes us out of the days of poisoning the patient and hoping that the tumour dies' (Rioux 2000: 896).

In talking to people who actually use Herceptin on a day-to-day basis, I discovered a variety of views regarding Herceptin's status as an exemplar of pharmacogenetics. Part of the problem stems from the kind of genetic test used. With Herceptin, the test for HER2 overexpression that determines one's eligibility for treatment is not a test of a person's genetic make-up, of the genome they inherited from their parents and share aspects of with their siblings. A HER2 test examines genetic changes in tumour tissue, somatic changes that are not passed on to children. Such changes are obviously quite different from inherited variation in drug metabolising genes.

Thus, roughly half of the people I spoke to were resistant to the idea that Herceptin is a form of pharmacogenetics: 'I think of pharmacogenomics as meaning something much more wholesale, large scale screening procedures' (CR 14). At best, Herceptin as an example of pharmacogenetics is 'very borderline, it's extremely borderline' (CR 6). Consistent themes refer back to 'traditional' pharmacogenetic issues, such as inherited differences – 'That's what I understood by pharmacogenetics, they're inherited differences' (CR 8) – or a focus on drug metabolism:

> what I know about pharmacogenetics could easily be written on the back of a first class postage stamp in quarter-inch felt-tip pen. But I suppose I don't see it as pharmacogenetics because what you're seeing is an abnormality in the tumour tissue itself, amplification of a gene not actually a mutation of a gene, just amplification, and you're targeting the protein . . . pharmacogenetics must mean something more to do with cytochrome P450 polymorphisms and handling of drug X, Y and Z.

> *(CR 4)*

For some, the point is that Herceptin and HER2 testing does not necessarily revolve around a gene, but around a protein: 'I would lean towards saying that it is a misnomer to call this pharmacogenetics. It is targeted therapy, if you

---

[11] Other commentators citing Herceptin as an example of pharmacogenetics/omics include: Cockett, Dracopoli & Sigal 2000; Ensom, Chang & Patel 2001; Hoban 2002; Sadée 1999; Mancinelli, Cronin & Sadée 2000; Murphy 2000; Shi, Bleavins & Iglesia 2001; Ferentz 2002; Bracco 2002; Johnson & Evans 2002.

like, which is pharmacologically based, it's based on a target, which is a protein target' (CR 18). This point of view is most clearly articulated by William Haseltine, chairman of the genomics firm Human Genetic Sciences, who suggests that labelling the drug 'pharmacogenomics' is 'off-base'. For Haseltine, 'A test for HER2 overexpression measures a phenotype that is not linked to genotype', noting that in this, the HER2 test is like that for oestrogen receptor status (Haseltine 1998; see also Tsai & Hoyme 2002). A response to this position from Lindpaintner and colleagues claims that Haseltine's is a 'difficult argument to follow', that it is probably quite likely that pharmacogenetic differences will manifest themselves in terms of gene expression rather than the underlying allelic variation (Lindpaintner *et al.* 2001: 77). Thus, HER2 overexpression, although 'only' a feature of the breast cancer tumour, may turn out to be a 'proxy' for some underlying genetic difference. Haseltine's objections are not widely supported in the literature. Perhaps one of the reasons why any debate over the status of Herceptin as pharmacogenetics seems to have died down is the drug's widespread success, both in terms of clearing licensing hurdles and of subsequent sales. With Herceptin possibly the only example of a pharmacogenetic drug in regular clinical practice, one would not expect widespread criticism of it from within industry.

For those who agree with the idea of Herceptin as pharmacogenetics, the emphasis on familial, inherited genetic differences is 'splitting hairs, really' (CR 7). The important point is that it counts as pharmacogenetics, since 'You can use a molecular biological test to diagnose the tumour that is likely to benefit' (CR 9). The appeal to basic molecular processes is also made by clinician researcher 13, who suggests that 'You get overexpression of a gene which leads to overexpression of a protein which leads to overgrowth of the tumour and then you're interrupting that pathway, so it's pharmacological alteration of a gene product; I suppose it's a reasonably good quasimodel, it's not too bad' (CR 13).

Thus there is a considerable degree of 'interpretative flexibility' around the idea of Herceptin being an example of pharmacogenetics; pharmacogenetics may, or may not, involve testing tumours for somatic, not inherited differences. An important part of clinicians' acceptance of Herceptin as pharmacogenetics relates to the creation of expectations around future developments. In the same way as commentators sketch out future scenarios of pharmacogenetic use to raise interest and construct markets, oncologists are keen to link developments in cancer drug research – 'another blanket term that you could use, which other people have used . . . individualisation of therapy' (CR 16) – with broader developments in pharmacogenetics and pharmacogenomics. For a number of my interviewees, it is *future* developments in cancer therapeutics that justify calling Herceptin 'pharmacogenetics' since 'that's the way things are going, it's not the other stuff [i.e. inherited genetics] . . . cancer's where the money is' (CR 15). This position seems to be saying that because cancer is an area where personalised medicine will play an important role in the future, this retrospectively 'boosts' Herceptin's status as an early example:

> genetic differences in cancers are going to be the future. Looking at the gene profile of patients' [tumours] . . . is going to determine our treatments . . . I think when you talk about inherited genes, that rather narrows the argument and I think it can be extended out to the situation so it's a reasonably good example and will become increasingly relevant in the future.
>
> *(CR 13)*

One risk of emphasising the way in which expectations about pharmacogenetics are constructed by industry and pharmacologists is that those who actually use the technology may be cast in a passive role, as 'consumers' of the expectations, 'buying into' the visions being outlined in commentary articles. Of course most people, certainly oncologists, should be seen in more active terms, as builders as well as consumers of expectations.

It is interesting to note that neither Genentech (the company that developed it) nor Roche (who market it in Europe) describe Herceptin as a example of pharmacogenetics. While Roche claim that 'Innovative, individualised medicines are the base for best possible therapy' (http://www.roche.com/home/healthcare/healthcare-therapy.htm), it does not explicitly push Herceptin as an example of this revolutionary approach. Despite this, Klaus Lindpaintner, Roche's Director of Genetics, is a high-profile supporter of pharmacogenetics and does cite Herceptin as a prominent example (Lindpaintner 1999; Lindpaintner et al. 2001; Lindpaintner 2003).

The final theme that emerges from discussing 'Herceptin as pharmacogenetics' with clinicians is the continuity that exists in breast cancer treatment, the idea that Herceptin is not quite the novel, revolutionary product it is sometimes presented as: 'But if Herceptin is pharmacogenetics so is, say, Tamoxifen and oestrogen receptor determination. But the term is only a word that's been created to suit somebody's purpose, and how it is used is up to what people choose it to be' (CR 3). As well as neatly summarising the interpretative flexibility of the term *pharmacogenetics*, this quote also makes the point that Tamoxifen can also be seen as a form of individual, or personalised, medicine focused on those tumours that are know to respond, identified through a laboratory test, a theme I will return to in chapter 8.

The uncertainty surrounding the question of whether Herceptin is an example of pharmacogenetics should not come as a surprise. As suggested earlier in this chapter, part of the creation of expectations around pharmacogenetics means that the term will mean different things to different groups. Yet despite the difference between the view from the clinic and that from outside, none of the people I spoke to denies that Herceptin is original and important in its mode of action, though as chapter 8 shows, there are questions over how effective it is. Many spoke of it as the first in a long line of new cancer treatments, focusing on individual variation in tumour genetics. It is also suggested that because of the serious nature of the disease, and the severity of the side effects in treatment, 'cancer is a field where pharmacogenomics will be embraced rapidly' (Ferentz 2002: 464). There is little dispute that Herceptin is 'tailor-made' or 'personalised' medicine, though of course some claim that it is not the first example of this.[12] Herceptin is presented as the first example of a therapy *deliberately* targeted at a molecular site: 'The ability of this targeted biologic therapy to provide significant antitumour activity is "proof of principle" for the concept that understanding the basic molecular alterations in cancer cells can directly lead to new treatment and better patients outcomes.' (Shak 1999: 76; see also Workman 2001a & b). As already suggested, there is considerable interpretative flexibility around the term *pharmacogenetics* and the form that such technologies will take. By thinking in terms of a broad, vaguely defined term such as *personalised medicine*, we can explore the issues these sorts of technologies will raise for healthcare systems clinicians and society as a whole, without having to align ourselves to one specific vision of pharmacogenetics.

Conclusion

Rather than seeing the rise of pharmacogenetics since the late 1990s and the subsequent debate over personalised medicine as unsupported 'hype', a more productive approach involves the sociology of expectations. From this point of view, speculative claims about a future technology play a vital role in both the development of the technology itself and in the shaping of the social, regulatory and economic environment into which the technology will emerge. Focusing on the creation of such expectations about pharmacogenetics has led to the two case studies used in the rest of this book. Alzheimer's disease and breast cancer, or more specifically, APOE4–Tacrine and HER2–Herceptin, are vital resources in the construction of expectations around personalised medicine. Yet in both cases, the way in which these examples are presented by supporters of pharmacogenetics simplifies uncertainties and obscures the complexities (both technical and social) inherent in the use of pharmacogenetic testing. The rest

---

[12] Jordan (2003) suggests that this honour should go to Tamoxifen.

of this book sets out to unpack these two case studies, to contrast the view of pharmacogenetics offered by those who would use the technology in the clinic with the visions and speculations proposed by academic and industry-based supporters of the technology. By rooting our expectations about pharmacogenetics in the lived experience of the clinic, this book sets out not to dismiss this sort of speculation as hype, but rather to show how central the social is to the complicated and fraught process of bringing a technology into existence.

3

Genetics, moral risk and professional resistance

'Ask a bunch of people on the street' is how we poll for politicians; we don't do the same thing for medicine. In medicine, you either know or you don't know, and the worst is if you *think* you know.

Clinician Researcher 12

Discussing the clinical application of pharmacogenetics in Alzheimer's disease is complicated, because as things currently stand there is considerable professional debate over whether Alzheimer's disease exists as a separate clinical entity at all. Since at least the mid-1990s the relationship between Alzheimer's disease and other forms of dementia, such as Lewy body dementia or vascular dementia, has been in a state of flux: 'Different forms of dementia are now known to have common underlying neuropathologies and histopathological studies have shown that mixed states (people presenting with features of more than one type of dementia) are probably more usual than pure dementia syndromes' (Ritchie & Lovestone 2002: 1759). For many of my interviewees, 'the dichotomy between vascular dementia and Alzheimer's Disease is probably artificial' (CR 10). Yet in the clinic Alzheimer's disease is still treated as a separate condition. In the NHS, for example, while clinicians can prescribe drugs such as Aricept or Rivastigmine for patients suffering from Alzheimer's disease, they are discouraged from doing so for Lewy body and other kinds of dementia.

For clinicians, Alzheimer's is a progressive neurological disease leading to the permanent loss of cells in parts of the brain associated with higher functions. It is the most common form of dementia in the western world, making up about two-thirds of all cases. The diagnosis of Alzheimer's disease is largely an exercise in ruling out alternative conditions. For example, although memory loss and cognitive impairment are the most obvious symptoms of AD, they can also be the side effect of prescription drugs. In addition to cognitive tests (such as recalling name and address or naming the parts of an object), clinicians look for personality changes (usually reduced emotional expression and increased stubbornness) and whether the patient experiences hallucinations. They may require blood tests (to rule out vitamin B12 deficiency) and computer tomography (CT) or Magnetic Resonance Imaging (MRI) scans of the brain (Geldmacher & Whitehouse 1996). Yet even at the end of this, one cannot be certain of a diagnosis of Alzheimer's disease, since the cast-iron, defining feature of the condition are the plaques and tangles in the brain that Alois Alzheimer first noted in 1907.[1] And they can only be found with an autopsy (Epstein 1999).

Origins of APOE[2]

The story of Alzheimer's pharmacogenetics is a story of professional resistance and industry suspicion, a story of what historian Thomas Hughes calls 'reverse salients' (Hughes 1983: 79–80). Alzheimer's, APOE and Tacrine is the story of how *not* to get pharmacogenetics into the clinic. The next three chapters show why pharmacogenetics is not in use in the Alzheimer's clinic, and why it is that there is such professional resistance to this new technology among clinicians and researchers.

The core problem for the 1995 Poirier result that linked varying response to the Alzheimer drug Tacrine to people's genetic make-up, the fact so enthusiastically adopted by supporters of pharmacogenetics, is that the gene involved, the gene that codes for the protein apolipoprotein E, already has a history in professional debates around Alzheimer's disease. Since the early 1990s discussion has taken place over whether a particular version of this gene, APOE4, should be used as a way of predicting risk of developing Alzheimer's.

> I think a lot of the debate about using it for testing has been, well, a lot of the fears have been misinformed. It's pretty useless as a diagnostic predictive test, as was obvious right at the beginning . . . there's a lot of fear I think of genetic testing that's out of proportion with the reality, for people outside the science. There's almost two bands of people: at one extreme there's the people hyping up genetics and what it's going to do, and at the other end there are the paranoid social

[1] The neurofibrilary tangles are made up of a protein called tau, and the senile plaques are accumulations of another protein called ß-amyloid.
[2] Terminology around APOE can vary, but the convention is that the protein, apolipoprotein E, is shortened to apoe (i.e., lower case) while the gene involved is always upper-case APOE, with its different alleles referred to as E, or epsilon, or ε. This book uses E.

scientists, sort of thinking 'oh my god, this is going to be the end of free will, and civilisation as we know it' . . . And of course somewhere near the middle is reality. Genetics is not, they're not going to be able to profile people and predict that they're going to get Alzheimer's disease on their 85th birthday. But you know you might be able to identify people whose risk is increased several fold.

(Researcher 2)

Resistance to the pharmacogenetic use of APOE genotyping is simply the most recent controversy to revolve around this gene. To understand why it is that the APOE4–Tacrine pharmacogenetic link has not made it into clinical practice, one has to set APOE4 in its context, both in terms of the science of Alzheimer's research, and the ethical debates that have taken place over the use of genetic testing.

An important, inescapable part of this context is the reputation and personality of the scientist most obviously associated with APOE4: Allen Roses, the same person we met at the beginning of chapter 1. As he himself puts it, 'the history of the APOE association with AD has been colorful', and it would not be unfair to suggest that at least one source of this 'colour' is Allen Roses himself (Roses 1998a: 43). Described by scientific news articles as the *enfant terrible* of Alzheimer's research (Larkin 1997), a rebel with a cause (Brower 1997) and a scientific street-fighter (E. Marshall 1998), Roses's powerful, aggressive personality could be summed up by the quote: 'I may be unpopular, but I'm not wrong' (E. Marshall 1998: 1001). Roses was a neurologist specialising in a form of muscular dystrophy, and had no background in Alzheimer's research when in the early 1980s he became head of Duke University's Alzheimer's Disease Research Center.[3] The late 1980s was a boom time for genetic research into Alzheimer's, with areas on chromosomes 21 and 14 being targeted by a number of different research groups. As Robert Cook-Deegan puts it, 'Two decades ago, the quest for the genetic origins of AD was a field in dire need of attention. It is now the subject of fractious rivalry, and the pathologies of hypercompetition have begun to appear' (Cook-Deegan 1998: 85).

When in 1990 Roses and his colleagues suggested that there was a link between Alzheimer's and a stretch of chromosome 19, his work was largely ignored by the research community, a position that John Hardy, a long-time critic of Roses, acknowledges as 'a mistake . . . For about 3 years, Allen was telling us there was something important on chromosome 19, but everyone

---

[3] In 1998 he left academia to join Glaxo Wellcome, and became a high-profile supporter of pharmacogenetics.

basically ignored him' (quoted in E. Marshall 1998: 1001). While the Duke team tried to narrow down its focus, Roses was involved in two vitriolic arguments over the naming of authors on papers to which he felt the Duke team had contributed, with lawyers being called in at least one case. Roses accepts that this incident 'caused a rift' in the research community (E. Marshall 1998: 1001–2).

In 1991 Roses and his team managed to narrow down their search, and by looking at proteins binding to the damaged parts of Alzheimer's brains, realised that the gene they were looking for was APOE, a well-known transporter of lipids and risk factor for heart disease (Cunning & Robertson 1984).[4] Roses describes this revelation as 'like a lightning bolt going off in my head . . . I knew APOE was in the middle of the region we were looking at, but there was no reason to consider it a candidate gene because it didn't do anything in the brain that anyone was aware of' (quoted in Larkin 1997). The result was viewed with scepticism by Alzheimer's researchers, whose response, Roses suggests, featured 'premature public announcements of nonconfirmations at international meetings, and frequent disparaging and sometimes personally hostile quotations in the lay press' (Roses 1998a: 42). When the Alzheimer's–APOE link was announced on the front page of the *Wall Street Journal* on 7 June 1993, and followed up with three academic publications, the research community began to take Roses and his team far more seriously. The initial unsupportive response from other researchers was swiftly transformed, largely 'because many practicing clinicians who treated large series of AD patients had APOE genotyping available to them locally . . . [as a result] . . . letters confirming the increased APOE ε4 association with AD started to appear in the *Lancet* and other journals in the year after publication' (Roses 1998a: 42–3).

This acceptance of the link between APOE4 and increased risk of late onset Alzheimer's disease is supported by my interviews with clinicians and researchers involved in this area: 'There are 40-odd genes associated with Alzheimer's disease in one study or another and only one of those has been replicated seriously and that's APOE' (CR 3). For Clinician Researcher 5, it is '[s]till the only generally applicable genetic marker we have for AD. It's the only one'. Researcher 2 describes it as 'a phenomenon, because it's really been the first genetic risk factor for a common disease. It was the first to be identified with molecular genetics. It's a very robust finding, and it's a very important finding; it's a hugely important finding.'

---

[4] The ethical problems raised by this overlap between APOE4 as a risk factor for heart disease and for Alzheimer's has been largely ignored (see Wachbroit 1998 for an exception). It goes largely uncommented on in both the literature and in my interviews. As such in this book it remains unexplored.

By November 1993 a conference report in *Science* could confidently claim that this result was 'not in dispute' (Marx 1993: 1210). In the mid-1990s what *was* disputed was the mechanism by which Roses and his colleague Warren Strittmatter claimed APOE was involved in Alzheimer's disease. Their model suggested that APOEs 2 and 3 were protective alleles, shielding a protein called tau from damaging changes that possibly led to neuronal death, and therefore Alzheimer's disease. In a test tube experiment APOE3 bound to tau, stabilising it, while APOE4 did not. Thus, E4's link to Alzheimer's would be not as a direct cause, but as a 'failure to protect'. Unfortunately for Roses, his colleagues and the APOE4 theory, this model leaves no room for the dominant approach to Alzheimer's causation, which revolves around another protein, called ß-Amyloid.

Roses dismisses the plaques of amyloid formed in the brains of Alzheimer's patients as symptoms of the condition rather than a cause, calling them 'scars' (E. Marshall 1998: 1003). Outlining his objections in a paper in 1994, Roses suggested that the presence of amyloid plaques in the brains of AD patients, which began as a convenient working diagnosis of the condition, had become elevated to the status of the 'gold standard'. In turn this had led to the tautological situation where 'Because all definite AD patients have amyloid plaques *by definition* . . . It is commonly stated that amyloid deposition causes AD' (Roses 1994: 429). This distinction between supporters of the amyloid hypothesis and the tau hypothesis has led to the half-joking religious designation of the two group: BAPtists versus TAUists. Although recent articles suggest that there may be something of a reconciliation between the two main groups (Mudher & Lovestone 2002; Trojanowski 2002), it is clear from talking to those working in this area that associating oneself too closely with the APOE4 causation hypothesis can be damaging to one's career. As one interviewee put it, 'The amyloid paradigm still dominates people's thinking, planning and publications. You don't get an APOE story published in *Nature*, but you do if its an amyloid story.' Allen Roses claims that his challenge to the 'amyloidists' led to him being 'blackballed' for National Institute of Health (NIH) research grants, and that once his main funding finished in 1995 he could get no more money for Alzheimer's research (Brower 1997; E. Marshall 1998). In a letter to *Nature Medicine* commenting on the role of anonymous journal referees, Roses suggests that 'the problem for journals is magnified by the major problem at funding agencies like the National Institute of Health (NIH). There it is now possible to have your science judged by patently conflicted individuals, and your career destroyed' (Roses 1997a). As the interviewee quoted above puts it, 'If I said otherwise about APOE4 as a risk factor rather than a cause, then they'd crucify me as they have Allen Roses.'

Consensus and debate

But Allen Roses's role as a controversialist extends beyond small groups of Alzheimer's researchers and geneticists, into much wider debates about the use of genetic testing in the clinic, the value of genetic risk estimates and the tensions between clinical judgement and research findings. Put at it simplest, Roses and a small number of other researchers are at odds with the vast majority of Alzheimer's professionals over the use of APOE4 testing for what is called 'differential diagnosis'. Roses's point is that although APOE may not be a good way of predicting who is going to get AD, once someone presents with symptoms of dementia, then APOE testing is a good way of helping a clinician work out whether a patient has Alzheimer's or some other, perhaps more treatable, condition. As one of my interviewees, who agrees with Roses, puts it, 'we had a number of patients who looked like Alzheimer's Disease but carried an APOE2 allele, and we looked especially hard at those patients when they would show up, and two out of three times they turned out to have something else' (CR 12). As a result of this differential diagnosis, 'I've already helped people who had reversible causes of Alzheimer's Disease when they were referred to me, and I was able to pick them out because they had a simple test that cost virtually nothing, compared to what they'd spent on consultant fees before . . . I've never seen a patient that's APOE 2/2 with Alzheimer's disease' (CR 12).

At the outset it must be made clear that, as far as I can tell, Roses has never supported the use of predictive APOE4 testing on *asymptomatic* people: 'apoE genotyping does not allow accurate prediction of whether or when an individual will develop Alzheimer's disease . . . On this point the literature is virtually unanimous' (Roses & Saunders 1997: 414). In a pithy summary of their position, Roses and his colleagues suggest that 'If a healthy 50-year-old is worried about Alzheimer's disease, contributing a bit more towards Alzheimer's disease research would be a more sound investment than learning an apoE genotype' (Roses *et al.* 1994: 1565). In my interviews, although most of the people I spoke to disagreed with the use of diagnostic genotyping, some clinicians were prepared to suggest that it might be useful: 'Where I could see the potential utility of it might be in patients with mild cognitive impairment and there is some work suggesting that it might predict so-called conversion rates to Alzheimer's disease. That could potentially then be useful because it's extremely hard to predict who's going to develop it and when' (CR 11). The usual response, though, is like that of Clinician Researcher 7, who said that

> at the end of the day, if you apply your clinical diagnostic criteria well, then you can get a good positive predictive value of about 93 per cent if you really work at it, if you really go by the book and this pumps it up to 95 per cent or something, but

you've lost . . . instantly, you're only going to a third of your population. So, it's not worth it. The cost–benefit ratio is not there, as far as I can see.

Professional concern about the clinical use of APOE genotyping was kick-started by the decision in early 1994 of the Genica Pharmaceuticals Corporation to mail 'to physicians across the United States a full packet detailing the $195 APOE test for susceptibility to Alzheimer's disease. A sticker on the envelope reads 'Rush! Here's the Genica Information you requested' (Post 1996: 112). Based in Montreal, Genica was trading on what was believed to be prior research on APOE carried out by Judes Poirier (of whom more in chapter 4). Although the company swiftly withdrew its testing offer, professional fears of inappropriate commercial exploitation spurred clinicians and the research community into action. In an editorial call to arms, cited by at least two of the subsequent consensus statements as the starting point for professional resistance,[5] Robert Butler, editor-in-chief of the journal *Geriatrics*, set out concerns that have shaped the debate around clinical APOE testing ever since. Noting that 'one enterprising company is already offering ApoE-E4 testing services to clinicians', Butler calls on his colleagues to be 'extremely cautious about testing your older patients or their families for ApoE-E4', to be aware that 'people who discover through testing that they have ApoE-E4 might decide to avoid marriage and having children', that 'Widespread testing could lead to insurance companies denying coverage to people who test positive for ApoE-E4'; in short, that 'The emotional toll on individuals . . . and on their families would be great' (Butler 1994). These concerns about the effect of genetic risk information on patients' families, the offspring and siblings who may be at increased risk of developing Alzheimer's, are a constant theme in the subsequent literature.

At least one of my interviewees has a clear recollection of the marketing of this test and how it was seen by the clinical community:

when it [the APOE test] first came out there was a company that marketed this test and they would go around to all the physicians and . . . basically the message was, subliminally the message was 'here's a test that'll make the diagnosis of AD'. That's how powerful the presentation was. Not just simply 'here's another test to measure a risk factor', but 'here's a test that's going to make the diagnosis so you don't have to worry about examining the patient'. Obviously that was very much frowned upon: nobody is ready to accept that.

(C 1)

---

[5] The Consensus Group Supported by the National Human Genome Research Institute and the National Institutes of Health (Post, Whitehouse, Binstock, *et al.* 1997) and the Stanford Program in Genomics, Ethics and Society (McConnell, Koenig, Greely & Raffin 1998).

The test being marketed was explicitly for diagnosis of Alzheimer's rather than predictive testing, yet, in this clinician's mind at least, even this kind of testing is ethically suspect. The Genica test was marketed as a diagnostic test since it claimed that the APOE4 result it produced 'should be interpreted in the light of other "clinical diagnostic information"'. Yet critics suggest that although 'this qualification rules out marketing of the test as predictive . . . nevertheless susceptibility was emphasized' (Post 1996: 112). Whatever Genica said the test was for, they were damned as marketing an Alzheimer's susceptibility test. In the meantime, Allen Roses and his colleagues at Duke University had applied for a patent on the use of APOE testing in Alzheimer's.[6] When this was granted in 1996, they licensed the test to a company called Athena Neurosciences, which introduced the ADmark ApoE Genetic Test 'for greater certainty in differential diagnosis of AD' (quoted in Post, Whitehouse, Binstock *et al.* 1997: 835). To ensure that the test was not used for predictive purposes, any sample had to be accompanied by a letter confirming that the patient was showing signs of dementia, signed by a doctor.

One suggestion made to me is that the licensing of the Athena test was deliberately done to 'spoil' the market for the Genica test, which Roses, who was then Chair of the Medical and Scientific Advisory Board of the Alzheimer's Association, and most other experts opposed as irresponsible.[7] An alternative view of the link between Roses and commercial APOE testing is that since it was Duke's policy of the time to pay 'its faculty inventors a healthy share (up to 50% after expenses) of the royalties of licensed patents', Roses's support for the clinical use of APOE4 testing is suspect, that there are ethical concerns that 'those who benefit financially from the performance of genetic testing . . . could be said to have a conflict of interests that might lead to aggressive promotion of those tests' (Merz, Cho & Leonard 1998: 1289). Not unreasonably, Roses is rather dismissive of this 'fact-poor attack', pointing out that 'More than 90% of the eight inventors' [of the APOE patent] portion of the Duke patent license income goes to the Joseph Bryan Scholars Endowment Fund at Duke University, the income of which has been used to support Ph.D. students in basic science departments, none of whom were students in my laboratory' (Roses 1998b).

Aside from the clumsiness of this attack on Roses, these authors seem to have rather a simplistic model of the relationship between science, patents and

---

[6] The patent was applied for in April 1994 and granted in 1996. For a discussion of the commercial issues surrounding the marketing of such a test, see Cook-Deegan 1998.

[7] This is supported by Athena Neuroscience's late 1994 announcement that it was planning on buying Genica Pharmaceuticals, renaming it Athena Diagnostic (Pharmaceutical Business News, 1994). What better way of preventing the use of an 'unethical' test than buying the firm that markets it!

industry. Fortun notes that when thinking about the relationship between industrial biotechnology and academia, we must be careful of 'Narratives of "selling
out" and "independence" ', suggesting that they are 'all too predictable in both
academic and public discussions of biotechnology' and that 'Such oppositions
are good mostly for moralistic posturing and sermonising' (Fortun 1998: 218).
It does seem too simplistic to suggest that Allen Roses's promotion of APOE
testing for differential diagnosis was somehow driven by commercial considerations. Far more credible is the idea that he genuinely believed that it was of
clinical value and that such testing could help patients and families. As I will
show, this does not mean that other experts could not take up very different
positions, on similar grounds.

Among my interviewees, the view seemed to be that the Athena test was to
have been marketed as a predictive test, but that resistance from the professional
community forced the company to 'downgrade' it to a diagnostic test:

> They obviously jumped the gun very quickly . . . When that failed, when they
> realised they couldn't use it as a predictive of who's going to get the disease or
> not, they then said well if you add it on to very robust clinical diagnostic
> criteria . . . which is running anyway at about 86–87 per cent, something like that,
> then it improves the positive predictive value tremendously. Which sounds great,
> but when you actually look at the numbers that you've got left by the end of that,
> you know, great, you've missed out more than half the population so you're down
> to a very small number of people and this is the trouble, every time you introduce a
> genetic test, you've reduced your market that it's actually of any value. So, if it's
> positive, great, it gives you an interesting result. But if it's negative, it doesn't really
> get you anywhere.
>
> *(CR 7)*

There is a degree of resentment over the way in which the commercial test was
marketed and its implications for clinical practice: 'these people who make
APOE4 kits and stuff like that, they give this impression that until you do your
blood testing, you don't know if you've got Alzheimer's disease or not, and
that's irresponsible because it's not quite the truth' (CR 8). At the same time,
there is an acceptance that clinicians are interested in the diagnostic test:

> It's partly driven by clinicians who are interested, and it's partly driven by
> companies. In particular there is Elan pharmaceuticals who own Athena
> Neurosciences and Athena have been for a number of years marketing a blood test
> based upon APOE as diagnostic test for Alzheimer's Disease in the States, but that
> commercial testing kit has never gained any foothold in this country because the
> consensus of Alzheimer's geneticists in the UK is, other than these specific familial
> autosomal dominant genes, there is no indication for testing.
>
> *(CR 1)*

Even setting aside the issue of commercial testing, there is a degree of personal dislike for the idea of predictive testing. For example, one researcher claimed that 'I think the literature's heavily biased by . . . one or two individuals who push it as being something that could predict disease risk but for obvious reasons you can't do that with that gene' (R 6). This interviewee seems to be suggesting that Allen Roses 'pushed' for APOE testing to predict disease risk, something for which I can find no evidence in the literature. I suspect that this response is partly in reaction to Roses's outsider status in the Alzheimer's research community, but also because the consensus position views both diagnostic and predictive testing as inappropriate, a view held by both UK and US clinicians.

A good example of the debate around the use of clinical APOE diagnostic testing can be found in a 1995 'point of view' article Roses provided for the journal *Annals of Neurology*: its title was 'Apolipoprotein E genotyping in the differential diagnosis, not prediction of Alzheimer's disease', and its purpose, unsurprisingly was 'to draw a clear distinction between use of APOE genotyping in differential diagnosis and prediction' (Roses 1995a: 6). In this paper, Roses points out that about 66 per cent of patients presenting at a clinic with symptoms of dementia 'can be diagnosed correctly by simply stating "AD", and one-third would be diagnosed incorrectly' (Roses 1995a: 8). If genotyping is introduced into such a situation, then 'if the patient is APOE4/4 genotype, the probability of that patient having AD increases to 0.94 [i.e. 94%] . . . In a similar manner, if a demented patient is APOE2/3, then the probability of AD is reduced by one-half. Thus there is double the probability that there may be another etiology for the dementia' (Roses 1995a: 10).

In an editorial response to this, Thomas Bird urges a cautious approach to diagnostic APOE testing, suggesting that many of Roses's numbers are 'rough estimates' and that 'Additional information is badly needed, is in the process of being obtained, and will undoubtedly change our perspective of the issues in the next few years' (Bird 1995a: 2–3). Responding to this, Kakulas and van Bockxmeer claim they wish to set the record straight, 'because of the unfortunate negative impression his [i.e. Bird's] views may give to the clinical neurologist' (Kakulas and van Bockxmeer 1995: 996). Bird replies that his main point was simply that

> It is my opinion that at the present ApoE genotyping is not of practical clinical use in the diagnosis of Alzheimer's disease . . . There are false positives and false negatives, that is, an error factor. The precise magnitude of that error factor is presently unknown . . . further studies and additional data will resolve this problem in the relatively near future.
>
> *(Bird 1995b)*

Building support

This exchange between supporters and opponents of diagnostic APOE testing is worth looking at not because it contains anything unusual, but because the themes and claims, on both sides of the argument, reoccur throughout this debate. Many statements made in papers published at the beginning of this controversy could be cut and pasted into discussions five or six years later, and one would be hard pressed to see the difference. One way of looking at this discourse is in terms of network-building. Between 1994 and 1998, when he moved into industry, Allen Roses and his allies, those who think that 'the use of *apoE* testing is clinically relevant in patients with dementia and suspected AD' (Growden 1998: 1054), attempted to build a network of support that would move differential diagnosis using APOE testing into the clinic. Like all 'heterogeneous engineers', they tried to enrol people, artefacts and ideas, translating various interests in such a way that they swung behind differential diagnosis. In the short to medium term, they did not succeed; the institutional and ethical hurdles were too great. Yet the network-building provided a vital context for Alzheimer's pharmacogenetics, shaping and helping to constitute the kinds of debates we can have over personalised medicine.

In a classic political move, Roses seeks to separate clinicians from researchers in terms of their relationship to clinical APOE testing. In contrast to his opponents' 'consensus view', which tends to see clinicians' and researchers' interests as closely linked, Roses's position is that their beliefs, needs and knowledge bases are quite different: 'A schism exists between part of the genetics community and some of the AD community, brought on by different attitudes towards patients and their needs' (Roses 1998a: 44). On the one side are clinicians and patients, who would like better, earlier diagnosis of Alzheimer's disease: 'According to interactive groups organized by chapters of the Alzheimer's Association, patients and families are "better off" with an accurate, early diagnosis' (Roses 1997a: 1155). On the other side, with influence over public policy, are genetics researchers and 'other sources unfamiliar with the detailed medical problems of AD patients and their caregivers' (Roses 1998a: 44).

At the same time, it would not make sense to alienate genetics researchers from clinical APOE testing; they are a very important constituency. It is just that if they are to be enrolled in the network, it must be on their own terms, separate from clinicians. Roses's solution is to associate his ideas with the need for research on patients that have been confirmed as having Alzheimer's disease; that is, patients who have undergone an autopsy. By building autopsy confirmed patients into his network, Roses ensures that researchers will also be enrolled:

'Discussions of the diagnostic value of all tests for AD should be based on prospectively ascertained, necroscopy-confirmed series, and not on clinically diagnosed groups with their inherently variable, unknown real frequency of definite AD' (Saunders *et al.* 1996: 93; see also Roses & Saunders 1997: 415). One cannot rely on clinicians' judgement, since it is their judgement that differential APOE testing brings into question. Yet at the same time, clinicians are central to the network, since without their agreement there is no context for clinical APOE testing. A difficult balancing act. Of course opponents of clinical APOE testing undermine this approach, by highlighting the difference between the populations encountered by researchers, based in specialist dementia clinics, and the average clinician who has to make the initial diagnosis: 'The predictive values in selective autopsy populations do not necessarily reflect those in clinical populations' (Whitehouse & Geldmacher 1996: 1998; also McConnell, Sanders & Owens 1999: 51). The effect of this is to reduce the clinical relevance of research into the sensitivity and specificity of APOE-based differential diagnosis carried out on autopsied populations.

This distinction between clinicians and researchers leads us to the central organising theme of Roses's position, which is the *clinical usefulness* or practicality of APOE differential diagnosis. While never explicitly spelled out, reading through Roses's writing on this topic allows one to 'sift out' those motifs that mesh together to make up this idea. First, there is the idea that clinical diagnosis of Alzheimer's is always only tentative and provisional. Until the patient dies and an autopsy is performed, a person can only be described as having 'probable' Alzheimer's disease: 'There is a profound difference between the differential diagnosis of cognitively impaired patients at the time *of initial presentation* and the results of autopsies after a long dementing disease with a course indistinguishable from Alzheimer's disease' (Roses 1995b). This tentative nature of an Alzheimer's clinical diagnosis justifies, in Roses's mind, the search for a way to improve diagnostic accuracy: an E4 genotype is just such a test. To be more specific, 'there are no reports of a case of probable Alzheimer's disease with an APOE4/4 genotype not meeting the criteria for definite Alzheimer's disease at autopsy' (Roses 1995b). Roses explicitly criticises the 'nihilistic suggestion that an accurate diagnosis may be unnecessary' (Roses 1998a: 44), arguing the case on behalf of the families of those with Alzheimer's, to give them increased certainty and reassurance. This is particularly important because it is argued that APOE genotyping will allow a differential diagnosis to be made earlier than is currently normally possible (Welsh-Bohmer, Gearing, Saunders *et al.* 1997: 323).

Beyond clinicians and researchers, Roses seeks to enrol 'responsible government agencies . . . managed care groups' (1997b: 1229), 'patients and relatives' (Roses 1997a: 1155), in short, anyone who funds healthcare. His point is that APOE testing is 'relatively inexpensive' and that 'Millions of patients are currently costing billions of dollars for diagnostic evaluations' (1997b: 1229). APOE4's diagnostic power is such it 'may result in a harder look at the continued use of some expensive, but non-specific technologies' (Roses, Strittmatter, Periack-Vance *et al.* 1994: 1564).[8] Linked to this is a third point, the claim that neuro-imaging using technologies such as CT or MRI scans 'in lieu of a reliable documented neurological examination infrequently provides additional diagnostic information' (Roses 1997a: 1156). Such technologies are often beyond the financial means of general practitioners, and tend to be used in an unfocused automatic way when the evidence supporting their use in diagnosis is equivocal (Roses 1996c; Roses & Saunders 1996; Saunders, Hulette, Welsh-Bohmer *et al.* 1996). Compared to APOE, 'No other test commonly used to diagnose dementia has been subjected to such a rigorous analysis of positive predictive value' (Roses 1998a: 51). As a result, 'the other diagnostic tests in common use need reevaluation with the same rigor as has been applied to *ApoE* testing' (Roses 1997b: 1229).

Those who reject Roses's attempt to enrol clinicians resist the idea that the increased accuracy gained from using APOE in differential diagnosis is outweighed by the complications an APOE4 result involves:

> The actual benefit you get of increasing the diagnostic accuracy by that small increment, both in cost benefit and benefit for patient, is rather small, considering what the fallout of that may be. You've improved your diagnostic accuracy by 3% but you've now burdened the family with the idea that this person's children have a higher risk of Alzheimer's disease: something that they may not want to know. So have you really done good? That's an open question.
>
> *(CR 6)*

From this point of view, 'clinical practicality' is about more than just whether the test concerned has high enough sensitivity and specificity figures: 'Diagnostic tests should be judged on the basis of their potential to change the opinion of the clinician regarding what should be done for the patient' (Van Gool 1996: 84). It is not clear that having information on sensitivity, specificity and predictive value 'allows for a proper evaluation of new tests from a *practical point of view*. It is not often that new tests are evaluated by their potential to increase diagnostic confidence . . . and studies on the utility for patients or caregivers of making a diagnosis of AD have never been performed' (Van Gool 1996: 85; emphasis added). What this emphasises is that for Roses's opponents, 'clinical practicality' includes an element of ethical and social consideration.

---

[8] See also: Roses 1996c (p. 1480); Roses 1996b (p. 53); Roses & Saunders 1996.

Since the ethical problems associated with an E4 status are unlikely to change in the light of new data about the accuracy of the E4 diagnostic test, one result of the absence of diagnostic sensitivity and specificity in this model is the repeated claim that 'further research is needed'. For example, Van Gool suggests that 'At present test characteristics such as sensitivity, specificity, and the predictive value of APOE ε4 presence are essentially unknown for clinical settings. No prospective clinical studies with subsequent follow-up in consecutive patients, investigated for suspected AD, have been performed' (Van Gool 1996: 82).

Similarly several consensus groups of professionals repeat the claim that more research is needed (Farrer, Brin, Elsas *et al.* 1995; Post, Whitehouse, Binstock *et al.* 1997), even after the results of such research have been published. Over the years, Roses and his allies have produced prospective studies on autopsied (i.e. definite) Alzheimer's populations, giving a basis for both the sensitivity and specificity of APOE differential diagnosis. In a 1996 paper, Roses's group followed 67 patients with 'probable Alzheimer's', 57 of whom were found to have 'real' Alzheimer's upon autopsy. In this study, APOE4 testing had a mediocre sensitivity of 75 per cent (meaning that if diagnosis was just based on E4 status, one would miss 25 per cent of the Alzheimer's patients) and a specificity of 100 per cent, meaning that none of the 10 patients clinically diagnosed with AD, but subsequently found not to qualify after necropsy, carried an E4 allele (Saunders, Hulette, Welsh-Bohmer *et al.* 1996: 91). Working with the Consortium to Establish a Registry for Alzheimer's Disease (CERAD), a network of over twenty specialist centres pooling patients and data, Roses and his colleagues also published the results of a preliminary study on 139 cases in 1997 (Welsh-Bohmer, Gearing, Saunders *et al.* 1997) and 1,833 patients in 1998 (Mayeux *et al.* 1998). This latter paper did not find that APOE genotyping necessarily improved upon the low specificity of clinical diagnostic criteria, but that when APOE4 testing is used 'sequentially' with such criteria (i.e. after patients have already been assessed for AD), this 'significantly improved the specificity of the clinical diagnosis . . . [which] . . . implies that APOE genotyping might be reserved for patients who meet the clinical criteria for Alzheimer's disease' (Mayeux *et al.* 1998: 509).

As suggested below, when opponents come to consider these studies, they tend to either ignore them or to suggest that there is still a need for more data on the sensitivity and specificity of the APOE differential diagnosis. The discursive stagnancy involved in simply calling for further studies is not because no new research has been published into the sensitivity and specificity of the APOE differential diagnosis, but because objections to the clinical use of APOE testing are fundamentally ethical. One of the few papers written in support of the consensus position to address these studies head-on tacitly accepts the role that ethical and other 'non-technical' factors play in deciding whether or not to use a clinical test: 'It is not possible to assign an arbitrary level of clinical validity that makes a diagnostic test useful. Instead, the utility of the resulting information must be evaluated based on whether it changes what is done for the patient' (McConnell, Sanders & Owens 1999: 50). These authors then go on to prove this point by admitting that 'for patients clinically diagnosed with AD, a positive test for an ε4 allele helps to predict with increased confidence the ultimate neuropathological confirmation of AD' but advise against the clinical use of APOE since such 'genotyping presents foreseeable, significant psychosocial consequences for family members that must be weighed against any hypothetical psychosocial benefits associated with a modest increase in diagnostic certainty' (McConnell, Sanders & Owens 1999: 52). Since these authors do not reference any empirical evidence in support of their claim that the negative effects of APOE diagnostic testing outweigh the positive, it is far from clear why the former are described as 'foreseeable' and 'significant', and the latter as only 'hypothetical'.

In addition to the way in which, for those opposed to Roses's network, the technical aspects of the APOE diagnostic test are inextricably linked to ethical issues, another source of resistance can be found in clinicians' tendency to resist any kind of external, non-clinical test, lest it undermine the validity of their clinical judgement:

> Clinically, when I see patients who come to me for a diagnosis, we never use it [APOE testing] . . . I consider my clinical assessment more accurate than the testing. So if I were to do that APOE4 and it's consistent with my clinical impression, voila! If I did the APOE4 and it was inconsistent I would throw the information away! . . . neurologists commonly have to deal with complex information – they have to decide what to keep and what to throw away, so in that case, if there was conflict, I'd throw it away. It wouldn't make any difference.
>
> *(C 1)*

Thus, despite Roses's attempt to enrol clinicians into supporting his position, their tendency to resist challenges to clinical autonomy, and the intertwining of the ethical and the technical when it comes to APOE testing, undermine the construction of the differential diagnostic APOE test as clinically useful. Of course, this does not mean that no clinicians support Roses's position. For those who do not accept the consensus view, their own clinical experience is the touchstone for their attitude towards diagnostic APOE genotyping.

I've already helped people who had reversible causes of Alzheimer's disease when they were referred to me, and I was able to pick them out because they had a simple test that cost virtually nothing, compared to what they'd spent on consultant fees before . . . So, you know, medicine is a little bit more serious, especially when you're dealing with a dementia. If you can do a thyroid test, to see if somebody's hypothyroid, you can certainly do an APOE test to see if they're carrying an APOE2, *not* that they're carrying APOE4.

(CR 12)

In addition to people like clinicians, patients and families, Allen Roses sought support for his idea of clinical usefulness from non-human actors. The most important of these, for my purposes, is pharmacogenetics, or more specifically, the putative link between APOE4 and reduced response to Tacrine. Pharmacogenetics was not an innocent bystander while Allen Roses tried to mobilise support behind clinical APOE testing. Rather, the idea of a link between APOE genotype and response to Tacrine and other anti-Alzheimer's drugs was a crucial element of this network. Even before the Poirier group had published their results, Roses and his colleagues were asking: 'If a drug is said to work in some Alzheimer's disease patients but not others, do either group of patients have a particular apoE genotype?' (Roses, Strittmatter, Periack-Vance *et al.* 1994: 1565). Once the initial Poirier paper had been published, Roses could note: 'If such reports are confirmed, then the use of APOE testing in clinical neurology supersedes its value in differential diagnosis, becoming instead a key adjunct to clinical management' (Roses 1995b: 969; see also Roses 1995a: 13). APOE pharmacogenetic genotyping would be both 'clinically useful' in its own right (Saunders, Hulette, Welsh-Bohmer *et al.* 1996: 93; Roses 1996a: 396) and in turn could 'only strengthen its [APOE testing as a whole] usefulness in clinical practice' (Roses 1997a: 1156). By building APOE pharmacogenetics into his network of clinical usefulness, Roses not only supports the use of clinical APOE testing, he challenges the consensus view that such testing is morally risky:

> APOE genotyping may play a future prominent role in treatment planning. Arguments against the early use of APOE genotyping for diagnostic purposes will need to be reassessed . . . if drugs have significant side effects that limit their general use, it will become standard of care to use APOE genotyping for the diagnostic information necessary for therapy. That circumstance supersedes concerns for usage based solely on genetic implications.
>
> *(Roses 1996b: 54–5)*

Thus, although later discussions of the Tacrine–APOE link and Alzheimer's pharmacogenetics as a whole have tended to ignore the role of APOE in predictive and diagnostic testing, they are closely intertwined. Admiration for

Roses's political skills only increases when one realises that this enrolment of the Tacrine–E4 result does not even need that fact to become accepted. As he suggests, 'Whether or not the efficacy data are accurate for Tacrine (or any other compound) is not the point of this discussion' (Roses 1998a: 53). This is because 'an alternative interpretation of the apparently better therapeutic effects of Tacrine in non-ε4-carrying demented patients might be that the drug works best in those $\varepsilon 3/\varepsilon 3$ and $\varepsilon 2/\varepsilon 3$ patients who do not have AD' (Saunders, Hulette, Welsh-Bohmer *et al.* 1996: 93). Thus, Tacrine's reduced effectiveness on E4 carriers may not be to do with an interaction between the drug and the gene, but because it is not a very good drug for Alzheimer's patients (as opposed to sufferers of other dementias). This allows Roses to enrol the Tacrine–E4 result without committing himself to its veracity as an example of pharmacogenetics.

Systems of resistance

As I have already pointed out, Roses's attempts to build a network around the use of APOE testing for differential diagnosis was not a success. Throughout the time he was mustering his allies, those who disagreed with him were undermining his attempts at heterogeneous engineering by seeking to relink those actors Roses tried to distance from each other (clinicians–researchers, diagnostic–predictive testing), to reclaim groups he sought to enrol (patients and families) and to introduce the actors he sought to exclude (the ethical implications of APOE testing). The tool used to destabilise Roses's network, or rather, prevent it from becoming stable in the first place, is a framework for decision-making called a 'consensus conference'. While consensus conferences have recently come into vogue as a way of allowing the public some sort of say over the governance of science (Guston 1999; Einsiedel & Eastlick 2000; Joss & Bellucci 2002), in US health policy-making circles, they have a longer heritage.

In 1977 the NIH set up a 'Consensus Development Programme' to organise meetings of experts on different topics to 'prevent hasty adoption or even misuse of new technologies, promote the adoption of technologies ready for clinical use, and phase out obsolete drugs, devices, and procedures' (Jacoby 1985: 477; for a history see Mullan & Jacoby 1985 and Ferguson 1996). Although none of the Alzheimer's–APOE consensus conferences were formally part of the NIH series, at least one explicitly states it used NIH methodology (Brodaty, Conneally, Gauthier *et al.* 1995: 182), three were funded by the NIH or one of its institutes (Relkin, Kwon, Tsai & Gandy 1996a & b; Post, Whitehouse, Binstock *et al.* 1997; Ronald and Nancy Reagan Research Institute 1998) and all adopt a similar approach to reaching a consensus, through review of the literature, debate in meetings and circulation of the final report.[9]

Although NIH-supported consensus conferences are influential and (sometimes) high profile, there are considerable reservations over this method as a way of regulating medical practice. At the heart of these problems is the very nature of consensus and its relationship to the scientific enterprise. As one critic puts it, 'most explorations of nature would have been stillborn if the scientists or navigators or climbers had heeded the advice of consensus panels' (Rennie 1981: 666). Even a former head of the NIH's programme admits that 'one of the most frequent criticisms of the program is that minority views are submerged or obscured, contrary to the original concept' (Perry 1987: 487). Interestingly, this is not necessarily the case in the Alzheimer's consensus conferences. Of the three groups of which Allen Roses was a member, two agreed to the use of APOE testing in differential diagnosis[10] and one did not (Post, Whitehouse, Binstock *et al.* 1997: 834–5). Since the possible evidence base for these conferences, in terms of what was published, was substantially the same, it suggests that the different consensuses were at least somewhat dependent on the membership of the meetings. This is reinforced by the knowledge that none of the four remaining groups, which Roses did not belong to, supported the use of APOE-based differential diagnosis. The influence of individual members over the direction a consensus conference takes is not limited to Allen Roses, of course. For example, Peter Whitehouse, a neurologist at Case Western Reserve University, who has written extensively on the ethical issues surrounding APOE4 testing was a member of the Alzheimer's Disease International committee in 1995, an advisor to the 1996 NIA–AA meeting and co-organised the 1997 meeting. Obviously such a prominent critic of clinical APOE testing may well have helped shape the final conclusions of these committees. Even if the consensus groups worked as originally intended, there is still the remaining problem of whether what an individual clinician regards as suitable practice should be overridden by broader community opinion. As Clinician Researcher 12, a

---

[9] The only group that does not obviously adopt this approach is the UK Alzheimer's Disease Genetics Consortium, which met annually for a number of years to discuss these issues. As such it does not fit the model of the one-off consensus conference which produces a report, but rather a series of letters to journals in the field, updating them on the group's opinion (e.g., Tunstall & Lovestone 1999). Since the majority of my interviewees belonged to this group, and since the group's opinions match that of the other, more conventional consensus conferences, it is included.

[10] The Ronald and Nancy Reagan Research Institute of the Alzheimer's Association and the National Institute on Aging Working Group willingly (Ronald and Nancy Reagan Research Institute 1998: 112), the National Institute on Aging/Alzheimer's Association less so (Relkin, Kwon, Tsai & Gandy 1996a: 156, 159).

supporter of Roses's position, puts it, 'if people vote and it's 99 per cent of the people think that you shouldn't use it like that, and I'm part of the 1 per cent, so be it'.

To date, seven different consensus groups have discussed APOE genotyping in the context of Alzheimer's disease, with a consistency of opinion suggested by one interviewee, who states: 'I've been a corresponding member of some of the advisory groups that have reported over the last ten years on APOE testing and whether or not APOE results should be given to people who seek genetic counselling, currently the consensus view is that these results should not be given to patients in whatever context that they present because there's no predictive value' (R 4). In 1995 the reports of two such meetings were published, one from a joint meeting of the American College of Medical Genetics (ACMG) and the American Society of Human Genetics (ASHG) Working Group on Apoe and Alzheimer Disease, and the second from the Medical and Scientific Advisory Committee of Alzheimer's Disease International (ADI), the umbrella organisation of Alzheimer's associations around the world. Like all of the consensus reports, both of these object to the use of APOE testing as a predictive test on asymptomatic populations. In addition, neither of them support the use of such testing for differential diagnosis between dementias. The ACMG–ASHG joint paper suggests that 'The use of APOE genotyping as a diagnostic test may not be as advantageous or cost-effective as has been suggested [ref. to Roses 1995a] . . . until appropriate studies are performed, the exact sensitivity, specificity, and predictive power of APOE epsilon-4 homozygosity are unclear' (Farrer, Brin, Elsas *et al.* 1995: 1628). The ADI statement claims that 'Studies to date suggest that sufficient AD patients have no E4 allele, and sufficient controls carry an E4 allele, to make sensitivity and specificity figures too low to enable E4 to be used as a diagnostic test' (Brodaty, Conneally, Gauthier *et al.* 1995: 184). Clearly the wording suggests that both of these positions could change in the light of new evidence, for example, the results of studies providing sensitivity and specificity figures.

Both of the 1995 consensus groupings were made up of clinicians and researchers, although Allen Roses was not a member of either. He *was* a member of the joint National Institute on Aging–Alzheimer's Association consensus group, which published a brief report of its meeting in the *Lancet* (Relkin, Kwon, Tsai & Gandy 1996b), with a fuller report in the *Annals of the New York Academy of Sciences* (Relkin, Kwon, Tsai & Gandy 1996a). Like all consensus groups and individual professionals, this group rejects the use of APOE genotyping on unaffected populations as a way of identifying risk. Yet unlike the two reports published in 1995, this group was more positive towards genotyping for use in differential diagnosis. Admittedly this issue was, as the full report diplomatically puts it, 'a source of lively debate . . . and is likely to provoke continuing controversy in the future' (Relkin, Kwon, Tsai & Gandy 1996a: 156). At the actual consensus meeting, held in October 1995, 'some participants expressed doubt that this supplemental diagnostic certainty was clinically meaningful given the relatively high diagnostic certainty that can be achieved by traditional methods of evaluation. Others saw little reason for seeking increased diagnostic certainty in the absence of an effective treatment for AD' (ibid.). Interestingly, from the point of view of Roses's construction of practical diagnostic APOE testing, 'Most practising physicians in the working group acknowledge the potential benefits that genotyping could offer' (Relkin, Kwon, Tsai & Gandy 1996a: 159). As a result 'The NIA/AlzA Working Group recommended that physicians consider using APOE genotyping as an adjunct to other diagnostic tests at their own discretion' (Relkin, Kwon, Tsai & Gandy 1996a: 159). Yet the *Lancet* article cautions that 'Any gain in diagnostic accuracy afforded by APOE genotyping in conjunction with other dementia tests must be weighed against the possible adverse effects of disclosing the genotype result' (Relkin, Kwon, Tsai & Gandy 1996b: 1092–3). This clearly links concern about APOE4 diagnostic testing to ethical issues; although the debate is couched in technical terms of sensitivity, specificity and how useful the test might be to clinicians, there is also the underlying theme that APOE genotyping is morally risky. It is only because the group could not reach agreement on diagnostic APOE testing that they devolve responsibility down to the individual clinician.

Exactly the opposite view of internal disagreement was taken by the 1997 consensus group supported by the National Human Genome Research Institute and the National Institutes of Health. The report of this meeting suggested that 'Since experts from our National Study Group cannot agree on the diagnostic utility of APOE genotyping, we must suggest that primary care physicians not yet consider APOE part of the diagnostic evaluation of dementia' (Post, Whitehouse, Binstock *et al.* 1997: 834). Rather than taking significant disagreement between its members as grounds for clinicians making up their own minds, this group made the opposite decision, that disagreement between experts requires more evidence to settle the arguments. Unlike previous consensus statements, the 1997 group had access to published work giving actual figures for the sensitivity and specificity for APOE in differential diagnosis (e.g. Saunders, Hulette, Welsh-Bohmer *et al.* 1996). The group accepts that this research 'suggests reasonable accuracy of diagnosis', but then states that 'The diagnostic applications of APOE testing are currently under debate' (Post, Whitehouse, Binstock *et al.*

1997: 834).[11] This report quotes Thomas Bird's 'cautious' view that there is not enough data to decide whether APOE testing should replace other diagnostic tests. Yet as I have already shown, Bird himself finessed this claim, made in 1995, suggesting that such caution was only needed until further research results gave sensitivity and specificity figures. The availability of such figures is countered with the hope that 'Further empirical studies should clarify the issue' (Post, Whitehouse, Binstock *et al.* 1997: 834), in the same way that the joint statement of the American College of Medical Genetics and the American Society of Human Genetics highlighted the need for 'appropriate studies . . . [on] . . . the exact sensitivity, specificity, and predictive power of APOE epsilon-4 homozygosity' (Farrer, Brin, Elsas *et al.* 1995: 1628), and that opponents of such testing, such as Thomas Bird, suggest that their views may change in the light of further data.

Two very different consensus reports were produced in 1998. The first was from the Ronald and Nancy Reagan Research Institute of the Alzheimer's Association and the National Institute on Aging. This group, of which Allen Roses was a member, addressed a whole range of different biological markers for Alzheimer's. When it came to APOE, this consensus statement simply noted that 'Testing for APOE is appropriate as an adjunct to the suspected clinical diagnosis of AD.' While 'The sensitivity and specificity of the e4 allele alone are low, indicating that this measure cannot be used as the sole diagnostic test for AD . . . when used in sequence with conventional clinical assessments . . . the presence of an e4 allele can add at least 5–10% confidence to the diagnosis of

---

[11] Here they reference Whitehouse and Geldmacher's response to comments on their review
     of the clinical criteria for evaluating dementia (Whitehouse & Geldmacher 1996). Thanking
     Roses and Saunders for new information on figures for testing given in their reply (Roses &
     Saunders 1996), they finish the same sentence by 'retstat[ing] our view that in clinical practice
     asymptomatic persons should not be tested', apparently ignoring that Roses and Saunders's
     data was explicitly *not* about asymptomatic testing (Whitehouse & Geldmacher 1996: 1998).
     Similar kinds of 'talking at cross-purposes' can be found in an exchange between Roses and
     Saunders and Bradley Hyman and Robert Wallace over research by Hyman and colleagues on
     an epidemiological study of a population of elderly patients and APOE levels. Roses and
     Saunders make familiar points concerning the way in which 'apoE genotyping does not allow
     accurate prediction of whether or when an individual will develop Alzheimer's disease' and
     that 'It is misleading . . . to confuse prediction for unimpaired subjects with diagnosis of
     demented patients' (Roses & Saunders 1997: 414 and 415). In their reply, Hyman and Wallace
     review their results, noting that 'These low positive predictive values limit the usefulness of
     apoE ε4 *in detecting or predicting dementia in the general population*' (Hyman & Wallace
     1997: 416, emphasis added). Roses and Saunders would probably agree with this claim, since
     they are interested in the value of E4 testing *not* as a predictive test in the general population,
     but as a diagnostic test in those people who already show symptoms of dementia. Hyman and
     Wallace's concluding line, that 'individuals with apoE ε4 have a good chance of living to old
     age without cognitive impairment' (p. 416) is compatible with Roses and Saunders's point that
     'a demented patient with an ε4/ε4 genotype almost certainly has AD' (p. 415).

AD' (Ronald and Nancy Reagan Research Institute of the Alzheimer's Association and the National Institute on Aging Working Group 1998: 112).

The second consensus report published in 1998 was produced by the Stanford Program in Genomics, Ethics and Society. This group, consisting of a mix of clinicians, scientists and bioethicists, suggests that the use of APOE genotyping in clinical diagnosis

> should not be encouraged. APOE status alone cannot establish a diagnosis. Indeed, a recent study showed that APOE genotyping is useful only when applied to people already diagnosed with probable AD by clinical evaluation [ref. to Mayeux *et al.* 1998]. The presence of an e4 allele in such patients increases confidence in the clinical diagnosis, although absence of an e4 allele does not rule out AD.
>
> *(McConnell, Koenig, Greely & Raffin 1998: 758)*

Of course, the claim that 'APOE status alone cannot establish a diagnosis' is hardly ground-breaking, when even Allen Roses is clear that it should only ever be used as an *adjunct* to clinical diagnosis.[12] This report accepts that, as an adjunct, APOE genotyping does increase diagnostic confidence (albeit by a 'small' amount) but this does not justify 'the burdens of testing' such as revealing information 'ripe for misunderstanding' by family members, and the possibility of 'social costs and psychological burdens' (McConnell, Koenig, Greely & Raffin 1998: 759). In diagnostic APOE genotyping, the benefits do not outweigh the costs.

For those who support the use of APOE4 genotyping in these circumstances, such emphasis on the needs of the family misses the point.

> Oh, I think that's nonsense . . . Do you know the Hippocratic Oath? You don't hurt your patient. If you can do something to help your patient, that's your first responsibility as a physician. Whether or not it has collateral information for other people in the family, can be handled by privacy, it can be handled by education, it can be handled by consultation, and it is very, very rarely a problem when handled with expertise.
>
> *(CR 12)*

In reaction to a draft of this report, Allen Roses sent a number of emails to Henry Greely, the Stanford panel's chair, accusing it of ' "loose analysis" and "misinterpreted data" and "repeating a lie" that physicians are already highly skilled in diagnosing Alzheimer's' (E. Marshall 1998: 1004). Roses's point is that the 'recommendations were not based on relevant data, but on incorrect notions and opinions based on traditional autosomal dominant genetics. They may be expert, but not in Alzheimer's disease' (Roses 1998b).

---

[12] 'We have suggested that APOE is useful as an adjunct in diagnosing cognitively impaired patients, never as a stand-alone diagnostic test' (Roses 1997a: 1155).

As the most recent, formal statement of the consensus, the Ethics Committee of the American Geriatric Society (AGS) classes both APOE genotyping for diagnosis and predictive testing as 'controversial': 'At the present time, the role of genetic testing for the prevention, diagnosis and treatment of late-onset disorders is uncertain . . . physicians should not routinely order genetic tests for late-onset disorders' (AGS Ethics Committee 2001: 225).

In addition to non-specific concerns about the psychological burden of knowing one's APOE status, a central ethical reason for not testing is the insurance implications for patients and their families.[13] A UK-based interviewee commented on the current voluntary moratorium on genetic testing in insurance, noting that 'Although the insurance industry is saying they're not going to be using the results of genetic tests, they might change their mind later on' (CR 1). Insurance issues have always dominated discussions about genetic testing, whether it be health insurance in the US or life insurance in the UK. But genetic testing in Alzheimer's disease raises issues about another kind of insurance altogether; long-term care insurance, where the policy pays for a person's nursing home care. In their discussion of the importance of such insurance in the US context, Binstock and Murray note that 'financing of long-term care for persons with AD through out-of-pocket payments or through government programs is likely to become more and more difficult in the years ahead . . . the use of private insurance care for persons with AD . . . may grow considerably' (Binstock & Murray 1998: 162). These authors conclude that the size of the ageing 'baby boom' cohort is such that there may well be powerful pressure on government to restrict long-term care insurers' access to the results of genetic tests.

In the UK, events have moved beyond speculation about the actions of industry. As Clinician Researcher 3 notes,

> There's a group called the Continuing Care Conference [CCC] which is a body established by the ABI [Association of British Insurers] together with BUPA [a major private health insurer], who are interested in long-term healthcare funding; when you go into a home, that kind of thing. And they looked specifically at APOE and they did a very serious actuarial analysis of the role APOE might play in insurance decisions for long-term care . . . But the actuarial analysis showed there is no role even in the provision of long-term care.
>
> *(CR 3)*

The CCC report certainly comes down against currently using APOE genotyping in setting insurance premiums, although it does note that 'For a small

---

[13] Insurance is mentioned as a concern by a number of the consensus statements: Brodaty, Conneally, Gauthier, *et al.* 1995 (p. 186); Relkin, Kwon, Tsai & Gandy 1996b (p. 160) and 1996b (p. 1093); Post, Whitehouse, Binstock, *et al.* 1997 (p. 835); as well as the AGS Ethics Committee 2001 (p. 226).

percentage of people with Alzheimer's disease, around 2 per cent [i.e. E4 homozygotes], there is a higher long-term care cost, at just over 10 per cent higher than the average for males.' Since 10 per cent is usually the threshold used by insurers to impose greater premiums, increasing rates for these people would be in line with current industry practice, although 'Many insurers are likely to absorb this degree of extra risk within the standard underwriting pool' (Warren 1999). Of course, Allen Roses is not naïve about the socioethical implications of susceptibility gene testing. Indeed he goes so far to suggest that 'consideration of the ethical, social, actuarial, legal and educational aspects of accurate disease prediction on an epidemiological scale must be viewed as a societal emergency' (Roses 1997b: 1229). His point is that we cannot deal with such challenges if we think of genetics in an 'old-fashioned' Mendelian paradigm. His criticism of the Stanford consensus group is that they thought in terms of 'traditional autosomal dominant genetics', when APOE is far more ambiguous and complex.

As already noted, rather than one-off consensus conferences, the UK Alzheimer's Disease Genetics Consortium, 'consisting of clinicians and scientists together with representatives from lay organisations', tended to meet on an annual basis (Lovestone *et al.* 1996: 1775). In a letter on behalf of the consortium, Simon Lovestone and colleagues describe the joint NIA–AlzA consensus statement as 'most helpful', although they do not spell out their own attitudes towards diagnostic testing. Writing later, Simon Lovestone, chair of the consortium, noted that 'The United Kingdom Alzheimer's Disease Genetics Consortium is concerned that the criteria to be expected from an adjunctive diagnostic test have not yet been met and that possible adverse consequences of diagnostic testing, although not as great as those of predictive testing, should not be ignored' (Lovestone 1998). In interview, one UK-based clinician researcher involved in the consortium described the motivations behind it:

> I think we have tackled it. The way we tackled it is that we were very concerned, I suppose about six or seven years ago now, when soon after the gene was found, in I think '94, and so at the time we were very concerned about the effects of APOE in relation to clinical genetic testing so we established a group called the UK Alzheimer's Disease Genetics Consortium, an informal consensus group of representatives from all of the major professional disciplines as well as the lay societies, the genetic interest group and the Alzheimer's society. And we were able to discuss the clinical implication for APOE and we very firmly came down that there was no role whatsoever for testing for diagnosis or prediction.
>
> *(CR 3)*

Clinician Researcher 13 suggests that at the time of interview, the consortium was dormant, since it had been so successful in imposing its consensus on clinical practice: 'we met several years in a row. We've stopped doing it now because we've gone as far as we can, but the view was consistent over a number of years' (CR 13).

Status quo

Back in 1997 Allen Roses, rather over-optimistically suggested that 'Considerable data on the utility of *ApoE* genotyping in AD diagnosis have developed over the past 2 years, essentially making the earlier consensus statements obsolete' (Roses 1997b: 1228). Yet the availability of more data, requested by both the 1995 and 1997 consensus statements, does not seem to have changed the way in which the professional community feels towards diagnostic APOE genotyping in the clinic. Despite the research published by Roses's group in 1996 and 1998, the consensus view is that there is still not enough evidence to support diagnostic APOE genotyping. First the problem was that there were no figures for the specificity and sensitivity of E4 as a diagnostic test. Once these figures were provided, the problem then became that a negative E4 test did not rule out Alzheimer's (whatever a positive E4 result tells you about a person with probable AD). Of course, a consensus does not imply unanimity. There are those clinicians who reject the resistance to APOE-based differential diagnosis.

> If you come to me at the age of 60, and you're having memory problems, and it looks like Alzheimer's Disease, and you have what looks like some mild cerebral atrophy, and you even have some PET scanning that shows decreased glucose utilisation, in – well – overlapping with the areas of Alzheimer's Disease, and you have an APOE2, I'm going to work you up for other things.
>
> *(CR 12)*

In 1998 Roses made another one of these slightly off-target comments regarding the relationship between the general professional consensus and his own ideas: 'The field of AD gives the outward appearance of uncertainty and conflicting messages' (1998a: 59). This does not seem to be the case. Since the mid-1990s the Alzheimer's community has given an outward appearance of certainty and very little conflict with regard to the use of APOE4 testing in the clinic. Genotyping should not be used to predict risk of developing AD (everyone agrees on that), and it should not be used as an adjunct to aid differential diagnosis (almost everyone agrees on that). While one occasionally comes across unusual reinterpretations of the current situation ('there is consensus that ApoE genotyping can be an integral part of the workup to establish the diagnosis of AD' – Paulson 2002: 640), the official position of the professional community, as represented by the American Academy of Neurology for example, is that 'Routine use of APOE genotyping in patients with suspected AD is not recommended at this time' (Knopman *et al.* 2001: 1149).

Professional resistance to the clinical use of APOE testing was kick-started by a commercially marketed diagnostic test, viewed as a surreptitious susceptibility test, which in turn produced a powerful moral reaction from many professionals.

> For a while there was more of a push to do this [i.e. testing], spurred on by the company that was selling the test . . . there was a private company that was marketing to doctors, that they should get this test for the patients. Not only to help the diagnosis, but to use it as a testing for a predictive procedure. I think that's terrible. To give people that kind of information. There's a such a commitment to explain to them exactly what it means. That's a very murky issue.
>
> *(C 1)*

There has never been any apparent crack in the widespread and unified professional belief that the predictive use of APOE4 testing on asymptomatic populations is both scientifically and morally wrong. Although Allen Roses and others have regularly claimed that APOE genotyping can aid diagnosis, and have presented data supporting these claims, the consensus resistance to APOE was never just about the technical details of the test's sensitivity and specificity. Integral to the 'anti-APOE' discourse are broader ethical concerns. Whatever data Roses and his colleagues produced would not address people's worries about the ethical impact of E4 results on patients and families.

However good Allen Roses was at building networks for the production of scientific knowledge – and his work with myotonic dystrophy and APOE suggests that he was indeed skilled – he was not an ideal candidate to marshal allies behind the clinical use of APOE testing. A self-confessed outsider among Alzheimer's researchers, with an abrasive personality, he was proposing a scientific model of Alzheimer's causation in direct competition to the dominant theory. From this position, gaining professional allies for a potentially controversial cause (clinical genetic testing) was very difficult. Drawn up against Roses were a majority of Alzheimer's researchers and clinicians, who managed to translate their weight of numbers into a strategy for destabilising Roses's network. The professional consensus conference is a wonderful technology for erasing dissent. By definition, it is based around agreement, and, although this is resisted by those who drew up the original rules for such meetings, such agreement tends to follow the majority view. There is no space for a minority report.

Conclusion

The 'pre-history' of the APOE–Tacrine link shows how such a pharmacogenetic test cannot be seen in isolation, without its historical and social context. In this light, the APOE–Tacrine result is firmly embedded in professional debates over the use of genetic testing in the clinic. The appearance of the pharmaco-genetic link between APOE4 and Tacrine at the same time as arguments over whether APOE testing should be used in differential diagnosis mean that one cannot separate APOE as a pharmacogenetic test from APOE as a disease sus-ceptibility test. After all, Allen Roses himself tied the two aspects together in his attempts to persuade clinicians to support his position. This obviously has broader implications for pharmacogenetic tests as a whole, requiring that we set such technologies in context before we try and understand resistance to their uptake, and the ethical implications that such tests may entail.

In addition, we can see just how powerful the clinical community can be when it comes to accepting or resisting a new technology. Considerable commercial and scientific support pushed APOE testing towards the clinic, yet clinicians and allied researchers were able to mobilise against the test, isolate it from clinical practice and ensure that policy debates were dominated by their perspective. Without the support of clinicians, it is hard to see how one can move a new technology into the clinic. Chapter 4 follows these themes by showing how the socioethical context around APOE4 has shaped clinician's responses to APOE-based pharmacogenetics, and explores further the basis for clinical resistance to such testing.

4

Clinical resistance to Alzheimer's pharmacogenetics

[I]t's not widely cited because it's an excellent bit of science, but because
it says what a lot of people want to hear, right now.

Researcher 2

At the same time as Allen Roses and his colleagues were trying to convince the research community that APOE4 was implicated in increased risk of
Alzheimer's disease, the pharmaceutical company Warner-Lambert was preparing to launch the first Alzheimer's drug treatment. Tacrine, as the product was
called, is one of a family of compounds called acetyl cholinesterase (AChE)
inhibitors, which delay the breakdown of the neurotransmitter acetylcholine,
thought to have a central role in thought processes and memory function. The
loss of the forebrain cholinergic system is characteristic of AD sufferers' brains;
therefore it was supposed that AChE inhibitors would slow the development of
symptoms of dementia.

These drugs have been around since the mid-nineteenth century, as variously:
glaucoma treatment, insecticides, nerve gas and finally cognition enhancers
(Taylor 1996). But, in a pattern which will be echoed later in this chapter,
Tacrine's development was far from smooth. Initial claims about the drug's
success in reducing the symptoms of AD were met with enthusiasm by other
professionals, patients and family members (Summers *et al.* 1986; Herrman,
Sadavoy & Steingart 1987). Over time however, questions were raised about
the study's validity, with the US Food and Drug Administration (FDA) taking
the unusual step in 1991 of publishing a report in the *New England Journal
of Medicine* which was highly critical of the methods, assumptions and conclusions of the original study (FDA 1991).[1] Despite this, the drug was finally

---

[1] For a discussion of this controversy over Tacrine, see Koenig 1991. The drug continued to be
controversial well into the 1990s: see the debate between Qizilbash *et al.* 1998 and Koepp &
Miles 1999 over the role of industry sponsorship in Tacrine trials.

approved by the FDA in 1993 (Krall, Sramek & Cutler 1999). Problems with Tacrine did not end there, however, when evidence was put forward of risk of liver damage associated with the drug (Watkins *et al*. 1994). As a result, within a month of the FDA approving Tacrine, Kaiser Permanente, a large US Health Maintenance Organisation (HMO), stated that the drug would not be placed on its list of funded products. The HMO felt that Tacrine's limited efficacy did not justify its expense ($1,280 – $1,447 p.a.) or the risk, and cost, of liver toxicity (Pharma Marketletter 1993).

This chapter looks at the possible pharmacogenetic link between APOE4, Tacrine and the second generation of acetyl cholinesterase inhibitors that arrived in Tacrine's wake and which are now standard anti-dementia treatments for Alzheimer's disease (Krall, Sramek & Cutler 1999; Frisoni 2001). As chapter 3 showed, the possibility of a pharmacogenetic link between APOE status and Tacrine was used by Allen Roses in an attempt to generate support for the clinical use of APOE-based differential diagnosis. Yet although, as suggested in chapter 2, the Tacrine–APOE study is one of the most heavily cited examples of pharmacogenetics in the literature, a vital tool for commentators constructing expectations about how this technology might develop in the future, APOE-based pharmacogenetics has not, so far, made it into the clinic. Thus we are faced with an intriguing discrepancy; the example of pharmacogenetics so relied on by commentators is a result which is so disregarded by Alzheimer's professionals that it barely registers as a topic of interest.

Resistance at the coalface

In 1995 'even before the term "pharmacogenomics" was invented' (Aerssens 2002: 71), a research team headed by Judes Poirier at McGill University announced that they had discovered a link between APOE status and response to Tacrine (Poirier *et al*. 1995). One problem with Tacrine was that there was a wide range of response, with up to 50 per cent of patients not improving significantly when treated with the drug (Farlow *et al*. 1992). What the McGill group had done was stratify the response rates from a clinical trial of Tacrine according to APOE status. They found that '>80% of apoE4-negative AD patients showed marked improvement after 30 weeks' whereas '60% of apoE4 patients were unchanged or worse after 30 weeks' (Poirier *et al*. 1995: 12260 and 12263). As a result, APOE E4 status 'may be a useful predictor to clinical outcome of . . . therapies' (Poirier *et al*. 1995: 12264). Without mentioning the word *pharmacogenetics*, the Poirier group had proposed a pharmacogenetic test for Tacrine, based on APOE status.

Targeting APOE made sense for this research team. They had been involved in some of the studies that confirmed Allen Roses's research linking APOE to increased risk of AD, and as one of my interviewees notes, 'APOE accounts for as much as half of the genetic risk for Alzheimer's Disease. And for one gene to have that much impact, from a pharmacogenetic point of view, it's certainly an attractive one' (R 3). Nor were the Poirier group the only ones interested in this area. Seven months prior to publication of this article, in May 1995, a number of papers at the annual conference of the International Psychogeriatrics Association in Paris suggested a link between APOE4 status and response to Tacrine. Two papers from a research group in Bristol presented preliminary results supporting this thesis (Wilcock *et al.* 1995; MacGowan *et al.* 1995). At the same meeting another group, this time based in France, failed to find lower response among E4 carriers, instead suggesting that E4 status predicts a *positive* response to Tacrine (Lucotte, Oddoze & Michel 1995). In the mid-1990s, then, the idea of APOE genotyping for response to Tacrine was a credible position to hold, with a number of different research groups exploring this area.

In 1996, the McGill team[2] repeated the original experiment using 460 patients rather than the forty used in 1995. Their results supported the original paper, with E2 and E3 patients responding best to Tacrine, and E4 carriers responding less well. This effect was most pronounced among women, and these researchers concluded that 'Future trials of cholinergic therapy in AD should include APOE genotyping' (Farlow *et al.* 1996: 108). This research team came to the same conclusion in a 1998 study of 528 subjects: APOE status affects response to Tacrine, this effect is most pronounced in women, and that 'it would be helpful to stratify patients in future drug trials by APOE genotype' (Farlow *et al.* 1998: 676). At the same time, the final results of the studies originally presented in Paris began to suggest that the relationship between APOE4 and Tacrine response was far from straightforward. The Bristol researchers published work concluding that E4 patients tended to respond *better* to Tacrine, as did women, but that the main predictor for response was gender rather than genotype (Macgowan, Wilcock & Scott 1998). Similarly, the French team followed up on their conference abstract with a paper again linking E4 status to *improved* response to Tacrine (Oddoze, Michel, Berthezene *et al.* 1998). Thus, by 1998 there was considerable uncertainty over exactly what the relationship

---

[2] The original 1995 research group was made up equally of researchers from McGill and the Indiana University School of Medicine: the 1996–1998 team was lead by Martin Farlow from Indiana (though Judes Poirier was one of the researchers), and the authors are predominantly from Indiana. In my interviews, this research network is usually referred to as the 'Poirier group' or the 'McGill group'. Therefore I have adopted the same, perhaps inequitable, terminology.

was between APOE status and response to Tacrine. The gene seemed to indicate both better and worse response to the drug.

One of the people involved in this research at the time noted their initially optimistic state of mind:

> We started out with high hopes, and Poirier was doing his work and we simultaneously were doing our own, and we tried a whole range of different markers to try and determine who might respond to Tacrine . . . – not just the genetic ones, but others – and most of them were disappointing . . . So we then moved into looking at genetic markers. APOE alleles seemed an obvious way to go and even then there was controversy. People like us, who had some findings that worked in the same way as Poirier but there was somebody . . . who . . . reported in exactly the opposite direction, and so it was very complicated.
>
> *(CR 13)*

The complexity they discovered was due, at least in part, to the variation in assumptions that underpinned the different research groups' work: 'When we looked into it in detail, we found that the populations of subjects that people were using were different, they had different numbers of females in them, they had different degrees of severity of dementia' (CR 13).

The result of this is that many Alzheimer's specialists give the impression that the original 1995 result has not been replicated: 'Lots of people have done APOE testing in clinical trials, and there's been a couple of trials that have come out with acetyl cholinesterase inhibitors showing that APOE4 status does predict response, but there are plenty of others that have come out not being able to replicate that' (CR 1). Stronger is the position that states 'the finding of APOE in relation to drugs again was found in one or two studies, and has never been replicated, and is almost certainly false' (CR 3). A similar view is expressed by scientists working for industry: 'The APOE4 result has not been replicated. There's no consistency with the results: for every study supporting the link there's one that disputes it' (Company 2&3).[3]

The range of reaction among specialists ranges from this rejection of the result, to less categorical opinions: 'I'm not sure that study's ever been replicated. In fact I don't think it has. I dimly remember reading someone tried to and failed' (CR 5). At the polite end of the spectrum are those like Clinician Researcher 11, who suggests that 'Personally I'm not very convinced by it, there's no particular rationale why it should affect treatment response . . . I'm not steadfast in my view, I'm prepared to be persuaded by further evidence but at the moment I'm not convinced that there are any real associations.' In a

---

[3] Company 2&3 are trained scientists working at the executive level in one of the firms producing second-generation acetyl cholinesterase inhibitors.

similar vein, Researcher 2 suggests that 'one always takes these sorts of studies with a certain amount of caution until there's a clear pattern of replication that's emerged'. It is important to note that my interviewees included those actively trying to test the relationship between APOE4 and Alzheimer's drugs. One researcher had recently done work, part of which had looked at the APOE4 as a pharmacogenetic target: 'We've just done a study which . . . looked at response to treatment rather like Poirier looked at. We found nothing with APOE4' (R 6). For some interviewees, the idea that the Poirier result has not been replicated is not a result of in-depth knowledge of the kinds of evidence presented in different papers. For them, such papers have not even been published: 'It's unpublished and fairly inaccessible data . . . I don't think it's been systematically examined . . . They've not disseminated the results. They've been mentioned in conference proceedings and that kind of thing . . . It's interesting that it hasn't been systematically written up' (CR 9).

At the same time, most of my interviewees were not resistant to the *idea* of pharmacogenetics. As Researcher 5 put it, 'I'm a great fan of pharmacogenetics as a general principle. I think that we will find that the very marked differences between patients and their response to drugs is largely genetically based.' But these clinicians' and researchers' experience of the complex nature of Alzheimer's genetics leads them to the conclusion that any *pharmaco*genetic solution will be equally complex. What would seem to be happening here is a version of Harry Collins's 'experimenter's regress'. Collins suggests that researchers trying to replicate others' results are faced with a problem: 'since experimentation is a matter of skilful practice, it can never be clear whether a second experiment has been done sufficiently well to count as a check on the results of a first. Some further test is needed to test the quality of the experiment – and so forth' (Collins 1985: 2). In the case of APOE4 and Tacrine, it appears that although the Poirier group and the other researchers working in this area in the mid-1990s were ostensibly working on the same topic, the differences between the populations they were looking at, in terms of gender ratios and extent of dementia, means that they could be seen as addressing different research questions. As one of my interviewees mused:

> Maybe they're doing studies in different populations, populations are the big problem I find . . . Those big studies on Rivastigmine, on Donepezil, on Galantamine now, and also the Tacrine studies it would be interesting to look at the populations and see what exactly is or isn't different. I know the international studies for Rivastigmine and Donepezil they are multinational. . . . So there are anomalies in the system there. Maybe that's why we're not getting a clean answer.
> *(CR 4)*

One solution to the experimenter's regress is to have a 'universally agreed criterion of experimental quality' (Collins 1985: 84). The problem with this in the case of Alzheimer's pharmacogenetics is not just that clinicians and researchers have to agree on how significant (in statistical terms) a particular relationship between E4 and Tacrine is. Beyond this, because so many of the researchers involved also have clinical interests, the results of the trial have to be applicable to clinical practice: 'it's an interesting scientific difference [between APOE genotypes] but it isn't any good in the clinic, because it isn't accurate enough to predict who's going to be responsive' (CR 13). 'I suppose that *might* be interesting data for clinicians. It's not getting into our minds really . . . on the street, it's not a major concern of ours' (C 4). And as suggested in chapter 3, such clinical usefulness is not just based on the statistics supporting a particular claim, but on a clinician's view of their social and ethical duty towards an individual patient and their family.

For the majority of Alzheimer's specialists, the failure of these studies to come to the same conclusion indicates that no replication has occurred, and that 'the most parsimonious explanation is that the original finding was a false positive' (CR 3). As I will show, there are a number of political reasons why the majority of AD specialists might want to reject the link between Tacrine and E4. At the same time, supporters of this research could reasonably claim that since these studies had been testing different things, the question of replication still needs to be settled.

By the time the Poirier group and other researchers were beginning to publicise the results of their work, debates over the clinical use of the pharmacogenetic relationship between APOE4 and Tacrine were, in the UK at least, moot. In the spring of 1995 the UK's Committee on the Safety of Medicines (CSM) recommended that Tacrine not be licensed for the UK (Hall 1995; Hunt 1996). Despite being available in the US and elsewhere in Europe, the CSM concluded that the risks associated with liver toxicity were too high: 'Yeah, we wouldn't even be thinking about Tacrine now. We don't prescribe it in this country, well I don't, we don't in here. I think you'd probably find very few people do, across the UK' (CR 7). This of course leaves the question of whether Tacrine is still in use in the US. The impression of one UK-based Clinician Researcher is that 'certainly in the States it's not used anymore. Patients on it have been taken off it' (CR 1). My three US-based interviewees confirmed this view: 'Tacrine is the least used [acetyl cholinesterase inhibitor], and the one that is the least attractive' (CR 6). Supporting this is the view of one recent review of Alzheimer's drugs, which claims that liver toxicity has 'all but removed the agent [Tacrine] from the marketplace', listing its market share at under 1 per cent (Lahiri, Farlow, Greig & Sambamurti 2002).

Second generation

In clinical terms, the refusal of the UK authorities to give Tacrine a licence was no great loss; a second generation of acetyl cholinesterase inhibitors was on its way, and these were regarded as being both more effective and free of the liver toxicity issues that had finally put paid to Tacrine. The first of these new drugs was Donepezil (marketed as 'Aricept'), developed by the Japanese firm Eisai and marketed by Pfizer, which gained US FDA approval in November 1996 and a UK licence in April 1997. This was followed by Rivastigmine ('Exelon'; Novartis) in April 2000 (May 1998 for the EU) and Galantamine ('Reminyl'; Janssen) in early 2001 (December 2000 in the UK).

For most of the specialists I spoke to, the arrival of these new drugs was final proof of the irrelevance of the E4–Tacrine hypothesis. They emphasised that the extensive clinical trials carried out on the second generation of AChE inhibitors would have revealed any underlying link between APOE status and response: 'there was one study with Galantamine . . . and they looked to APOE and said that the response wasn't affected by APOE genotype at all . . . I mean I can't think offhand of studies with Donepezil or Rivastigmine but I'm sure that they must be there' (C 2). Clinician Researcher 8 attributed the decrease in support for the original Poirier result to these later trials: 'subsequent work with Galantamine, there's been no association with E4 in response, so it's [the Poirier result] probably fallen by the wayside a bit'.

Ironically, it was the recommendations of the Poirier group that lead to this position: both the 1996 and the 1998 papers suggested that in the light of the Tacrine results, future trials for Alzheimer drugs should use E4 testing (Farlow *et al.* 1996 & 1998). One of my interviewees admits to encouraging industry in this point of view: 'I was one of the number of people who actually were pushing the companies to do this. We persuaded two of them, and in fact all three companies, in fact there were more than three – not all the drugs actually got through to licensing – but they all did this' (CR 13). Industry people I have spoken to agree there was pressure on them to use E4 testing in their trials: 'In 1995, when the [Tacrine] result came out, everyone said that we had to do APOE genotyping in trials. Most pivotal trials of our drug had already been done. Later, there was a one-year trial where APOE was included, but there was no effect' (Company 2 & Company 3).

The failure of the trials for other AChE inhibitors is seen by at least one of my interviewees as a vindication of the scientific method: 'It's done now, I mean they've kind of shot themselves in the foot slightly because they recommended it. It was done, and it's disproved their hypothesis. Good science really' (CR 3). The power of these trials lies in the sheer numbers of participants they involved.

Interviewees emphasised the size of the databases these trials used, and hence the strength of their conclusions: 'the big databases on Rivastigmine and Donepezil have not borne that out and their databases will be bigger' (CR 4). For example, the coalition of researchers who tested Galantamine (the Galantamine-1 International Study Group) tested over 650 patients based in eighty-six clinics across Europe and Canada (Wilcock *et al.* 2000). The so-called 'Nordic' study on Donepezil, which found no link between APOE genotype and drug response, used over 280 participants (Winblad *et al.* 2001). But, and this is a point I will return to later in this chapter, while the initial studies on the Tacrine–E4 hypothesis were small-scale, work such as Farlow and colleagues' 1996 or 1998 papers used over 400 and 500 patients respectively. If the size of a trial is the deciding factor for Alzheimer specialists, then they should have been convinced of the Poirier group's results in the late 1990s. Yet it was the *original* studies that set the tone for Alzheimer's professionals' reaction to the Tacrine–E4 hypothesis:

> The sample size of those original studies is relatively small, in the order of 100, 150 or so . . . It's subject to multiple testing; they're often divided into responders, non-responders, APOE4 carriers, non-carriers, and then subdivided again into gender. If you look carefully I think you'll find that none of the studies have appropriate controls for multiple testing. And if you do those kinds of association studies, you know that they are extremely vulnerable to false positives.
>
> *(CR 3)*

Of course negative results on other drugs do not in themselves *necessarily* undermine the original Tacrine result. One does not have to espouse the experimenter's regress, to see that

> What you could be getting into is 'horses for courses' of course [i.e. different effects with different drugs]. So Tacrine is a different molecule although it's an AChE inhibitor. Why should there be any difference in responders to Tacrine compared to the other two? But there could be, and part of that picture could be the gene profile of an individual in terms of how the molecule will fit in.
>
> *(CR 4)*

Yet despite professional scepticism about the Tacrine–E4 hypothesis, the practice of clinical trials for Alzheimer's drugs has changed in the light of the original Poirier paper. As a result, several other drugs have been mentioned as having putative pharmacogenetic stratification according to APOE status: Xanomeline, reduced efficacy with E4/4 (Poirier 1999 a & b); and S12024 (Richard *et al.* 1997), Citicoline (Álvarez *et al.* 1999) and Deprenyl all showing improved efficacy with E4 (Riekkinen *et al.* 1998). It may be significant that none of these drugs is currently licensed for the treatment of Alzheimer's, nor are they undergoing current clinical trials. Xanomeline, for example, an Eli Lilly product, has been withdrawn from clinical trials (Pharma Marketletter 1999), and S12024 was withdrawn from Phase II trials due to toxicity (Cacabelos *et al.* 2000).

Yet the limited support the Tacrine–E4 hypothesis has received from Alzheimer's professionals has not stopped either Judes Poirier or other researchers from linking E4 carriers to a lower response to Tacrine. In 1999 Poirier published a couple of review articles, the titles of which leave the reader in no doubt as to where he stands concerning the importance of APOE4 as a pharmacogenetic target: 'Apolipoprotein E4, cholinergic integrity and the pharmacogenetics of Alzheimer's disease' (1999a); and 'Apolipoprotein E: a pharmacogenetic target for the treatment of Alzheimer's disease' (1999b). In each of these papers he reviews both his own work on Tacrine and Xanomeline, as well as others' results which conform to the hypothesis. Since then, a number of papers have been published, either supporting the Tacrine–E4 hypothesis (Sjögren *et al.* 2001; Almkvist *et al.* 2001), rejecting it (Rigaud *et al.* 2000), or linking E4 to better (Oddoze, Michel & Lucotte 2000) or worse response to Donepezil (Borroni *et al.* 2002).

Poirier's most recent comments on the pharmacogenetics of Alzheimer's disease come in an edited collection published in 2002. Here he restates the original Tacrine–E4 results from 1995, and reviews the work of others, such as Oddoze and colleagues, and the Bristol group, which overlap with his own. He reanalyses the data from the Galantamine-1 IPA study group, who concluded that 'Galantamine was effective regardless of patients' apolipoprotein E genotype' (Wilcock *et al.* 2000), suggesting that E4 homozygotes displayed the greatest improvement compared with non-E4 carriers (Schappert, Sevigny & Poirier 2002).

Sources of resistance

As previous work on scientific controversies would lead us to expect, the debate over the relationship between APOE4 and response to Tacrine and other anti-Alzheimer's drugs cannot be settled by the publication of a single research paper. Complaints about the small sample size used for the original 1995 result can be countered by later studies which use far more participants. The arrival of second-generation AChE inhibitors, with their apparent non-link to E4, can be countered by reference to the differences between Tacrine and other drugs, the publication of other studies implicating E4 in varying response to, say, Donepezil, and the reinterpretation of studies such as that of Wilcock and colleagues (2000), to highlight the variations caused by genotype.

Yet in the face of this, specialists in Alzheimer's disease have largely turned their backs on the idea of response to Tacrine and other AChE inhibitors depending on APOE genotype: reviews of the clinical use of Tacrine or the other AChE inhibitors make no mention of APOE genotyping (Frisoni 2001) or actively suggest that it has no clinical value as a predictor of response to these drugs (Siest *et al.* 2000; Cummings 2003; Lanctôt, Hermann & LouLou 2003); a review of drug targets for Alzheimer's disease, co-authored by Martin Farlow (lead author on the 1996–1998 Tacrine supporting papers) claims that 'Currently, there is no known way to predict whether one will benefit from these drugs [AChE Inhibitors]' (Lahiri, Farlow, Greig & Sambamurti 2002: 273). Another author sums up the clinical position when he states: 'The APOE4 allele was once suggested as a marker of poor response, but subsequent studies suggested no correlation' (Bullock 2002: 135).

Like so much sociology of science, the focus here is not on those things that unite Alzheimer's specialists, but on those things that divide one group (Poirier and other supporters of the Tacrine–E4 link) from another (the vast majority of professionals). As I have already shown, the scientific tension between supporters of APOE research and more mainstream 'amyloiders' is still present in professional circles. One consequence of this is that despite Poirier and his colleagues sketching out plausible 'routes' for how APOE alleles interact with the cholinergic system and hence AChE inhibitors (Poirier 1999 a & b), it is still legitimate for others to suggest that such a link 'doesn't quite make sense from a biological point of view from what we know about APOE' (CR 3). But beyond this, for the clinicians and researchers I interviewed, resistance to the Tacrine–E4 hypothesis is not just based on a lack of supportive clinical trial data or unclear biochemical pathways. There are at least two 'non-technical' sources for this resistance. The first is the limited clinical usefulness of the kind presented in Poirier and colleagues' 1995 publication:

> I think probably the reason why you don't see any anything coming through is that . . . clinicians tend to take their judgement as being the most reliable indicator. With pharmacogenetics being a relatively new subject, the impact of anything that's going to be more reliable [than a clinician's judgement] simply hasn't got down to the clinician just yet.
>
> *(R 6)*

To be more specific: 'it's an interesting, scientific difference but it isn't any good in the clinic' (CR 13). Clinicians' interest in a pharmacogenetic test is going to depend to some extent on the level of discrimination it provides between different groups.

The second source of resistance to the Tacrine–E4 hypothesis is APOE4 itself. Chapter 3 has shown how a consensus has arisen among Alzheimer professionals that restricts APOE testing to the research setting and prevents such genotyping from making its way into the clinic. It also showed the different ways in which this consensus is 'policed' by the clinical and research community, through networks of collaboration, publications and contributions to policy debates. In this context, where the use of APOE testing in the Alzheimer's clinic is seen as dangerous for patients and their families, it is hard to see how the community of Alzheimer's specialists could have reacted differently. Researcher 6, who has significant contact with his/her clinical colleagues suggests that 'the same sort of reservations that have been applied to disease risk are now being applied to any purely pharmacogenetic application of APOE in that, rightly or wrongly, people are saying, "well, it wasn't much good for specifying disease risk, therefore why should it be any good for specifying responses to treatment?"' In essence, APOE is still embedded in the ethical debates over prognosis and differential diagnosis. And as such, this restricts its pharmacogenetic use. Clinical resistance to Alzheimer's pharmacogenetics derives from what are seen as a number of technical and scientific issues. But, as the rest of this chapter explores in more detail, underpinning these are ethical concerns about access to treatment and control of genetic information. As Researcher 1 put it, 'the biggest ethical issue, if you're going to test people for APOE4, they're going to know the APOE status, and no genetic testing, in our view, should be done without genetic counselling alongside it'. Just as in chapter 3 it was shown how separating diagnostic APOE testing from the ethical issues raised by predictive genotyping is far easier said than done, it is not clear how easy it would be to present an APOE test as being purely about pharmacogenetics. This 'overlap' between the ethical issues associated with the predictive/diagnostic test and the pharmacogenetic test is clearly spelt out by Researcher 3:

> The box that's being opened is the ramifications, not for the patient, who's already demented, because you're talking about treatment . . . The potential ramifications are because the nature, because this is a genetic molecule, is inadvertently predicting among relatives of this individual, this patient, their APOE genotype. And that's regardless of whether it's used in pharmacogenetic testing or as a diagnostic marker. If this information becomes known to others in the family, then you are entering this realm of putting information out there that may need some further thought.

The dilemma facing clinicians was neatly demonstrated by Clinician Researcher 4, who presented the following scenario.

> Supposing you know that lack of APOE4 predicts response, if you do this, and depending on what age group, etc., you do their APOE4 and you find out they're 3/4 or 2/4 or 4/4:
>
> 'Right, sorry you're not getting treatment.'
> 'Well why am I not getting treatment?'

'Because of your genotype, that doesn't respond.'
'Well what is that genotype?'
'OK, so it's 4/4.'
'What does that genotype mean then?'

You won't get this from the patients sometimes when it's Alzheimer's, you get it from the family:

'What does that mean then?'
'OK, APOE4 is associated with a worse vascular outlook and, really, worse prognosis in AD, I think, maybe that's been shown or been suggested.'

Even if you don't tell them, if they know the genotype, the family will be away [mimes typing at computer], downloading from whatever site. And we see that and you can't blame them for that.

As Clinician Researcher 7 succinctly puts it, 'that's the problem with the E4, it's not just a pharmacogenetic tool, it's also a risk factor for the disease'. And in a clinical culture where the use of such risk factors is resisted, it should come as no surprise that clinicians reject APOE-based pharmacogenetics. Perhaps the ethical problems are less than in the case of predictive testing, since the patient is already assumed to have Alzheimer's, but this does not reduce clinicians' concern for patients' families: 'The problem is you test patient X and you find he's E4/E4, well then you immediately know that all his children are carrying an E4 allele. So you immediately know they've all got a four times increased risk of getting AD. Do you actually have to provide genetic counselling for those individuals?' (CR 1).

The most obvious ethical problem with APOE pharmacogenetics – that an APOE test for drug response is still an APOE test – is singularly underdiscussed in the pharmacogenetic literature. Firstly, those papers that cite Poirier's original result rarely, if ever, acknowledge that this particular pharmacogenetic test carries broader ethical issues with it. Even those commentators who discuss the potential ethical problems surrounding pharmacogenetics (e.g. Anderson, Fitzgerald & Manasco 1999; Chamberlain & Joubert 2001; Roden & George 2001; Akhtar 2002) or those who admit that APOE4 is also a risk factor for late onset AD (e.g. Lau & Sakul 2000; Maitland, Boer & Leufkens 2000; Vesell 2000), neglect to explore the specific problems raised by APOE as an 'overlapping' pharmacogenetic/predictive test. An honourable exception to this is Patrice Rioux, who notes in his section on ethics, that 'a person's apoliopoprotein E genotype could have an impact on drug treatment by acetylcholinesterase inhibitors but also seems to be a risk factor for early onset of Alzheimer's disease' (Rioux 2000: 896). Of course the difference between commentators and specialists in attitudes towards the *ethics* of APOE pharmacogenetics mirrors the differences in attitudes towards the *scientific* status of the Poirier result, since the specialists' scientific position is constituted in part by these kinds of ethical concerns. Some discussion of pharmacogenetics by ethicists has tended to pick up on this possible overlap between pharmaco- and disease genetic testing (Robertson 2001; Buchanan *et al.* 2002; Lipton 2003), though there is little in-depth analysis of the issues involved. An exception to this is Issa and Keyserlingk's work (2000), which emphasises the problems raised for pharmacogenetic research in Alzheimer's disease. Whether, as these authors suggest, these problems are 'unique ethical quandaries' (p. 918) to the pharmacogenetics of AD, is something that will be drawn out at the end of this chapter.

To understand the failure of scientific commentators to get to grips with the ethical problems raised by the APOE–Tacrine link, one needs to note that there is broader discourse within the literature, which suggests that pharmacogenetics needs to be seen as ethically distinct from more traditional disease gene ethics. While not all commentators take this position, those that adopt the 'ADR vision' of pharmacogenetics tend to stress that it is 'important to make a clear distinction between the ethical implications of testing for disease predisposition . . . and those surrounding tests whose goal is simply to predict the effectiveness of therapies for existing conditions' (Pfost, Boyce-Jacino & Grant 2000: 337). Such claims tend to be made by senior industry figures, such as Sir Richard Sykes, then chairman of GlaxoSmithKline: 'Pharmacogenetics applications will only measure how a patient will respond to a medicine. Thus they are quite distinct from those [genetic] tests considered over the past two decades' (Sykes 1999). Perhaps unsurprisingly, Allen Roses also enters in to this debate, in his role as vice-president for Genomics for the same company: 'Clear language and differentiation of respective ethical, legal and societal issues are required to prevent inaccurate vernacular usage creating a confused public perception of "genetic testing"' (Roses 2000a: 1361). Obviously in terms of an approach focused on the ADRs, where pharmacogenetics is distanced from disease mechanism, ethics is just another area where lines need to be drawn. But of course it is also important that if the ethical issues surrounding pharmacogenetics are seen as less threatening that those involving 'normal' genetic testing, then the regulatory burden on those developing and using pharmacogenetic tests may also be quite different. And this is a viewpoint that has already been tacitly accepted by at least some regulators. The European Medical Evaluation Agency (EMEA) suggests that 'It is important to distinguish between genetic testing for the diagnosis or prognosis of disease and the form of genetic testing performed for pharmacogenetics . . . [which] . . . generally carries a different magnitude of social, legal and ethical considerations for the patient' (EMEA 2001). The Consortium on Pharmacogenetics suggests that 'It would be a mistake to require an informed consent process for PGx [i.e. pharmacogenetic] tests modelled on what is appropriate for genetic testing for serious, untreatable genetic disorders such as Huntington's disease, for susceptibility to serious disease such as breast cancer or colon cancer' (Buchanan *et al.* 2002: 28). Yet these same authors are happy to suggest that while 'other clinical facts' (such as a patient's condition and the accuracy of the test) have to be taken into account 'to determine whether or not use of a particular drug is wise, as now occurs with the use of Tacrine for Alzheimer's patients with the APOε4 allele', the role of APOE4 as a risk factor for AD is apparently not relevant (Robertson *et al.* 2002: 161).

Clearly such a position does not hold in the case of APOE-based pharmacogenetics. One of the reasons why such testing has not made it into clinical practice is because, in this case, we *cannot* distinguish between 'genetic testing for the diagnosis or prognosis of disease and the form of genetic testing performed for pharmacogenetics'. While APOE testing for Tacrine or other acetyl-cholinesterase inhibitors may not be an issue, it is quite possible that a newer Alzheimer's drug may well vary in response rates due to APOE status, if only because APOE genotyping is so prevalent in Alzheimer's clinical trials (see chapter 5). It is peculiar that the obvious (to clinicians at least) ethical issues raised by one of the most heavily cited examples of pharmacogenetics barely get a mention by supporters of this technology, and are apparently hardly on the horizon for regulatory agencies in this area.

Distrust in numbers

As already suggested, the other major theme in my interviewees' ethical concerns about Alzheimer's pharmacogenetics revolves around the strength of the association between a gene and response to a drug; in essence, how good are the numbers? The original Poirier paper from 1995 suggested that 80 per cent of non-E4 carriers responded to Tacrine, while 40 per cent of E4 carriers did so. A common response from my interviewees to this was: 'Using the numbers you cited, if it were your father, and you saw those numbers? . . . Shall we try it? Of course you would try it. There's no other options' (C 1), or 'Let me turn it round the other way; how would you treat your mother if she had the unfavourable genotype?' (CR 5). For these professionals, 40 per cent is not strong enough to rule out treatment. Clinician 3 points out that

> I'd have thought that if I got a 40 per cent response in my kind of field, that would be good. You're saying to me, think of that as a threshold, no, I'd still be using it, I'd still be going clinically and still be prescribing it and looking for a clinical effect because when you've moved with Alzheimer's disease from no treatment whatsoever to get, say, a 40 per cent response, it would be pretty good . . . and I guess that's the classic history of doctors and prescribing, we'll give it every chance, which isn't tied in with the statistics necessarily.

One obvious question would be, how high do the numbers have to get for clinicians to accept the use of pharmacogenetics to rule out treatment? For some, numbers in the high nineties would be acceptable: 'if you're going to have something you have to have it up in the mid to high nineties in terms of your sensitivity of your test if it's going to be helpful' (CR 1), a point accepted by Clinician Researcher 11:

> In terms of predictors of response to drugs, obviously if you had a really good predictor, that would be excellent, it would help you to target therapies but I think there's also a counterside that would worry me, which is that if it's used as a way of rationing drugs, particularly if it wasn't an extremely good predictor, so if you had something which was a 99.5 per cent accurate predictor, then great but if you've got something which may be 70 per cent for people with the characteristic response, and 30 per cent of people who don't, then you still have some people without that characteristic who respond, so it seems unethical to withhold it on that basis.

Thus a consistent theme for my interviewees was a reluctance to rule out treatment on the grounds of numbers. How much of this is due to the nature of Alzheimer's disease is not clear. As Clinician Researcher 5 puts it, 'Well, the Alzheimer's diseases are relentlessly progressive. If you don't do nothing, nothing will happen. It'll go on getting worse. Even if there was a 20 per cent, a 10 per cent chance of someone going to get a benefit, well if you were that individual, or closely related to that individual, you'd probably take your chance.' While supporters of pharmacogenetics might point to the numbers involved to make their case, in many ways clinicians view statistics as being on their side: 'if someone shows signs of dementia, you give the drugs anyway; a clinician is not going to deny drugs on the basis of such a test. Statistically there is always a chance that it will work' (CR 2). Any individual patient could respond, even if they are a E4 homozygote. This ties into current clinical practice, emphasising the point that an assessment of pharmacogenetics can only take place in the light of the way clinicians currently make decisions about treatment.

> So if you're 20 per cent less likely to respond to a drug, are you going to be refused it because of your genome? That seems to me to be wrong in principle and in practice because we already know there are people who are 20 per cent less likely to respond to all sorts of things, but we always give the hope that they might. So at what point does it become clinically acceptable not to give a drug to somebody who is marginally less likely or even significantly less likely to respond?
>
> *(CR 3)*

This theme, that pharmacogenetics needs to be seen in the context of other treatments, and not regarded as somehow 'special', crops up in the second half of this book in the debates around Herceptin. The danger is that descriptions of pharmacogenetics as a revolutionary approach to healthcare, as seen in the launch of the UK's Genetics White Paper, for example, will obscure the problems that arise when such technologies arise in the clinic, the problems of ordinary technologies. The language of revolution and novelty needs to be seen in the context of clinical practice, the particular disease being treated and the nature of the genetic test. To abstract APOE testing from its scientific, historical and ethical position in the debates of the mid to late 1990s is to pretend that somehow pharmacogenetics appears out of nowhere, free from the cultural and moral baggage associated with other forms of genetic testing.

The nature of the drugs involved in Alzheimer's disease is also part of the story when it comes to clinicians' resistance to APOE-based pharmacogenetics:

> would you really want to do APOE testing if number one, the benefit of the drug is fairly small to begin with and the side effects of the drug are fairly minimal, and if the difference between the responders and non-responders is not black and white; you know some people in the APOE negative groups don't respond and some in the positive do respond, then how cleanly does the APOE distinguish the groups for a drug that is not that expensive when compared with all the other things we do, and quite benign to try. Usually you can tell if the drug is working in a few months.
>
> *(CR 6)*

Variable response rates to acetyl cholinesterase inhibitors are nothing new to these clinicians; as a result they have ways of dealing with such variation, mainly by treating everyone with the drug, and withdrawing those who, after a period of time, do not seem to be responding. Since acetyl cholinesterase inhibitors are currently the only treatment available for AD, clinicians are reluctant to deny them to patients. If pharmacogenetics lead to a choice *between* treatments (rather than between treatment and non-treatment), then it is quite possible that clinical resistance would drop: 'Now, if it turns out, at some point in time, you could say that based on this profile, either Drug A will have a 90 per cent chance of helping or drug B – there's a double dissociation if you will. Then it's valuable' (C 1).

As the next chapter will show, industry may well be very reluctant to allow retrospective pharmacogenetic tests that rule out groups of patients on the grounds of efficacy. Clinicians have a similar point of view, though of course the motivation is quite different:

> The trouble is . . . it's too late; these are treatments which have already been developed and have not been pharmacogenetically worked up. So it's a sort of *post hoc* analysis if you like and as such, I think pharmacogenetics is going to have a limited use. So, you've already got a treatment out there which works in a particular way, trying to work out the pharmacogenetics of that is going to be difficult.
>
> *(CR 7)*

'Working out' the pharmacogenetic link may not be as much of a problem as getting clinicians to accept that they should deny patients a treatment on the basis of a statistical test. While personalised medicine may be about targeting drugs at some people, these clinicians suggest that there is another side to it: 'My concern is that drug targeting, the opposite side of the same coin is drug denying. I'm concerned even by the concept of denying the drug to somebody based on a percentage response . . . I think that the win/win situation is not a win/win situation for those people who don't get a drug because they're rather less likely to respond' (CR 3).

At least one of the genetic researchers I interviewed experienced a degree of frustration with his/her clinical colleagues. When talking about a link between AChE inhibitors and another gene, butyrylcholinesterase K (BCHEK) Researcher 6 suggested that

> speaking to the clinicians, their idea was, 'What's the point of using pharmacogenetics in the clinic because we're going to give this to the patients anyway, we will give them the cholinesterase inhibitors anyway because they just might respond'. Even with some very clear-cut results that we have, which were based on a double-blind placebo controlled trial, and applying pharmacogenetics to that, we still can't convince the clinicians to take up genetic testing.

In this case the gene concerned does not have the ethical 'baggage' that plays such an important role in clinicians' response to APOE, yet they are still unwilling to adopt pharmacogenetics. Researcher 5, who has carried out similar research, suggests that

> An example of that is the gene that we found associated with Alzheimer's, which is butyrylcholinesterase K variant, and we've just published a meta-analysis which shows that the vulnerable subset, the relevant subset, is actually quite small; it's male APOE4 carriers greater than 75 years – those people are highly vulnerable so there's great significance for both prevention and therapy in the long run even though it's a small subset.

And as already suggested, BCHEK status is not just related to increased risk of Alzheimer's disease, since it 'was shown to be a predictor of response to the drug, S12024, that work, however, has never been published'. As a result, 'I think that we're going to discover that it's much more complicated and one has to take into account interactions such as the interaction between APOE4 and BCHEK. I'm sure people will find ways of predicting drug response better by looking at people's genes' (R 5).

The debates around, and clinical resistance to, APOE-based pharmaco-genetics looks less like a one-off aberration and more like a regular feature of Alzheimer's treatment. Whether this case tells us anything about possible reactions to pharmacogenetics in broader medicine, in other clinical speciali-ties, is not clear. In conditions where there are more treatment options, where the 'double dissociation' mentioned by Clinician 1 would come into play (i.e. choosing between treatments, rather than whether to treat or not), then perhaps clinical resistance would be much less of an issue. What does hold true for all clinical specialties, of course, is that while decisions about treatment are made by clinicians, they function within a framework of rules and regulations, which may conflict, or at the least shape, the kinds of clinical decisions available.

> I could also see that if there were definitive tests that would predict response on a genetic basis, you would get a pressure on from above, at health authority and government level, to focus prescribing. That would work and it might be easier for clinicians to work with that one, if it was categorically there: 'Here's your test.' Because we're trained that way – 'Here's the test, here's the treatment. It will work in these people and you don't give it to the other people.' So there would be advantages in that. At a practical level. Having said that you're still going to have to screen the patients, make a diagnosis of probable AD and then you're going to have to do the genotyping for response to treatment. So it won't eliminate the workload. But it will eliminate that final process of the decision-making bit. My view of it always was that the authorities would be quite happy with it [pharmacogenetics].
>
> *(CR 4)*

In this excerpt, Clinician Researcher 4 highlights how larger structures can define policy in such a way as to remove the element of choice from clinicians. While they may resist such top-down interference in their clinical judgement, it is not clear what clinicians could do to prevent such policies being implemented. Clinician 3 claims that she/he 'wouldn't feel comfortable with it', but also questions whether

> would I still, nevertheless, collude with it, would it become practice in five to ten years? I'm trying to think of examples where, do I unconsciously do that already? It's interesting, it's not a good analogy but because it popped into my head, I'm just going to say that looking for eligibility for the anti-Alzheimer's meds now, I'll do scanning in order to exclude strokes so you could say I'm screening out by another method there. I feel quite comfortable with that. Is it the usual hypocrisy?

Because acetyl cholinesterase inhibitors are currently only approved for use on Alzheimer's patients, clinicians have to get a clear diagnosis of AD before they can prescribe these drugs, even though there is growing evidence that they are also extremely effective on other kinds of dementia. The issues raised by the prescribing rules for AChE inhibitors neatly illustrates the way such regulations impact on clinical practice:

when I used to see people let's say five years ago at the community, first contact, mild early dementia, I would say 'it's mild early dementia, probably Alzheimer's disease', tell the family, communicate the prognosis, which is untreatable, downhill and all that stuff, say 'you'll need social services at some point' and walk away, almost. *Now* a person with 'mild dementia, probably Alzheimer's disease', is a candidate for drugs. I may need to do a fairly comprehensive assessment and, of course, they'll be on my books for years potentially, so it's having huge resource implications that we haven't addressed yet . . . Yes, and also medical monitoring because NICE says we've got to keep an eye on them and we've got to initiate the prescribing and all that, so as opposed to doing a one-off 'raid', saying this is the diagnosis, this is what's going to happen, goodbye, or maybe I'll see you in three years' time when there's a major physically deteriorated, grossly demented person, I've now got to review them on a regular basis . . . and it's changing our lives.

(C 3)

Claims about the impact of these drugs on clinical practice are supported by Clinician 4, who states that 'Things have changed because of the anti-dementia drugs, but now everybody who comes with dementia is fairly fully assessed, which includes blood tests and scans, etc., and physical tests . . . if somebody gets referred with dementia, we go through this whole process.' As the second half of this book will show, the formal structures and regulations surrounding a technology shape to a large extent the options open to clinicians and, in turn, what we can consider ethical clinical practice.

At the same time, my interviewees acknowledge the reality of current medical systems and policy and the impact that has on clinical practice.

If on the other hand you were commissioning services and you were trying to accommodate need on the basis of a limited budget, as everyone, you probably would be persuaded to have the pharmacogenomics, genetics influencing policy decisions in terms of population stratification and the decision to treat certain populations, and that needn't necessarily be congruent with the wishes and needs of the individual, or people closely related to that individual . . . Statistics is a population – it ain't me, necessarily.

(CR 5)

Or as another interviewee put it:

A lot of what pharmacogenetics is is really just pharmacoeconomics. It's really a matter of can you deliver healthcare to a select group because you don't want to try it on everybody for reasons of expense. That's not the only reason of course, you also don't want to hurt people, but pharmacoeconomics plays into the story, no doubt about it. You really need to be able to get the balance sheet right.

(CR 6)

In short, from a clinician's or a researcher's point of view, 'We're looking for indicators for success, I think Policy's looking for indicators not to give and the level of evidence and the effort that goes behind it is proportional to which side of the fence you're coming from' (CR 8). This perspective on 'Policy' should be tempered with the knowledge that when the National Institute for Clinical Excellence (NICE), about which much more can be found in chapter 7, set out its rules for the use of AChE inhibitors in the NHS, it noted that 'not everyone treated appears to benefit [from the drugs] and no analysis has been presented which would allow patients who will benefit the most to be identified before treatment is commenced' (NICE 2001: 4). Although NICE relies on industry to provide much of its information, it is the sort of organisation that would readily adopt a pharmacogenetic approach if it thought that the evidence was strong enough.

In the light of this deep-rooted resistance to APOE-based testing among Alzheimer's professionals, where does this leave the broader issue of pharmacogenetics and personalised medicine for this condition? Researcher 6 suggests that

> this idea of personalised medicine whereby you're going to treat each individual patient is going to become a reality but it's not going to be a reality based on genetics. It's going to be the clinician with experience saying, 'Well, normally when I get an 85-year-old with Alzheimer's Disease in front of me, and I know that their MRI's telling me there's a bit of vascular pathology, they'll do best with [drugs] x and y whereas if I'm presented with a 70-year-old who doesn't have this vascular pathology, I'll give them the cholinesterase inhibitor because this is the group that does best on them.' But [this will] not [be] based on anything like he carries gene x, y and z . . . it's going to be more clinical experience than anything else.

This muted endorsement of pharmacogenetics is from a geneticist who would 'love it to be the other way round, since we could genotype to our heart's content and say, "Well, there you go, I think you should treat them with x, y and z." I think however it's going to be down to clinical experience. Realistically, unless there is *really* a quantum change in how clinicians see genetics' (R 6).

Conclusion

What is clear from this chapter is that those people who are most likely to use APOE as a pharmacogenetic test in the clinic are also most dismissive of this result, regarding it as scientifically and ethically dubious. Thus, clinical resistance to this technology lies not just in the perceived scientific flaws of the original research, but crucially in the ethical and social problems that APOE-based pharmacogenetics would introduce into clinical practice. As chapter 3 showed, clinical resistance to a new technology can play a vital role in preventing it from moving into the clinic. While, as I will show, industry also has a role to play in the failure of Alzheimer's pharmacogenetics to become a clinical reality, the core problem for those seeking to encourage the use of pharmacogenetic testing is the need to gain the support of those who would use the technology.

This clinical resistance is all the more surprising when we consider the picture painted of the APOE–Tacrine result in the reviews and commentaries that cite Poirier and colleagues' original 1995 paper. In chapter 2 I showed how central this result is to many people's claims about the applicability of pharmacogenetics to common disease and even its value as an example of personalised medicine in current clinical practice. In addition, almost all commentators demonstrate some sort of 'blind spot' when it comes to the high-profile, widely recognised ethical difficulties associated with APOE4; for most of those writing about pharmacogenetics, these issues do not seem to exist. This reinforces the idea that the construction of expectations uses references in a way quite alien to the traditional view of scientific citation. In essence, the Poirier result becomes a political marker, 'a paper which may not itself be read carefully . . . but which can serve a political purpose by being spoken *about*' (Collins 1999: 187).

Clearly, pharmacogenetics can overlap with disease genetics, and this overlap can itself form an important source to resistance to pharmacogenetic testing. While the extent of overlap between disease gene and pharmacogenetic testing in Alzheimer's disease is unusual, this is not the only case where this happens. Another frequently cited example of pharmacogenetics, that of reactions to the heart drug Prevastatin varying according to alleles of the CETP gene, has a similar pattern. In this case, the allele associated with best response to the drug is also linked to increased disease risk (Kuivenhoven *et al.* 1998). At the moment, too little is known about the future of possible SNP profiles to categorically say that such overlaps are a rare subsection of pharmacogenetics. Given the resistance resulting from clinicians' association of APOE pharmacogenetics with the problems of APOE predictive testing, it is hardly surprising that a consistent theme in the pharmacogenetic literature is the ethical difference between the two kinds of testing.

But at a more general level, differences between the coalface and expectations around pharmacogenetics raise questions about who counts as an expert, who do policy-makers, for example, consult with? If debates around pharmacogenetics are restricted to commentators, the geneticists, pharmacologists and industry scientists involved in generating expectations, then the kinds of ideas about the clinical use of pharmacogenetics that policy-makers will get will be very different from the positions that might be put forward by those who have to use the technology. Whether policy-makers want the kind of uncertain, messy account that talking to clinicians produces is another matter. But what is clear is that by talking only to those engaged in the creation of expectations, policy-makers ensure that regulations are shaped to fit the needs of those expectations, in the same way as the EMEA seems to accept that pharmacogenetics does not involve the same ethical problems as more traditional ethical tests.

5

Research, industry and pharmacogenetic literacy

I think a more honest interpretation of their data would be to say, well there's no evidence either way. But they've obviously interpreted it in a way that's market-wise, more sensible for them.

(Clinician Researcher 13)

The previous two chapters have shown how the current consensus view of clinical APOE4 testing for both differential diagnosis of Alzheimer's and the prescription of Tacrine and other acetyl cholinesterase inhibitors has come about. In general, there is significant reluctance to introduce APOE testing into the clinic, a reluctance based on a complex mesh of technical, social and ethical factors. At the same time, there is widespread APOE genotyping in the research setting, both academic and commercial, and increasing interest in bringing APOE into the clinic. This final chapter on Alzheimer's disease explores the role of APOE genotyping in current pharmacogenetic research and how this relates to industry concerns. It also uses theoretical ideas from the sociology of science to explain the differences between expectations and the coalface in Alzheimer's pharmacogenetics, and to get to grips with the source and solutions to clinical resistance.

APOE testing in research and the clinic

Although resistance to clinical APOE4 testing is strong, there is a great deal of genotyping going on in specialist Alzheimer and memory clinics throughout the US and the UK. While the location for such testing may be the same as for clinical treatment, the motivation of this work is ostensibly quite different. As Clinician Researcher 9 puts it, 'do we APOE4 test people in the clinical service? No. As part of the research programme, routinely? Yes.' And it is as part of routine research that this widespread genotyping is taking place. Most of the clinicians I spoke to agreed that such testing was commonplace in their centre: 'Well, we APOE4 test everybody, but as a research procedure only, and we then anonymise the data so we can't link it to people'(CR 13); 'Every patient we get through here will consent to having DNA testing done' (CR 4). The widespread use of APOE genotyping in clinical trials was predicted by Allen Roses at the height of debates around the clinical use of testing: 'In the future . . . it will probably not be possible to perform a clinical trial without testing for APOE genotype as a biologic risk factor for AD' (Roses 1995a: 13). This form of genotyping is certainly not regarded as dubious or unethical. Clinician Researcher 3, who is vigorously opposed to clinical testing, suggests that 'I think that's perfectly reasonable, we all do that, as long as the people who gave the consent know what's going to happen, that's a very reasonable thing to do.' Since the information is not going to be fed back to patients, one does not have to worry about the impact of the patient's APOE status on them, and the consequent psychological impact and insurance concerns.

Such widespread APOE testing is used in a number of ways. Sometimes it is used to explore the relationship between APOE and other forms of dementia, as outlined by Clinician Researcher 11.

> We've got a previous dementia cohort that we followed up and collected autopsy material on quite a few of them, so we had about 350 patients in that series and we've got genotyping on all of those including APOE4. We've got APOE4 genotyping on a large group of elderly stroke survivors that we're looking to see whether they develop cognitive impairment, and on a new dementia cohort as well, so we certainly routinely do it as part of our genetic screen . . . The sort of questions we've looked at with it are more to do with does it predict the amount of Alzheimer's pathology in Lewy body dementia or vascular dementia, does it predict the development of Alzheimer's type changes in stroke patients, is it related to the amount of amyloidal deposition? It's more those kind of questions rather than drug response.

In this context, testing is for a number of different genetic markers: 'we don't just do E4 . . . DNA's extracted and saved and used repeatedly for different reasons' (CR 9). While in some cases APOE's role in Alzheimer's pathology is the reason for research, pharmacogenetic drug trials lie behind much of the current vogue for taking DNA samples from Alzheimer's patients: 'It's a long time since I've seen a clinical trial protocol that hasn't definitely included APOE testing, it's one of the things they get consent for' (CR 1). Even those who do not use APOE testing in their studies are aware of the way in which research in this area is going: 'And I don't genotype for my studies, as yet. But, I'm aware that they do in the international drug trials, they always take DNA there . . . I think it's going to go like that, sure' (CR 7).

APOE testing serves two different purposes in clinical trials for Alzheimer's drugs. Firstly, it allows you to 'separate out risk groups, so that if you are doing research on large groups of patients you can increase your yield, or you can stratify based upon the presence or absence of these alleles. It's used as a marker to improve the strength of your analysis' (C 1). As Allen Roses suggested in the mid-1990s,

> Clinical trials can now be designed to allow more rational interpretations: with the ε4 positive group containing AD patients, and the ε4 negative group containing both AD and non-AD patients. Treatments that are effective for AD would be expected to be observed in both groups, perhaps better in the ε4 positive group since the ε4 negative group contains most of the non-AD patients.
>
> *(Roses 1996c: 1480)*

As Clinician Researcher 12 put it, 'for doing that kind of enrichment comparison, clinical research, on anything that's related to Alzheimer's disease, it's useful'. But obviously trials for Alzheimer's drugs also routinely use APOE genotyping to decide whether there is any pharmacogenetic link between drug response and APOE status. As noted in chapter 4, since Poirier's original 1995 result, a number of other drugs have been reported as having variable response according to APOE status. Thus, despite professional dismissal of the link between APOE status and response to Tacrine and the other acetyl cholinesterase inhibitors, considerable work continues to go on, exploring APOE's role in Alzheimer's drug response.

The impression given in both the literature and many of my interviews is that there is a clear distinction between clinical practice (which obviously does not involve APOE genotyping) and research, where APOE status (and that of other genes) is determined and the results are anonymised. Yet it is clear that in some centres APOE results are being fed back to clinicians:

> patients who are seen in the clinic often get APOE4 testing done. It goes back to the clinician. The clinician takes a look at it, says fine, and puts it to one side because, so far, there haven't been the [large-scale] prospective studies that allow you to say with any certainty what would happen to a patient if they carry any one of the genes.
>
> *(R 6)*

In the case of Clinician Researcher 4, there is not even the physical separation between the clinical site and where the research is carried out: 'this is reflected in the amount of people who would do APOE testing for diagnosis. Some of the bigger centres wouldn't do it at all, but we would do it routinely. There's a lot of people I think, this would not sit easy with them' (CR 4). Of course this does not mean that the results of APOE testing are being 'fed back' to patients and families, but it does suggest that the consensus view is not present in all clinical centres in the UK. At least one group of clinicians carries out APOE genotyping specifically for differential diagnosis, and in another case, APOE information is included in patients' medical notes.

At the same time, previous experience suggests that this line between the clinical use and the research use of APOE testing sometimes becomes blurred, and that despite people's best intentions, ethically ambiguous events do occur. This can be clearly seen if we look back at clinical practice during the mid to late 1990s, while the consensus position around testing was being pulled together; however coherent and immediate the consensus on APOE testing might appear now, it took a while for the principles and values underpinning these ideas to sink in. At least two of my interviewees described use of APOE testing in the clinic that would now be out of the question, but that during this period of debate over testing, seemed less problematic. Clinician Researcher 4 outlined what happened at his/her hospital when equipment arrived that allowed testing:[1]

> We set out, one of our first M.D. fellows, and we did the E4; we didn't do the genotyping, we were phenotyping at that stage, but we all went blithely and had ourselves phenotyped, housemen and everybody, if we needed volunteers for a control, for a pilot scheme. And I know I'm APOE E3/E3. My colleague who was doing the study is very happy cause he's 2/3 [i.e. very low risk]. But there are housemen we identified, younger people, who are 4/3 and 4/4 – so we suddenly [thought] we don't really want people to know this. So I think our knowledge and approach to the whole genetic thing has been very much influenced by our involvement in the area.

The problem here is, of course, one of interpreting what the APOE information means. The complexity of the relationship between APOE status and the chances of developing Alzheimer's make explaining an E4 result very difficult.

> When you say vague things about relative risk . . . [at] . . . individual case level, and all you can say to somebody is, you're three times more at risk than you would have been if you didn't have one E4 allele, or you're six or eight times more at risk if you didn't have two E4 alleles, but then since I don't know what your risk was individually before, it's three times more. People can't understand that, they say, no, it must be three times the population risk. We say, no, it's not. Even with very bright people, you end up in a position that is not helping them, I think.
>
> *(CR 9)*

---

[1] These were blood tests for the APOE phenotypes, i.e. the proteins coded for by the APOE alleles, though of course the implications of this information are the same.

A similar position is taken by Researcher 5:

> in my view, for most people, that self-knowledge will be dangerous because in my
> experience most people don't have an educated understanding of risk, the concept
> of risk is actually quite difficult. Every time I discuss this with an intelligent,
> well-educated friend, I have problems and I actually know of friends who are dead
> worried because they have relatives with senile dementia in some form, and in my
> view are probably worrying more than they need because they don't understand the
> genetics.

An obvious consequence of this is that 'either you have all this self-knowledge or you have a situation where your professional advisors, your doctors, patronise you because they know secret things that you don't know and I don't think I would like that. So where do we go?' (R 5). For my interviewees, it is difficult to explain complexity, not just to 'bright' lay persons but also to other medical professionals: 'it's difficult for me to even impart the information to psychiatrists. In fact, just before you came, someone said "Oh, I've got someone who's got a family history, can we do their E4?" And I said "Well, why?" Literally they've got the blood in their hand and I said "Well, why are you doing it?" And I'd just given a talk on this, a week ago. They can't work it out, they can't work out why I'm saying it's of no value' (CR 7). Thus Clinician Researcher 4's experience of his/her hospital's slightly careless use of APOE technology reinforces the concerns apparent in the growing professional consensus.

Another example of clinical APOE testing contrary to the consensus involves its use as a diagnostic adjunct.

> The only time we really thought seriously about using E4 as a predictor was in the
> memory clinic about four or five years ago; we set up an early diagnosis
> service . . . until about four or five years ago dementia was being diagnosed at a
> relatively late stage when people were presenting with behavioural problems or
> care needs, and then I guess because of cholinesterase inhibitors largely, people
> were referring themselves to GPs a lot earlier saying, 'I think I've got a memory
> problem, is it possible that . . .?' We set up an out-patient clinic-based service then
> which . . . and for a while, about the first 100 to 150 cases we saw, we did E4s or we
> did APOE typing and we didn't get consent because we thought this was clinical
> practice. Then we looked at the ethics of it and we looked at the consent
> procedures, we thought, no, we shouldn't be doing this, this is research activity, so
> now we've stopped.
>
> *(CR 9)*

Here the problem relates to the APOE test's status as a research rather than a clinical procedure. What started out as a straightforward addition to clinical practice became problematised at around the same time as the consensus position among Alzheimer's professionals began to come together against clinical

APOE genotyping. It may just be coincidence of course, that ethical considerations led this team to shut down differential APOE testing at the same time as
the majority of Alzheimer's professionals turned against such testing, or this
may just be an example of how the formation of the consensus position has
influenced clinical practice.

The line between research setting and clinic is blurred in a number of different ways. Often they are the same building (or are physically co-located on the
same site). In old age psychiatry and memory clinics, clinicians and researchers
tend to work very closely together, to the extent that a large number of clinicians
have significant research interests (though they may not be lab-based geneticists). And there is the object of such research. As Clinician Researcher 3, a
vocal opponent of clinical APOE testing, put it: 'I don't screen for APOE4 in
clinical practice, so if you extrapolate that, it shouldn't be changing pharmaceutical industry practice would be my view.' This acknowledges the fundamental
problem, that APOE-based pharmacogenetics will bring APOE testing into the
clinic.

The way in which DNA is sampled and stored in such pharmacogenetic clinical trials has been the focus of ethical debate. Clinician Researcher 1 suggests
that 'Just about every clinical trial we get invited to participate in, wants to
take blood samples from patients, to store them for undetermined pharmacogenomic work.' It is this storage of genetic material for an indefinite length of
time, and for undetermined reasons, that raises concerns. Two broad approaches
to such testing can be found in the literature. On the one hand, epitomised by the
publicly funded DNA bank run by the US Department of Veterans Affairs, is
a view that requires a separate informed consent form for the taking of DNA
within a clinical trial (for which consent has already been given), referral back
to the participant should researchers want to link additional phenotypic data to a
DNA sample, and more consent to be given should there be a follow-up study or
a search of other databases. This cautious approach to consent and what is done
with participants' DNA samples 'helps to ensure that the participant's specimen
will not be used in research against his or her wishes' (Lavori *et al.* 2002: 225).
The final fall-back for the participant is the knowledge that 'If a subject chooses
to withdraw consent, the Bank will destroy the subject's specimen and delete
linking information from its databases' (Lavori *et al.* 2002: 226).

A very different perspective on consent is offered by the Pharmacogenetics
Working Group, 'a voluntary association of pharmaceutical companies involved
in clinical drug trials and genotyping whose goal is to advance the understanding
and development of pharmacogenetics' (Anderson *et al.* 2002: 284). These
authors complain that in some jurisdictions, informed consent (IC) regulations
require pharmacogenetic studies to explicitly spell out which genes will be

studied: 'Such IC requirements have the important disadvantage of limiting the use of DNA or other genetic materials for pharmacogenetic evaluations in a way that will not allow researchers . . . to maximize the value of donated samples in light of future knowledge or hypothesis' (Anderson *et al*. 2002: 285). In addition, the 'requirement for recontact or reconsent . . . is not always practical or even possible' (Anderson *et al*. 2002: 285). For these authors, the bottom line is that 'pharmacogenomic data collected and/or analyzed up to the time of a request by a study subject to withdraw should be maintained by the sponsor as it is not consistent with good clinical practices to delete individual data from stored data sets' (Anderson *et al*. 2002: 286).

Obviously these two positions are far from compatible, though both are couched in terms of ethics; the public DNA bank focuses on informed consent and participant autonomy, and the industry perspective limits such individual rights in a context of broader 'meritorious goals with potentially positive health implications' (Anderson *et al*. 2002: 285). It is not at all clear under which of these broad regimes Alzheimer's patients' DNA is being sampled. On the part of the professionals I spoke to there is very little concern about these issues, save a general need for 'informed consent'.

The ethical worries presented by the increase in the amount of genotyping tend to fit into the framework of problems that have already grown up around the current consensus on clinical APOE testing. For example, Clinician Researcher 3 is 'concerned, that its [pharmacogenetic APOE testing] is done ethically and appropriately'. Sometime before this interview:

> we became aware . . . that there were very large clinical trials going on in the UK where they were taking blood for genetic testing without due consent and feeding the information back to clinicians when they wanted it. It was done naïvely rather than through any kind of malintent, but it was done because people didn't realise the complexities of genetic research. And we very easily put a stop to that. We published a letter in [a journal] explaining what we thought was good ethical practice in relation to clinical trials in genetics and my experience is that drug companies are now very sophisticated about that aspect and are also very happy to take advice, and as far as I can tell a specific consent form during genotyping is now taken.
>
> *(CR 3)*

As the same interviewee puts it, when genotyping moves into clinical trials, 'one of the problems with that is that it spreads genetic research to people who are naïve about the ethics of doing genetic research' (CR 3). Obviously for this interviewee, feeding back the results of APOE4 testing to clinicians, even if patients are still not informed, is not in the spirit of the current consensus on clinical genotyping. Beyond this, Clinician Researcher 3 clearly thinks there is a need for professionals to 'police' the use of genetic testing in both trials and the clinic. There is a need for companies and trialists to 'take advice' from genetic professionals, from people who are aware of the 'complexities' of this kind of research. Clearly, we can see an attempt here to enrol these new actors (pharmaceutical companies and academic clinical trials experts) into the pre-existing network, to translate their interests in terms of ethics, responsibility and keeping the APOE test out of the clinic.

Even the consensus position against the use of APOE genotyping on asymptomatic populations has recently come under pressure. At the heart of this is the consensus position's reliance on supposition. It is assumed that learning one's APOE status will be harmful for asymptomatic people and families of patients. Yet as already noted, there is little if any evidence either way. Surveys of the public in the US (Neumann *et al.* 2001) and the UK (Frost, Myers & Newman 2001) are equivocal. The authors of one of these studies interpret their findings that 'most respondents . . . were prepared to learn whether they carried a gene for Alzheimer's disease' as supporting the consensus position against the clinical use of APOE testing (Neumann *et al.* 2001: 258). Both studies accept that more research is needed. In the case of first-degree relatives of Alzheimer's patients, another study found 'a high level of interest in predictive testing among individuals at risk of AD', but going on the experience of Huntington's disease, where actual take-up of testing was far less than surveys predicted would be the case, these results 'should thus be taken with a grain of salt, given that they are likely to be much greater than actual rates of utilisation' (Roberts 2000: 49).

Given the lack of research in this area, the National Institutes of Health have funded a project called the Risk Evaluation and Education for Alzheimer's Disease (REVEAL) study, which aims to 'provide healthy adult children and siblings of Alzheimer's Disease (AD) patients with genetic susceptibility testing and risk assessment for AD . . . to determine if it is beneficial to educate people about their potential genetic risk for AD'.[2] The study is based around a 'primary intervention drug studies model . . . where the "intervention" here is the information about APOE' (R 3). The procedure is that 'subjects are enrolled in the study, they all know they're going to get counselling on the basis of family history, they're all at increased risk, they're all ascertained because they have an affected first degree relative . . . . and then they're, in a double-blind fashion, the subjects are randomised into what we call treatment groups, the treatment being whether or not they get information about their APOE status' (R 3). At the time of this interview (October 2001), the research team did not

---

[2] http://www.bu.edu/alzresearch/reveal.html

see any adverse problems using it, but this has been in a controlled research
environment, and the aims of this study are several, which include evaluating what
the demand for this is, and figuring out what is the best construct for a programme
to deliver results on a mass scale. It's one thing when you have a small-scale
operation where you've got genetic counsellors and neurologists and all of that, but
what about when this really gets into the hands of the primary care guys?

(R 3)

The consensus view has tended towards avoiding these issues. At the very least,
the REVEAL study is trying to get to grips with a topic that may well be vitally
important (if APOE testing is creeping towards the clinic); as Researcher 3
notes, 'It is important for us to see how this kind of genetic information is
interpreted, does it have meaning for people?' At the same time, running against
the consensus (even if you have NIH funding) may be difficult.

Thus we have a complex, uncertain picture of the Tacrine–E4 hypothesis.
For Alzheimer's specialists, the link between Tacrine and APOE4 is almost a
non-issue; an unreplicated result, suggesting a clinically unhelpful relationship
between an obsolete drug and an ethically problematic allele. A number of
commentators, mainly from industry and academic pharmacology and pharmacy, tell a quite different story. In this story, the result is, largely, undisputed;
a useful scientific fact helping readers see the potential of pharmacogenomics
in the future of healthcare provision. Yet this picture is incomplete. A third
way of looking at the Tacrine–E4 hypothesis is through the eyes of industry. If
companies are so keen on sampling DNA from clinical trial participants, what
might they be interested in finding out?

Follow the money

A number of the clinicians and researchers I spoke to discussed industry's
willingness to get involved in pharmacogenetic testing. On the one hand were
those specialists who were convinced that if there was a link between one of the
newer AChE inhibitors and E4, then industry would have found it and exploited
it for profit:

what's puzzling me a little bit is that the pharmaceutical industry which has
probably about 50,000 to 55,000 APOE types from clinical trials and cholinesterase
inhibitors around the world, there's not, to my knowledge, a single publication
come out . . . I would have thought if there was a positive link, they would have got
it out into the public domain.

(R 4)

A similar point is made by Clinician Researcher 10, who suggests that

> the pharmaceutical companies have got a large amount of information tucked
> away on the status of APOE versus acetyl cholinesterase inhibitors and if it
> looked promising they would have released it by now. The fact that nothing has
> been published since then suggests to me that there's not a very interesting story
> there.

In contrast there are those specialists, usually those with more experience of
industry, who question whether it would be in a company's interest to link E4
to response to AChE inhibitors:

> [I'm] not sure how happy the drug companies on the other hand would be [to
> discover a link]. The big picture is that the more people they get on treatment the
> better, so are they *really* interested in predicting the genetics of response, in some
> of these areas? All of a sudden you could find your cholinesterase prescribing
> returns reduced by a factor of 60 per cent. I've always said this to them, 'Why are
> you bothering? You're taking all this DNA in these studies and what happens if you
> come up with something, you shoot yourselves in the foot. Your shareholders won't
> be happy'.
>
> *(CR 4)*

This concern about splitting the market for a drug was made following the
rise of pharmacogenomics in 1997 and has been a consistent source of worry
for a number of commentators on the pharmaceutical industry ever since. As
Ken Conway of the biotechnology firm Millennium pharmaceuticals, puts it:
'What we are seeing again and again . . . [is that] . . . pharmaceutical marketing
departments don't want to narrow their markets, even though they know their
drugs aren't applicable to everyone taking them' (quoted in Regalado 1999: 40;
see also Economist 1997 and Murphy 2000). How can companies deal with the
financial threat caused, not by ADR-centred pharmacogenetic testing (which
makes good business sense), but by efficacy testing, which threatens to 'weed
out' non-responders? Clinician Researcher 13, who is one of those who originally encouraged companies to adopt E4 testing in clinical trials, proposes
a slightly cynical solution: 'None of them could find a result and they didn't
want to find a result, because if they'd found a result, it meant that that further
depleted the number of people who would take the drug, do you see? So they
gaily say in their literature, there was no . . . the results were independent of
APOE.' Such caution on the part of companies has been noted in the context of
Alzheimer's disease trials: 'Interestingly, some companies are not examining
the effect of APOE, perhaps not wishing to reduce the size of the potential
sales market by identifying factors that might exclude some individuals from

receiving therapy based on a marker that predicts low responsiveness to their drug' (Whitehouse 1998: 77).

Other interviewees imply that industry resistance to E4 pharmacogenetics goes beyond the realms of wishful thinking, of not *wanting* to find a result, into the suppression and manipulation of clinical trial data, to prevent the splitting of lucrative drug markets. Clinician Researcher 15 claims that several years ago she/he 'wrote a paper on the E4 response with [an anti-Alzheimer drug]: it still hasn't been published because the company will not let me release the data'. Even when academics are allowed to publish the results of such a trial the summaries of the data usually come from the companies themselves, and are not designed to highlight possible pharmacogenetic links: 'You have to deliver a full data set if you want to convince people about pharmacogenetics; yet much of what comes out of marketing departments is "nuanced" data' (CR 15). The statistics used in such summaries are such that any variation in drug response according to APOE status is masked. The idea that companies control the data coming out of academically linked clinical trials is not new, of course. As Michele Brill-Edwards notes,

> in general, academic clinical researchers do not design and implement drug trials in an environment free of influence by the manufacturer of the product being studied. Data collection, interpretation, analysis and publication are generally in the hands of the company, and the physician investigators are very often just along for the ride because they are the people with access to patients.
>
> *(Brill-Edwards 1999: 45)*

Clinician Researcher 15 suggested that companies still carry out APOE testing on Alzheimer's drugs because 'European regulations now require E4 genotyping for Alzheimer drugs.'[3] Within companies, the site of resistance lies not with R&D departments, which are largely in favour of pharmacogenetics, but in marketing, where people are 'too busy hiding the pharmacogenetic reactions' (CR 15) to interact with researchers. As a result, such R&D departments 'have been told not to contract pharmacogenetic studies outside their companies – to keep control of the results in-house' (CR 15).

In addition to these claims about industry practice regarding its own research, some of my interviewees were involved in an independent trial of one of the second-generation acetyl cholinesterase inhibitors. This trial was about more than just pharmacogenetics, it tried to assess the effectiveness of the drug in real world situations and was looking at a range of factors, such as age of

[3] This claim is *partly* borne out by the European CPMP's 'Note for guidance on medicinal products in the treatment of Alzheimer's disease' which lists APOE genotype as one of a number of possible prognostic factors to take into account when running a clinical trial.

onset, gender and APOE status, to see whether they predicted response. The interviewees could only offer limited support to the idea that APOE status predicts drug response.

> there's some support for previous claims about the presence of APOE alleles reducing cognitive response, but it's not wholly convincing, and what is probably needed is a meta-analysis of all the available evidence to try and confirm or refute it. There's certainly not a lack of evidence out there, but we need to get hold of all the data for an unbiased assessment of the predictive value of APOE . . . We've seen a trend towards it, but looking in subgroups is quite difficult statistically and it's not, in my view, at all convincing.
>
> *(R 8)*

More important was the response of the company that manufactured the drug being tested. Although the trial was independent of industry, the researchers obviously needed to get hold of the drug in order to test it. Unfortunately the company concerned 'delayed the supply of the drug, preventing [us] from buying it, almost to the extent of derailing the trial' (R 7). Since the trial was already up and running, staff costs were being incurred and there was a danger that too much time would elapse before the trial got started properly. The second problem was that of the placebo. In order to test the effectiveness of the drug, the researchers needed to compare it against a placebo. To ensure that the doctors administering the treatment did not know whether they were giving the placebo or the drug, the placebo needs to be packaged in the same bottles and boxes as the drug concerned. Again the company 'refused to provide us with placebos originally and we can't manufacture a placebo that says [drug name] on the one side and [company name] on the other, because it would be like forging a five-pound note, so unless the company provides the placebo then it's very difficult to run independent trials' (R 8).

This brings us back to the question of whether there is a pharmacogenetic link between APOE and anti-Alzheimer's drugs? Chapter 4 showed how Alzheimer's clinicians and researchers have resisted the idea that there is a link between APOE status and response to AChE inhibitors. Running in parallel to this are issues around whether industry is likely to allow such data to be made public. The majority of clinicians and researchers in this area would say that there is no link, that the original result has not been replicated, that newer drugs do not respond in the same way. Yet supporters might reply that there *have* been replications, that there is some evidence of links to the second generation of AChE inhibitors, and that research supporting this pharmacogenetic link has been suppressed by the pharmaceutical industry.

The issues surrounding independent drugs trials cut to the heart of the goals of the British government's Genetic White Paper. The interest in adopting retrospective tests for drugs already on the market is highlighted by the government's willingness to invest 4 million pounds in research on the genetic basis for variations in response to currently available drugs. Yet at the same time, the government is putting in place regulations which may prevent this kind of research being carried out. In 2001 the European Union adopted its Clinical Trial Directive (2001/20/EC), which became European Law in member states over 2003, with compliance required by 1 May 2004. The nature of European law is such that individual member states have considerable control over how such directives are actually implemented on the ground. In the case of the UK, academic scientists and non-commercial research funders have become concerned that the form the directive is taking in the UK is too geared towards commercial clinical trials. While there are a number of concerns about the new law (see Medical Research Council 2003), for pharmacogenetics research, the most important aspect is that to carry out research on a drug, an investigator will need Clinical Trial Authorisation (CTA), but as Researcher 8 notes, 'to do that you need to have all of the development paperwork about how the drug was first developed and tested. The company are the only people who have access to that. If they refuse access they can effectively suppress any clinical trial they disapprove of.' The fear is that once the directive is in place, such an independent trial would not just be difficult, it would be illegal. Of course, it is not just pharmacogenetic trials that would be restricted: 'The pharmaceutical industry rarely provides support for trials in some populations, such as children, or in pregnancy, because of the potential risks associated. This could have major implications for the production of the information required for CTA application' (MRC 2003: 17).

It is perhaps because Researcher 8 was involved in the independent trial of an Alzheimer's drug that the manufacturer of which did so much to block, that she/he may have an overly concerned point of view. Current discussions as to the exact form of the final legislation may well introduce some flexibility into this system, limiting the amount of control manufacturers have over independent trials. But this does highlight both the central role pharmaceutical companies play in getting a pharmacogenetic drug into market, as well as the need to see pharmacogenetic trials in the same terms as other clinical research.

The politics of APOE

When I started interviewing clinicians and researchers, my own expectations about specialists' views of Alzheimer's pharmacogenetics had been shaped by the review articles and commentaries I had read. I was expecting discussions about the practical issues of using APOE genotyping in the clinic, about the

day-to-day problems involved in applying pharmacogenetics in a clinical setting. Instead, I came up against scepticism, uncertainty and resistance. In many
ways, this disparity between the literature and what scientists say in interviews
relates to core themes in the history and sociology of science over the past
twenty-five years (Collins 1999: 188). Although Harry Collins is concerned
with a different kind of 'mismatch between publication and influence', he is
quite right to suggest that those outside a particular scientific community are
easily mislead by the written literature as to that community's beliefs and attitudes regarding specific scientific facts. Collins suggests that a visiting alien who
wanted to learn about science by reading the peer-reviewed literature would end
up with a very different view of science from that held by most human scientists
(1999: 163).

Collins's division of the scientific community into several groups can help
us to understand why it is that there is such a discrepancy between pharmacogenetic commentators and Alzheimer's professionals regarding the value of the
APOE–Tacrine result. At the centre of any scientific controversy is the core set
'of scientists who are actively engaged in experimentation or important theo-
rization at the heart of a scientific controversy' (Collins 1999: 164); in the case
of the current example, this is all those involved in Alzheimer's research. Within
the core set, a core *group* emerges, which embodies the dominant view regarding the controversy (i.e. those who resist the link between APOE and current
Alzheimer's drug response), leaving marginalised outsiders at the periphery of
the set (Poirier and those who, like him, think that there is some link). Beyond
the core set of active researchers is the wider scientific community, most of
whose members 'are in no position to understand the meaning of controversial
claims in specialisms other than their own' (Collins 1999: 164). This case study
focuses on those in this group I have called 'commentators', the pharmacologists, pharmacists and industry researchers who tend to write the review articles
and commentaries that cite the APOE4–Tacrine result so assiduously. Beyond
the scientific community are policy-makers and funders, and beyond them, the
public. Thus, adopting and adapting Collins's 'target diagram', one arrives at
fig. 5.1.

One well-acknowledged reason for the differences in attitude between these
groups is Collins's widely accepted point that 'distance lends enchantment';
the further away from a scientific fact a person is, the more certain and straightforward that fact seems. But while this may underpin some of the differences,
it is too passive an explanation to describe the extent of the variation in attitude
towards the APOE–Tacrine link; and surely such enchantment should side with
the dominant view held by the core set. Yet what we have here is support for the
minority view among the wider scientific community. Thus a fuller description

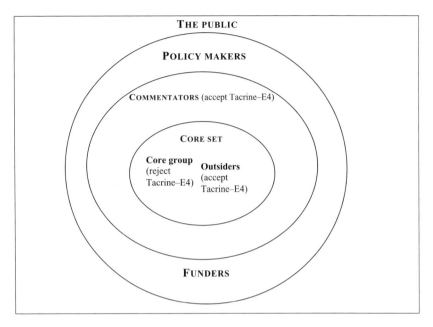

Figure 5.1 The core set and surrounding groups in Alzheimer's pharmacogenetics.

would incorporate ideas about the social, ethical and political culture of the core set and its relationship with the remaining members of the core group, as well as considering the use to which commentators put the APOE–Tacrine link in their construction of expectations.

As the previous three chapters have shown, the culture of the core set in Alzheimer's research and clinical practice is characterised by resistance to the use of APOE testing in the clinic, whether it be for disease risk prediction, differential diagnosis or for pharmacogenetics. The roots of this resistance lie in a complex mixture, a seamless web of the technical and the ethical: the APOE-causation hypothesis is in direct conflict with the dominant amyloid approach and was originally proposed by an outsider to the research community; clinical APOE testing is seen as being driven by commercial concerns, presents an emotional and psychological risk to patients and complicates clinical practice; APOE-based pharmacogenetics carries with it ethical baggage and provides little clinical benefit.

The commentators, so far outside this culture that they can unproblematically mention that APOE4 is a risk factor for AD without rushing to make clear that it is of no clinical use, have quite different concerns. As chapter 2 showed, they are engaged in a process of bringing about the conditions which will allow a promissory science, personalised medicine, to come into being. The APOE–Tacrine result is an important tool for the construction of expectations around this new technology. It is an example of pharmacogenetics in a common disease which is proving expensive for healthcare systems and will only become more so. The APOE–Tacrine result has been black-boxed, for use as a discursive resource. Yet instead of the 'losing' argument in the controversy being *inside* the black box, as is normally the case, it is outside, and it is Alzheimer's professionals' 'victorious' concerns that are within, out of sight and the commentator's mind.

It is, I think, largely a result of historical contingency that commentators have not noticed that they are relying, for much of their persuasive power, on so disputed and questioned a result. It is certainly not a good way to convince Alzheimer's clinicians that pharmacogenetics has a future. For at least one of my interviewees, the continual citation of the APOE–Tacrine result raises questions about the pharmacogenetic project as a whole: 'it's always cited as the big example, and . . . it's being cited by people who are advocates of pharmacogenomics, and the fact that they keep citing it makes me question whether there is very much in pharmacogenomics as a clinical, as opposed to a drug discovery, tool' (CR 3). But because interest in pharmacogenetics and pharmacogenomics took off in 1997, and because in 1997 the core set had not yet fully formed around the rejection of this result, when the APOE–Tacrine result entered pharmacogenetic discourse, it was a reasonable result to cite. The rejection of the APOE–Tacrine result was gradual and low-profile, a series of non-replications and contradictory papers and a steady growth in the belief that there was no link between APOE status and response to anti-Alzheimer's drugs.

One obvious question to ask at this point is what do Alzheimer's specialists think of the citation of a result widely dismissed by people 'in the know'? Some of my interviewees were just bemused. For most of my interview with Researcher 4, she/he had been confused by my interest in the Tacrine–E4 hypothesis: 'You seem slightly preoccupied with APOE because there's no good theoretical reason to presume that cholinesterase inhibition involves the role of APOE in the brain; I can't think of a plausible biological link.' When I pointed out that the result was well cited in the literature, Researcher 4 turned to their computer (this was a telephone interview) and began to check up: 'I'm looking at where it's been cited, at least 216 times, you're dead right, it's been cited in 2001 I'm up to, dozens of citations but not one of them is a replication, so far any way . . . I never knew this . . . I've actually read some of these references but never spotted that they cited it.' Researcher 4 concluded by encouraging me to highlight the discrepancy between specialist opinion and the citation record, asking me to send pre-print copies of any articles based on this research and suggesting that 'You're about to do us [i.e. Alzheimer's specialists] a great service, you know. I'm delighted to have spoken to you.'

Other interviewees were less surprised, displaying a neat, political view of scientific citation. For Clinician Researcher 3, 'There's so much invested by the pharmacogenomics people in the concept that I think they're rather reluctant to throw it [Tacrine–E4] out because the baby might go with the bath water.' Researcher 2 even speculates about the creation of expectations when she/he suggests: 'I suspect that the reason that people cite it is as an example of what might happen in the future . . . There are very few examples at the moment, so I suspect this has been picked on because it was an interesting finding . . . They are saying what everyone wants to hear, right now. So it's going to be widely cited.' Like the scientists studied by Greg Myers, with their sophisticated, rhetorical view of scientific writing (Myers 1990a), my interviewees belie the notion that scientists are sociologically naïve about the practice of knowledge construction. While none of them seemed pleased by the continued citation of the Poirier paper, it was not seen as particularly unusual: as Clinical Researcher 3 put it, the fanfare around the Tacrine–E4 hypothesis and its subsequent failure 'is absolutely typical of the way in which genetics progresses'.

One of the reasons this case study is so interesting is that one of the major actors in Alzheimer's research, Allen Roses, is also one of the most high-profile supporters of pharmacogenetics. Thus his ideas provide a useful way of testing the relationship between the opinions of the core set and those of the commentators. As I have shown, Allen Roses is an outspoken supporter of the adoption of APOE4 testing in the clinic, and would seem a likely champion of the Tacrine–E4 hypothesis. His review articles would seem an obvious place for Poirier's research to be cited. Chapter 3 showed how important the pharmacogenetic link between APOE and Tacrine was, as an element in his attempt to get support for APOE-based differential diagnosis. But his last mention of this result, in 1998, was equivocal, and emphasised that 'Whether or not the efficacy data are accurate for Tacrine (or any other compound) is not the point of this discussion' (Roses 1998a: 53).

Writing from within industry, Roses has speculated about what the pharmacogenetics of Alzheimer's disease might look like (Roses 2000a: 864; Roses 2000b: 1358), and has described the 'proof of principle' research Glaxo-Smith Kline has done using SNPs to locate the APOE4 allele on chromosome 19 (Roses 2002a, b & c). He has even co-authored a paper called 'The role of apolipoprotein E in Alzheimer's disease: pharmacogenetic target selection' (Saunders *et al.* 2000). In these papers, Roses has discussed everything to do with the pharmacogenetics of Alzheimer's disease except mention the one example of Alzheimer's pharmacogenetics that his fellow commentators are happy to cite.

Clearly Roses signs up to the dominant view of the core set, which disputes a link between APOE4 and Tacrine (or other drugs). Despite his disagreements with the majority view of APOE in differential diagnosis, it is still possible for him to be a member of the core group regarding pharmacogenetics. In addition, the overlap of pharmacogenetics and disease genetics is in direct contrast to his approach to pharmacogenetics, centred as it is on ADRs, rather than on efficacy and disease mechanisms.

The previous three chapters have explored the debates around clinical APOE testing (in various guises) and have highlighted the political relationship between genes and drugs. Different groups form up around different interpretations of the value of a particular genetic test forming sites of dissensus and contestation. The kinds of political manoeuvrings these groups undertake, whether it be clinicians using formal consensus conferences, Allen Roses building networks or companies undermining clinical trials, highlight the intrinsically political character of a pharmacogenetic test's route from lab bench to clinic. Or not (as the case may be). Attempts to bring APOE-based Alzheimer's pharmacogenetics to the clinic were hampered by a number of factors: attempts to replicate the original result varied; later attempts with large data sets were too late to change specialists' opinions and conflicted with industry concerns; the Tacrine–E4 result did not provide good enough numbers for patient discrimination in a clinical setting; and the hypothesis proposed the clinical use of a genetic test the Alzheimer's specialist community had spent the best part of a decade keeping out of the clinic. In terms of 'science as politics by other means', the story of Alzheimer's pharmacogenetics is quite conventional. Of course, for commentators trying to construct expectations about personalised medicine, using Tacrine and APOE4 as an example of current clinical practice may not be ideal. It highlights the gaps in the commentators' accounts, particularly in terms of how clinicians are expected to uncritically adopt new technologies.

Deficits and resistance

A consistent concern on the part of those who write about pharmacogenetics is that clinicians may be too ignorant to accept the new technology and thus need to develop 'genetic literacy'. For example, the Consortium on Bioethics suggests: 'Perhaps the greatest single factor affecting the penetration of PGx [pharmacogenetics] into clinical practice and the pace at which it will occur will be the knowledge and acceptance of physicians. Studies indicate that many physicians lack basic knowledge of genetics . . . It is therefore now commonplace to call for improved physician education in genetics, and this, no doubt, is essential' (Buchanan *et al.* 2002: 25).

The basic equivalence between genetic 'knowledge' and 'acceptance' of genetic technologies is not just restricted to pharmacogenetics. One result of the broader developments in genetics has been an intense debate in the medical and scientific literature over the role of general practitioners and other medical professionals with regard to the 'new' genetics. Some authors claim that although GPs have the right kinds of experience and interpersonal skills to present genetic information to patients, time constraints and the limited occurrence of Mendelian genetic disease justifies resistance on the part of GPs to the introduction of clinical genetics into primary care (Kumar 1999; Kumar & Gantley 1999). The alternative point of view claims that more complex genetic technologies (led by pharmacogenetics) will inevitably enter primary care, and there is thus a need for GPs 'to become genetically literate' (Emery & Hayflick 2001: 1027). To support their case that 'pharmacogenetics may be a much greater driving force for the application of genetic medicine in primary care than specific genetic screening programmes', Emery and Hayflick mention the pharmacogenetics of Alzheimer's disease, citing not Tacrine, but the almost as discredited association between E4 and response to the experimental, abandoned drug S12024. In this case, Alzheimer's clinicians might reasonably complain about these authors' own lack of scientific literacy.

It is not that educating health professionals about genetics is a bad idea, but that the assumptions underpinning this perspective, linking education, knowledge and acceptance, are simplistic and discredited. This appeal to 'education', to the development of 'genetic literacy' of both the broader public and the medical profession (whether GPs or specialists), is merely the deficit model of the public understanding of science in new, post-genomic robes. The deficit model posits that the reason the public mistrusts and resists scientific and technological developments is because they do not know enough about them. Educate the public, the model goes, and they will learn to accept new technology. Unfortunately the deficit model underpins such disasters (in public acceptance terms) as nuclear power in the 1970s and genetically modified organisms in the EU in the late 1990s. Despite its intuitive appeal, the deficit model flies in the face of a considerable amount of empirical research which highlights how complex publics' reactions to new technologies are, and how their scientific understanding needs to be seen in the context of background knowledge and everyday experience (e.g. Irwin & Wynne 1996; Miller & Gregory 1998).

The professionals I interviewed about Alzheimer's disease, have no knowledge deficit when it comes to this condition, its treatment or its genetics. A number of the researchers I spoke to know as much as anyone does about the function of APOE in Alzheimer's disease, and its perceived value in the clinic. The clinicians I spoke to also have considerable understanding of the genetics of Alzheimer's disease, as well as their daily contact with patients. To suggest that these people need to improve their 'genetic literacy' to smooth the passage of APOE-based pharmacogenetics into clinical practice is laughable. The uncertainty and doubts they expressed regarding the replication and validity of the original APOE–Tacrine result were not because they did not know about important research in their discipline, but is rather a marker for how this result is perceived by Alzheimer's professionals. If these professionals' resistance cannot be blamed on ignorance (as the deficit model requires), then perhaps supporters of pharmacogenetics need to accept that getting a technology into the clinic is not just a case of educating people. To blithely propose APOE-based pharmacogenetics as a driver for clinical uptake of this technology, as Emery and Hayflick do, is to display one's own deficit, not just in terms of disciplinary knowledge, but also in terms of the social and ethical contexts which surround and constitute any such test.

As Jon Turney points out, 'genetic literacy' is a rather broad, amorphous term, and that what is needed is a more nuanced debate over what clinicians need to know, lest 'the technical experts . . . continue to advocate education programmes based on an unexamined notion of genetic literacy' (Turney 1998: 138). Of course, the inverse of this is that those who are proposing a revolution in healthcare need to get to grips with how clinicians view new technologies such as pharmacogenetics. Resistance may not be due to ignorance, but to genuine social and ethical concerns about changes to clinical practice and harms to patients and broader society.

The final word is best left to Researcher 6, who was so keen to genotype, but who accepted his/her clinicians' resistance as a legitimate part of clinical practice.

> A lot of the biotech companies that I have contacts with, their whole ethos now has changed to this personalised medicine state. They see five to ten years down the line, a little personal chip that will check you for gene x, y and z, and will tell you whether you'll respond to dementia treatment or aspirin's going to work for your colon cancer, etc., etc. They're thinking that way but whether people, certainly the clinicians at the coalface, are going to take them up on that, is a different thing. . . . [L]ooking at it in terms of, from the clinician's standpoint is, they're getting pressure from the end-users, the patients or the patients' relatives, is to try anything, just try it, certainly in terms of dementia where you've got basically a terminal disease. They're saying, try it, it may just work and never mind whether you've got this lovely data that says it works or it won't work. They just want something to grab on to.

Conclusion

If chapters 3 and 4 showed that clinicians have clout, that they can resist a new technology, then this chapter shows how they are not the only ones. Industry too has considerable power when it comes to moving pharmacogenetics into the clinic, or preventing its use. Clearly companies do not reject the idea of APOE-based pharmacogenetics in Alzheimer's disease; the extensive, if unspecified, genotyping that accompanies any current drugs trial highlights the importance of personalised medicine in industry's thinking. Yet industry will only accept pharmacogenetic tests if they are on industry's terms. Not only are companies not interested in developing pharmacogenetic tests for drugs that are already on the market, they may well actively resist the introduction of such tests. Despite industry's excitement about personalised medicine, one cannot assume that companies will be interested in every example of pharmacogenetics that comes up. They are far more likely to pick and choose cases for development.

This commercial resistance combines with clinical resistance to pharmaco-genetics, the roots of which lie not in the realm of knowledge deficit but ethical concern, to suggest that it may be far harder to make personalised medicine a clinical reality than many commentators assume. Most expectations about pharmacogenetics tend to suggest that companies will automatically adopt pharmacogenetic tests simply because of the weight of investment that is going into research in this area. Yet it is marketing costs, not R&D, that account for the largest part of pharmaceutical companies' expenditure (Relman & Angell 2002). It is quite possible that marketing concerns, such as loss of market share, may dominate over research interests. Similarly, the simplistic idea that informing clinicians about pharmacogenetics will reduce resistance may well lead supporters of these new technologies to suspect that they need not address clinicians' social and ethical concerns. This would be a mistake.

6

Engineering the clinic – getting personalised medicine into practice

There's no point in doing diagnostic tests that don't advance your care of the patient; it's a waste of money and it's waste of the patient's time.

(Pharmacist 2)

Herceptin, breast cancer and drugs

If the story so far has been about resistance to personalised medicine, how not to get pharmacogenetics into the clinic, then the next three chapters are an example of pharmacogenetics that did successfully make that move. In 1998 the US Food and Drug Administration (FDA) licensed a new drug called Herceptin. Aimed specifically at women with metastatic (i.e. severe) breast cancer, the drug was rushed through the FDA's licensing procedures using a special mechanism. With little or no effective treatment for this kind of cancer, Herceptin, like so many other drugs, was heralded by the popular press as a breakthrough. Beyond the headlines, it is an extremely interesting drug if you happen to be interested in the way in which pharmacogenetics moves into the clinic, because, depending on who you talk to, Herceptin may just be the first example of a pharmacogenetic drug in regular clinical use.

The story of the development of Herceptin, its shepherding through clinical trials and the internal company politics that almost killed the drug off make a fantastic narrative about the role of the contingent and the social in techno-science. But this is not the story I am going to tell, for two reasons. First, the story has already been told, by the science journalist Robert Bazell, whose 1998 book *HER2: The Making of Herceptin, a Revolutionary Treatment for Breast Cancer*, presents a wonderfully detailed, occasionally unflattering portrait of the drug development process, and all those involved. Bazell highlights the con-tingent, almost random way in which Herceptin made it through development, and the way in which larger political forces impacted on the process.

99

My second reason for not discussing Herceptin's development is that my interest is in what happens when the artefact 'Herceptin' has been produced. How does it come to be used by clinicians? How do the structures already in place, and those that come afterwards, serve to act on the shape a new drug takes in the clinic? The first half of this book covered some of the ways in which pharmacogenetics can get stalled and sidetracked. We now need an example where the technology works. Thus, this chapter highlights the challenges and problems facing those who would get such a drug to market, and the issues faced by those clinicians who use this example of personalised medicine on a day-to-day basis. As already emphasised, a successful technology exists as a network of actors whose interests support its promotion and who are allied against those who might resist it.

Breast cancer is the most common form of cancer affecting women in the developed world, with up to 32,000 new cases being diagnosed every year in the UK and with US incidence at about 210,000 new cases a year. It is also one of the most politicised of diseases, with breast cancer research and treatment proving a fertile site for political activism and public interest, to the extent that as Barbara Katz Rothman notes, 'To even suggest that breast cancer isn't an out-of-control epidemic is positively heretical' (Rothman 1998: 128). The politicisation of breast cancer is such that the debates that took place in the US in the late 1980s and early 1990s between patients, activists, doctors and politicians over breast cancer funding are referred to as the 'breast cancer wars'.[1] As one might expect, for a drug developed in the city with the world's highest breast cancer rates (Anglin 1997: 1407) and a highly vocal activist population, the role of patient groups in the political shaping of Herceptin cannot be underestimated.[2]

Surgery has been the standard intervention for breast cancer since at least the early 1900s, when the Halsted (i.e. total) mastectomy began to be used on a regular basis. The logic behind this and other similarly radical approaches which were unchallenged until the 1960s were theories about breast cancer development. The assumption was that breast tumours started out small and confined to the breast. Then came a phase where the tumour spread to the lymph nodes in the chest, followed by the spread of the tumour to the rest of the body. Given this reasoning, the removal of all breast tissue and lymph nodes, as well as aggressive radiotherapy, makes sense (Williams & Buchanan 1987: 60). Over the past thirty years, an alternative view of breast cancer as a systemic disease with

---

[1] This is the title of at least one history of breast cancer activism (Lerner 2001), with three others referring in their titles to the 'politics of breast cancer' (Batt 1994; Altman 1996; Casamayou 2001). For a more traditional history see Olson 2002.

[2] For accounts of the impact of breast cancer activists on Herceptin's development see Bazell 1998 and Anglin 1997.

the tumour spreading before diagnosis, has come to the fore, undermining the basis for more extreme interventions. As a result, 'There has been an insidious encroachment of medical oncologists into areas once regarded as the preserve of the surgeon' (Fentiman 1998: 161), with chemotherapies steadily gaining ground as first line treatments.[3] While mastectomy is still a treatment option, many women are now offered a lumpectomy (i.e. removal of just the tumour tissues) followed up by adjuvant radiotherapy and chemotherapy. The changes in approach over the past twenty years are such that 'we are now entering a phase where the very usefulness of surgery is being questioned' (Margolese 2001: 185). The value of radiotherapy is unclear in the case of less radical, surgical interventions, though it is still recommended in the case of those women who are deemed likely to relapse (Houghton & Tobias 2001).

As well as becoming more popular as a first choice anti-cancer treatment chemotherapy is now used on a fairly regular basis as an adjuvant, or follow-up, treatment after surgery. Chemotherapies are drugs that kill cancer cells through a variety of mechanisms. There are over fifty different drugs currently in use, either on their own or mixed with others in combination treatment.[4] These drugs interfere in the way cells divide, so they affect not just rapidly growing tumour cells but also normal cells such as bone marrow. Since cancer cells cannot repair the damage and normal cells can, hopefully the body can recover while the cancer dies off. Although chemotherapy can be extremely effective, the well-known side effects (e.g. loss of hair, nausea and loss of appetite) can obviously make treatment both physically and psychologically tiring. As will be seen, one of the 'selling points' for Herceptin is that its novel mechanism means that these kinds of side effects are absent.

In the past fifteen years a common choice for treatment has become endocrine therapy, the best-known example of which is Tamoxifen. Initially developed as part of a late 1950s contraceptive programme, Tamoxifen has emerged as a vital adjuvant treatment for breast cancer, as well as a possible prophylactic against the disease. It has become 'probably the most prescribed anticancer drug in the world' (Wiseman 1994: 35). It has long been acknowledged that there is a link between the operation of the ovaries and the development of the breast. The view steadily developed that certain forms of breast cancer are stimulated by

---

[3] Cancer doctors divide into three broad groups depending on the kind of treatment they specialise in: surgical oncologists ('surgeons') are those who look to remove cancer tissue with a knife, leaving healthy tissue behind; clinical oncologists are trained in all aspects of cancer care, though they mainly use radiation treatment; medical oncologists are trained to administer chemotherapy. Obviously, because of my interests, the majority of my clinical interviewees were medical oncologists.

[4] For a detailed history of the development of one of the more recent forms of chemotherapy, see Goodman & Walsh 2001.

oestrogen, leading to Antoine Lacassagne's 1936 speculation that 'if increased sensitivity to oestrogen was responsible for the hereditary susceptibility to breast cancer, then perhaps an antagonist of oestrogen accumulation could prevent the disease' (Jordan 2003: 206).

Although Tamoxifen was licensed for clinical use in the UK in 1973, it took over a decade before clinical trials started showing its effectiveness as an adjuvant treatment in breast cancer (Jordan 2003: 210). As an anti-oestrogen, Tamoxifen prevents the growth of oestrogen receptor positive tumours, which are stimulated by the hormone (Wiseman 1994). Most interestingly for a study of Herceptin, since Tamoxifen is targeted at those tumours that are oestrogen receptor positive (ER+), before a woman is treated with Tamoxifen, her breast tissue has to be tested to see whether it is ER+. This has led some to claim that Tamoxifen 'evolved into the first targeted medicine for breast cancer' (Jordan 2003: 205; Miles 2001). From this point of view, Tamoxifen is personalised medicine, and Herceptin an example of ordinary, rather than revolutionary, technology.

The importance of these older methods to Herceptin is that this new treatment is very often defined in terms of its difference from the 'slash, burn and poison' of traditional approaches. As one of my interviewee's put it,

> an Australian Herceptin expert summed up the other day at a meeting I was at and he said that the beauty of Herceptin is the woman can have it in the morning, it takes about an hour, she can then go to lunch with her friend, and then she can go to the hairdressers in the afternoon, you can't do that with chemo as you're feeling sick and your hair falls out.
>
> *(C 1)*

The protein HER2 is one of a family of four growth factor receptors involved in the normal growth of breast tissue, in cell proliferation, migration and differentiation (Leyland-Jones 2002: 137).[5] Human epidermal growth factor receptor 2, or HER2, plays a key role in the molecular pathways that control normal cell growth and division. The gene that codes for this protein, also known as HER2, plays an important role in the development and spread of certain breast cancers. Normal breast epithelial (i.e. surface) cells contain between 20,000 and 50,000 HER2 receptors, as well as two copies of the gene (one on each copy of chromosome 17). Tumour cells on the other hand, because their HER2 genes are 'overexpressing', can contain up to 2 million HER2 receptors. For some reason, currently unknown, tumour cells generate more than the expected HER2 genes;

---

[5] The HER2 gene was originally discovered in 1979 in the laboratory of Robert Weinberg, a leading cancer geneticist. He named the gene 'neu' (because it was discovered in the neurological system) and then forgot about it. Following his (re)discovery of the gene in 1987, Denis Slamon named it Her2. Often it is referred to as Her2/neu to acknowledge its double discovery (Bazell 1998: 16–18). It is also sometimes referred to as ErbB2.

more than five and the cell is regarded as 'amplified', and more than ten copies of the gene is not unusual. The result of too much HER2 is increased growth of these cells, and a more aggressive form of cancer (Kaptain, Tan & Chen 2001). In addition, various studies have suggested that HER2 overexpression is a predictor of lower response rates in the cases of a number of chemotherapy drugs and endocrine treatment such as Tamoxifen (Hamilton & Piccart 2000; Mokbel & Hassanally 2001; Yu & Hung 2000). At the same time, the disputed nature of these results leads many clinicians to conclude that 'a rational view would be that no active therapeutic option should be disregarded based solely on the HER-2 status of a patient's tumour' (Miles 2001: 381).

In 1986 a UCLA oncologist called Denis Slamon ran a small, highly speculative project with a molecular biologist called Axel Ullrich, who worked for a San Francisco-based biotechnology company called Genentech. Using Slamon's collection of tumour tissue, gathered over a number of years, and Ullrich's list of cancer-causing oncogenes, they looked to see whether particular genes occurred within particular kinds of tumours. Slamon found one gene that seemed to reoccur with certain breast and ovarian cancers: HER2/neu (Bazell 1998: 38). Since then it has become widely accepted that HER2 overexpression, which occurs in between 20 and 30 per cent of tumours, is an indicator of worse prognosis and outcome in breast cancer patients (Ross & Fletcher 1998; Lohrisch & Piccart, 2001; Mokebel & Hassanally, 2001). For example, one study found that women whose tumours overexpressed HER2 had an average survival of three years, compared to six to seven years in those women with normal HER2 levels (Leyland-Jones 2002: 138).

Once Slamon and Ullrich had highlighted the role of HER2 in breast cancer, the issue then arose whether a treatment could be produced. Attention turned to monoclonal antibodies, the original biotechnological 'magic bullet', an elegant and clever way of turning the body's immune system against cancer cells (Reichert 2001). The 'exquisite specificity' of monoclonal antibodies (MABs) comes from their targeting of individual antigens (parts of cells that are recognised by the immune system) and reacting in a variety of different ways to kill the tumour cell (Green, Murray & Hortobagyi 2000).[6] After testing a number of different options Genentech settled on a MAB called 4D5, which was then 'humanised' to avoid immune response to mouse proteins.[7] The result, the recombinant humanised Monoclonal Antibody Trastuzumab (marketed as

---

[6] For a detailed history of the development of monoclonal antibodies, see Cambrosio & Keating 1995.

[7] It was this reaction to mouse tissue that caused such problems for the early biotechnology industry; of the forty-nine mu-MABS that entered US clinical trials between 1980 and 2000, only one, Muronmonab-CD3, was ever approved. And this is probably because it treated kidney transplant patients taking other immunosuppressants (Reichert 2001: 819).

Herceptin) had the efficacious benefit of 4D5, without the side effects. Herceptin entered clinical trials in 1992, both as a single agent and in combination with various chemotherapies, and it was targeted at those patients with the severest form of the disease, metastatic breast cancer (where tumours have spread to elsewhere in the body) (Shak 1999). The focus on metastatic patients is largely driven by the lack of any effective treatment for this group of women (Shak 1999): 'Metastatic breast cancer is considered to be a chronic disease . . . most patients will ultimately die due to their cancer' (Piccart & Kaufman 2001). At the same time, just because a drug has been approved for patients with this advanced form of cancer, does not mean that at some time further on, it might not be used on women with non-metastatic tumours, and even in other, non-breast cancers. Even before Herceptin had been approved by the FDA, Genentech was planning trials to test the drug's efficacy in non-metastatic breast and other cancers (McNeil 1998).

In clinical trials Herceptin was hailed as a success, both as a combination treatment and as a monotherapy:

> results indicated that the combination of Trastuzumab and chemotherapy increased both the percentage of patients having an objective response and the duration of the response. The addition of Trastuzumab prolonged the time to treatment failure significantly compared with chemotherapy alone.
>
> *(Baselga 2001: S21)*[8]

It is important to note that in the case of these (and many other) cancer trials success is not measured in terms of an actual cure, but in the delay in 'Time to Progression' of the tumour and other ways of assessing the spread of the disease. The median survival rate for women taking the combination Herceptin and chemotherapy was 25.4 months, as opposed to 20.3 months for those women just on chemotherapy. But in the case of metastatic breast cancer, even such an apparently limited improvement is regarded as a significant step forward for treatment options.

In terms of side effects, Herceptin is often described as relatively benign: there is none of the nausea and hair loss associated with chemotherapy. After the first dose of Herceptin, up to 40 per cent of patients report a fever or chill, but this is usually a one-off, rather than a recurring feature (Stebbing, Copson & O'Reilly 2000). More seriously, Herceptin has also been associated with heart failure. In one of the phase III combination trials, 'congestive heart failure' was noted in 16 per cent of patients (as opposed to 2 per cent in the chemotherapy alone arm). The general opinion is that heart failure is a significant risk

---

[8] For other reviews of the trial results, see Ross & Fletcher 1998, Miles 2001 and Lohrisch & Piccart 2001.

when Herceptin is either combined with a type of chemotherapy called anthra-cyclines, or is prescribed to patients who have received anthracyclines in the past (Lohrisch & Piccart 2001). The majority of the people I spoke to seemed relatively unconcerned about these risks; patients can be monitored and heart problems that arise can be treated with medication. For my interviewees, the risks of Herceptin are far outweighed by the benefits of its use in a condition where there are very few other treatment options. Despite the risks of heart problems, Herceptin was generally viewed as a low toxicity drug:

> If this had lots of horrible side effects, you would say, let's not get overexcited about this, but it is pretty non-toxic, so the idea that you can give it for individual patients you do get very long periods of remission in twelve, eighteen months, two years, which at that stage in the disease is impressive.
>
> *(Pharmacist 2)*

In a theme that will be explored more fully in chapter 7, Clinician 1 suggested that it is Herceptin's low toxicity which makes it an economically valuable product. Although products like Herceptin will

> be very expensive . . . patient's quality of life will be brilliant and they won't actually have to stop work. I've got a load on my desk now, insurance claims and people who are giving up work because of the side effects of treatment and now they're claiming it from their insurance company, earnings and all that sort of stuff, you know. That's a cost that's never taken into account in quality of life measurements. So it may not be as expensive as it seems if you take a broader view.
>
> *(C 1)*

It is worth noting, of course, that current Herceptin use is largely in combination with chemotherapy, so although women treated with such a mix may not get sickness and hair loss from Herceptin, the chemotherapy drug may well pro-duce the same effects. For activist Sharon Batt, Herceptin's use in combination therapy is a fundamental flaw: 'If a selling point for genetic treatments is that they are more targeted and less toxic than cell-kill chemotherapy, this advan-tage is somewhat academic if the drug is given in combination with a cell-kill regimen' (Batt 2000: 12).

As one might expect, some cardiologists are not quite as sanguine about the risks associated with Herceptin as oncologists. In a highly critical piece, Feldman, Lorell and Reis note that long-term survival of women with conges-tive heart failure is worse than that of women with limited metastatic breast cancer and certainly than those whose cancer has not yet spread. They state that 'although the warning in the package insert suggests that trastuzumab be discontinued in patients with a "clinically significant" decrease in ventricu-lar function, the descriptor "clinically significant" remains undefined, and no information is provided to identify which clinical tests would be appropriate for assessing cardiac function in these patients' (Feldman, Lorell & Reis 2000: 273). They view the 'extension of trastuzumab use to patients with less invasive forms of breast cancer' as 'imprudent in view of the untoward cardiac effects' (Feldman, Lorell & Reis 2000: 274). Elsewhere, Feldman suggests that the willingness of clinicians, patients and even regulators to use Herceptin is driven, in part, by fear of breast cancer and claims that a heart drug with a 1 per cent cancer rate would never be approved by the FDA, while Herceptin, with a 28 per cent incidence of heart failure, is seemingly okay (Gottlieb 2000). A recent editorial in the *Journal of Clinical Oncology* agrees that there is 'a clear clinical association between Trastuzumab and cardiomyopathy, and one must assume that a causative relationship exists' (Speyer 2002: 1156).

Testing cultures

When you finally have your new pharmacogenetic drug you are, of course, only half way there. The production of such a complex and expensive artefact required prodigious network-building on the part of Genentech, or to be more accurate, a number of researchers and executives within Genentech as well as some researchers external to the company. But then the challenge facing manufacturers of such a novel product was to get people to use it. The rest of this chapter, as well as chapter 7, shows the heterogeneous engineering involved in actually getting a pharmacogenetic product to market, in this case the UK's National Health Service.[9]

To decide whether a patient should receive Herceptin, a clinician must determine the levels of the HER2 protein, which the drug acts upon, in the patient's tumour. Two main ways of testing a breast tumour sample for HER2 status are a basic histopathological test called ImmunoHistoChemistry (IHC), and a more complex DNA-based test called Fluorescence In Situ Hybridization (FISH).[10] Both methods are used to test tumour samples, which may have been taken

---

[9] There are a number of reasons why I focus on the NHS. First, as a UK-based researcher, NHS or related staff formed the vast majority of possible clinical interviewees. But beyond the pragmatic, the NHS is an intensely political organisation, both in terms of party politics and in terms of internal, institutional politics and its relations with industry (Salter 1998; Klein 2001). In addition, the NHS is a model for the way others might approach healthcare funding, judging by the interest shown by other countries in the National Institute for Clinical Excellence (NICE), which, as chapter 7 shows, played a major role in moving Herceptin into the clinic (Paul & Trueman 2001).

[10] Interestingly, there appears to be a variation in terminology around FISH, with some authors using 'Fluorescence' and others 'Fluorescent'. The latter appears to be favoured by UK-based authors.

months, or even years, earlier, but which have been preserved by embedding in paraffin wax. One appeal of both these approaches is that they measure HER2 levels while 'preserving the tissue architecture' (i.e. not breaking up the tumour cells) (Rampaul *et al.* 2002).

In IHC, samples of the tumour are sliced and heat-treated to revive the HER2 antigen, and then stained with the testing antibody. The antibody reacts with the HER2 protein, so that those samples with more protein, which are overexpressing, appear darker when looked at down a light microscope. IHC is extremely attractive because it is a standard testing method, cheap and widely used in pathology laboratories. It also directly tests the levels of protein in a tumour, which is, after all, what Herceptin actually acts upon. As in IHC, FISH works on slices of tumour tissue that have been treated to remove the fixative agents and paraffin and attached to a slide. This is then washed with a solution including HER2 DNA probes, which have also had fluorescent markers attached. The DNA probes bind to HER2 genes in the tissue sample; the markers mean that the binding sites glow under special light. Thus IHC tests for protein overexpression while FISH indicates gene amplification.

One of the main things that shaped the way in which Herceptin was introduced into the UK is what we might call the 'culture of testing' that existed among oncologists prior to the arrival of the drug. I am not claiming that this culture exists in other medical specialties (though it may), or that it is unique to the UK (though it seems to be). I am claiming that the strength of this culture was such that it required Roche to totally rethink its strategy for the introduction of Herceptin to the UK. In essence, this culture forced a change in the shape of this new technology as it arrived in the NHS. Put simply, the effect of this culture is such that in 'no other country, bar Ireland, are [Roche] providing free of charge HER2 testing' (Company 1).

This different culture became apparent to Roche, who have the European marketing rights for Herceptin, when they looked at the availability of HER2 testing across Europe:

HER2 testing has been quite routine in Europe for quite some time, but we looked at some market research data for Spain, France, Italy, Germany and the UK at the end of 1999, so a year before we launched our drug, only 6 per cent of patients with metastatic disease were being tested for HER2 [in the UK]. We looked across the rest of Europe and that figure was closer to being about 40 per cent.

(Company 1)

In the UK, 'we started with a very low base . . . There were very few centres that were routinely doing HER2 testing in breast cancer at that time . . . This contrasted with the States where I think it was close to 90 per cent' (CR 18). Thus 'the UK was very much a unique situation'; although 'People were identifying, reading more about HER2, learning more about it at meetings', they were 'not necessarily going back and changing practice in the UK' (Company 1). For Roche, the underlying reason for this inertia was that 'the UK is one of the worst countries in Europe for putting funding behind cancer drugs'. One result of this funding problem was that clinicians 'were saying at the time, "I will not test because I am morally obliged to give that patient Herceptin, so if I don't test, I don't identify them and therefore I don't treat them" and then it doesn't put them [the clinician] in a moral dilemma' (Company 1).

Intriguing as this ethical position is, it does not fully explain the testing culture in the UK prior to Herceptin's availability. UK clinicians seem particularly resistant to testing, unless there is some practical purpose: 'In this country there has been, and I think there persists, a thought that you don't do testing unless there is a real reason to do the testing' (CR 18). It is not clear how this culture expands beyond the community of oncologists and pathologists who work with them, but it does seem as if it is not a HER2-specific resistance, but rather a broader feature of UK oncological culture. For example, prior to HER2 being an issue, there was similar resistance to ER testing for Tamoxifen: 'I was astonished to find that up until just five years ago, less than 50 per cent of patients around the country were getting tested for oestrogen receptor and now that is close to scandalous' (CR 18).

Clinician Researcher 18 was closely involved in the debates around HER2 testing and the introduction of Herceptin, and, like Roche, emphasises the contrast with

> the States and in much of Europe, where the view seemed to be that if some thing's considered to be of prognostic significance . . . they'll measure it . . . Some places in Europe are doing all sorts of intricate things, P-27, P-21 [different oncogenes]. None of these have been evidence-based in their application to breast cancer management and sometimes I think it actually ends up with a bit of quackery . . . the patient is treated badly as a result of having too many data points.[11]

For Roche, the value of HER2 testing extended beyond the indication for Herceptin:

> The only thing that we can probably deduce . . . before the introduction of Herceptin, if a patient was HER2 positive she would have a much more aggressive disease . . . So there seems to be some resistance to types of chemotherapy if you are HER2 positive, so it's a prognostic indicator but also a predicative indicator and may be responds to therapy even before Herceptin came along.
>
> *(Company 1)*

---

[11] The American Society of Clinical Oncology (ASCO) recently recommended that HER2 'overexpression should be evaluated on every primary breast cancer' (Bast *et al.* 2001: 1871).

Yet despite the apparent strength of the testing culture opposing this view of HER2 testing, care has to be taken lest this 'testing culture' appear too monolithic. HER2 testing was going on in the UK, but only in a small number of big research centres. Even within a single NHS Trust, there could be variations:

> the way things have been done have varied, so obviously this Trust had two breast units at one point. There was a breast unit at the [other site] and there was a breast unit here and then they were all merged on this site. The breast unit at the [other site] had traditionally done CRB 2 onco-protein [i.e. HER2] testing on everyone since about 1994 or something like that. But when everything moved here, that wasn't actually as readily available.
>
> *(C 2)*

The difference between the UK culture and that of other countries where there is more willingness to test, is that from the UK point of view, HER2 is extremely limited as a prognostic factor. As a way of giving information about a patient's prognosis, 'It's largely irrelevant. In a way, in this context, it's more how the lymph nodes are positive, how aggressive is the tumour, what grade, what size is the tumour' (CR 2). For these clinicians, one thing that would make HER2 testing relevant to their clinical practice would be the availability of Herceptin: 'if it wasn't for Herceptin, it [HER2 testing] doesn't really help you to make decisions about treatment' (CR 3).

In terms of the *formal* hurdles to the acceptance of Herceptin, Roche was aided by the Department of Health when it decided that Herceptin should be appraised by the National Institute for Clinical Excellence (NICE). A positive appraisal from NICE would give Herceptin formal, institutional support within the NHS: how that support was gained, how NICE was enrolled in the Herceptin network, is covered in chapter 7. Yet such official acceptance is not enough. Truly effective heterogeneous engineering involves enlisting the support of more than just the bureaucrats; it requires support, or at least reduced resistance, from those at the coalface. In the case of Herceptin, Roche was faced with two 'reverse salients' that the UK's testing culture presented its expansion. Roche was faced with a 'chicken and egg' problem: in order to promote the use of Herceptin in the clinic, Roche needed to increase the levels of HER2 testing. Yet in the UK, HER2 testing was not seen to be of prognostic or diagnostic value. It only made sense if it could be used to aid treatment decisions. But the only drug where UK clinicians accepted HER testing was of use was Herceptin. And this needed widespread HER2 testing to make it into the clinic.

The rest of this chapter shows how Roche overcame the resistance of the testing culture within UK oncology, promoting HER2 testing and preparing the landscape for Herceptin.

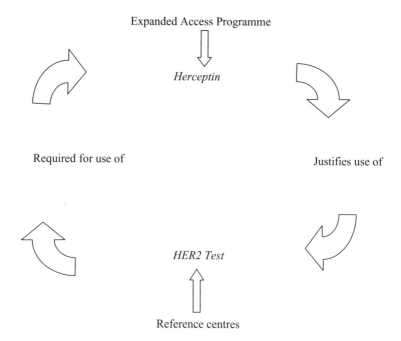

Expanded Access Programme

Herceptin

Required for use of

Justifies use of

HER2 Test

Reference centres

Figure 6.1 The chicken and egg problem

Reference centres

Ideally, Roche needed to get UK oncologists using HER2 testing even before Herceptin was introduced into clinical practice. In essence, 'there needed to be a service provided very quickly to support some of the trials which we wanted to get into' (CR 18). Testing needed to be made available to clinicians. Roche's solution was to decide to fund all HER2 testing in the UK for a period of time running up to and past the NICE approval of Herceptin.

Roche underwrote three HER2 'reference centres' based in hospitals in Nottingham, Glasgow and London. From October 1999 to the end of March 2003 Roche paid 'free of charge testing for all patients and allowed every centre in the country to send the samples through' (Company 1). The establishment of such reference centres is a clear example of Roche enlisting the help of pathologists to their cause, of enrolling them in a network of support for Herceptin. Rather than getting help from the Department of Health, or any other official body, the status of reference centre 'is a self-appointed position . . . It's not as if it was the government or anybody else turned around and said this, or the Royal College of Pathologists. We said we've got the resource; we will actually get a quality control system done between ourselves' (CR 18).

Pathologists at labs round the country sent in tumour samples to these centres for FISH testing, or even IHC, although most local labs could do that. With Herceptin being made available through an expanded access programme (see below), and free testing provided by the reference centres, Roche set about changing the way oncologists viewed HER2 testing.

Although the company had planned to stop testing at the end of March 2002, such a programme 'is hugely expensive as you can imagine' (Company 1), the NICE decision was delayed, and Roche continued funding the reference centres until March 2003. One aspect of this decision to carry on funding testing was the continued resistance from the testing culture: by March 2002, 'the testing situation had gone up to about 27 per cent in the UK, metastatic breast cancer patients being HER2 tested, but the rest of Europe was ahead of 70–80 per cent, so we were still quite far behind, so we felt that we should support it for a little longer' (Company 1). Roche explicitly set out to change the testing culture in the UK, and they realised 'that the only way really we were going to . . . almost educate some of the doctors or persuade some of the doctors that this is a valid test, [was] perhaps by funding it' (Company 1).

While it might be easy to criticise Roche's actions in setting up the reference centres as a commercially driven attempt to increase uptake of their drug,

> I must say that my experience with Roche on this has been that they've been perhaps more responsible than I would have imagined they would be. They've been entirely focused on getting good-quality testing out there I think probably with the recognition that if it was messy it would bring the whole business into disrepute. Whether or not they were altruistic is a good question. Nonetheless, they've been keen to get good-quality testing done.
>
> *(CR 18)*

This is worth considering: while it makes sense to be concerned with the effect of industry on the health service and the independence of clinicians,[12] at the same time it is possible that companies can act in their own best interests while at the same time providing a useful service. The commercial reasoning underpinning the reference centres is quite clear to clinicians. Although Roche have 'been very reasonable in appointing these three reference labs' (CR 4), their decision to fund the reference centres is 'not a tenable position long term, and I think it's being done really to get the use of Herceptin off the ground' (CR 2). Although Roche regard the expense as not inconsiderable, it was pointed out to me that 'for them to pay for some testing until funding of that gets through [from the NHS] is pretty commonsense for them in terms of the amount of money they're

---

[12] See a themed issue of the *British Medical Journal* for examples of this: 31 May 2003, volume 326, issue 7400.

going to return on one patient being treated with Herceptin; it will probably pay for God-knows how many hundred IHC tests' (CR 13). The commercial reasoning behind Roche's decision was regularly stressed: 'I guess they are making a very commercial decision and say well it might be better that we continue to support a couple of labs around the country doing it because it's better that someone's doing it than everyone doesn't do it' (CR 4). Put plainly, interviewees saw the cut-off date for funding the reference centres to be NICE's decision on whether to approve Herceptin for NHS funding or not: 'They're not going to do it indefinitely. If it doesn't go through NICE, they'll stop doing it immediately' (CR 16).

Being fair to Roche, one could note that NICE approval for Herceptin was gained in March 2002, and that they continued to fund testing at the reference centres for another year. Yet despite this unexpected extension, from the point of view of my interviewees, clearly the winding down of funding could have been handled better:

> The warning that was available to labs in the country wasn't anywhere near as long as it might have been. That proved difficult for some of them because obviously business plans have to be written to get new activity in place many months in advance of actually taking them on and really people weren't warned more than a couple of months [in advance]. It was in the background that it could actually happen, but until we actually got the news from Roche that it definitely wasn't going to go ahead with any further free testing from April 1st, we weren't in a position to tell the other labs. And that was a little unfortunate . . . we're only two to three months after that actually happening and I've not had too many grumbles about that, but we've had quite a lot of grumbles in the early part of the year as people said that we need to know and I said, yes I know you need to know, I'd like to tell you but I just don't have the information.
>
> *(CR 18)*

By funding the reference centres and working with the oncological community, Roche has succeeded in swinging professional support behind HER2 testing, in overcoming the conservative culture of testing that existed in the UK. In this sense, Roche acted as a 'heterogeneous engineer' seeking to 'dissociate hostile forces and to associate them with their enterprise by transforming them' (Law 1987: 121). Although such support often requires continuous nurturing to maintain, Roche seem to have organised their enrolment of the clinical and pathology community in the UK in such a way that support for HER2 testing and the use of Herceptin continue even after they have withdrawn financial support for the centres.

But simply funding HER2 testing in the UK was not enough for Roche. While it might work in the short term, building networks of clinicians, pathologists, labs, hospitals, tests and drugs is an unpredictable process. Such networks are inherently unstable, unless you can introduce some degree of formal regulation. While regulations can always change in the future, they do give heterogeneous engineers, like Roche, a bit more control over the shape of the network, and hence the final technology. In the case of Herceptin, an important part of network stabilisation involved quality control: 'we've supported this for a long time, we've maintained the quality assurance, we've constantly checked between the three centres to ensure that there is concordance between the results. We don't want it to then go out to some of the smaller labs and they start giving Herceptin inappropriately' (Company1). Within the scientific community there is considerable debate over best practice in terms of HER2 testing, as well as more complex arguments over whether IHC or FISH testing should be considered the 'gold standard' for the HER 2 test (Mitchell & Press 1999; Pauletti *et al.* 2000; Lebeau *et al.* 2001; Schnitt & Jacobs 2001; Birner 2002; Rampaul *et al.* 2002; Yaziji & Gown 2002). It was obviously not in Roche's interest for there to be widespread debate over the validity of HER2 testing, especially since getting UK rates of such testing up to European levels took such large amounts of time, money and effort. By emphasising and formalising quality control in HER2 testing, Roche managed to avoid many of the problems of the controversies surrounding HER2 testing.

In the UK at least, Roche's desire for improved quality assurance was helped, by of all things, the conservative testing culture, which was the source of such low HER2 testing levels in the first place. Such low levels are an advantage since in the UK '[we] haven't got bad practice ingrained in the pathology community' (CR 18). The obvious answer for Roche's quest for quality was the use of just three reference centres, to cut down on the possible 'economies of performance', to use Jordan and Lynch's helpful phrase (1998), that could exist in UK HER2 testing. With the majority of HER2 testing being carried out by these centres, the variety of possible testing contexts is severally constrained. Very few of my interviewees expressed detailed concern about these controversies over HER2 testing. Although aware of some of the issues, the reference centres seem to act as a means of 'black boxing' these problems for clinicians: 'The policy is that we will use an external laboratory because there are serious quality control issues in the histochemical testing and the superior insitu-hybridisation test is a special thing anyway' (CR 8). Thus, quality assurance supports the need for such centres: 'basically what you need is centrally approved agents/testing centres that have been fully validated, good quality control because there's too much poor quality out there; if you look at differences between different centres, you can often find marked variation so quality control's absolutely vital in this' (CR 13).

Since 1 April 2003 reference centres have ceased to be funded by Roche, but the company's control over the UK oncological testing culture has deep roots. Most obviously:

> we've also worked with [reference centre], because after March 2003 they will provide a test, but it will have to be paid for. So we're working and negotiating with [reference centre] on the prices that can be made available, so any local centres that aren't able to do it locally or within the network or local network, we will still be able to send it through as they are doing now.
>
> *(Company 1)*

Thus it is that via one of the reference centres, Roche will maintain some control over the quality of testing for many small path labs. In addition, Roche is working with the UK's National External Quality Assessment Services (NEQAS), an independent body that provides quality assurance testing for clinical laboratories in the UK. For at least one of my interviewees, the speed at which quality control was implemented was less than satisfactory: 'I don't think we really got a quality control scheme up and running as early or as intensively as I would have liked it to be, to ramp out to the rest of the country' (CR 18). This point of view suggests, of course, that there is more to quality control than simply setting up reference centres and encouraging pathologists to send in their samples. While for the company, quality control is best served by centralised testing and encouraging reference centres to keep to their standards, for this interviewee, quality control is about the spread of knowledge to other centres.

Nonetheless, Roche overcame the initial resistance of the UK's oncological culture towards HER2 testing through mobilising a variety of supporters: the three laboratories that were to become the reference centres; histopathologists (both within and outside the reference centres); and the idea of 'quality control' via surrounding structures such as NEQAS. While histopathologists and even some clinicians may debate the pros and cons of different versions of the IHC test, and IHC versus FISH, with the reference centres using Roche-approved 'validated IHC (HercepTest) and FISH techniques (PathVysion)' (Ellis *et al.* 2000: 892), the company has severely limited the range of debate and practice surrounding their drug. And it is Herceptin itself, which was the most important point in Roche's network to change the testing culture.

Expanding access

The chicken and egg problem shown in figure 6.1 shows two points where the cycle can be broken. Funding the reference centres broke the cycle with regard to HER2 testing, but to fully change the UK's testing culture, Roche needed to ensure that clinicians were used to prescribing Herceptin, even before the drug was approved for NHS use by NICE. Roche wanted to get the drug 'out there', to get clinicians using Herceptin, so that if and when NICE approved it, there would already be a degree of clinical experience. While a small number of my interviewees were involved in the 'pivotal' European trials of Herceptin, not all of them had used the drug by the time it had been approved by the licensing authorities. Roche's solution was to initiate an expanded access programme.

The idea of compassionate access to experimental drugs is largely a result of AIDS activists in the late 1980s, who pressured companies into allowing them to take drugs before they had received FDA approval. The epicentre of such AIDS activism was the San Francisco Bay area, and it is here, the home of Genentech, that the concept of compassionate use programmes for Herceptin arose (Epstein 1996). In the early 1990s breast cancer patients and activists in the Bay area began hearing about Genentech's new 'wonder drug', Herceptin. Attempts by activists to contact staff at Genentech were rebuffed, with meetings granted only with security staff or PR people. The company's position was simple: 'Genentech had no interest in giving out the [at the time] unproved drug to a few dying women . . . [an action that] wasted resources, time and money' (Bazell 1998: 117–18). But the rumours coming out of the treatment rooms, where women receiving the drug as part of the trial reported significant improvements, were boosting activist interest. On 8 November 1994, ACT-UP/Golden Gate (the lead activist group in the area) borrowed tactics from the AIDS activists of the 1980s and launched a phone and fax 'zap' against Genentech, clogging up the direct lines of as many company staff as possible (Anglin 1997: 1409). Following the routing of a dead activist's funeral cortége through the Genentech campus in December, a failed meeting between the company and ACT-UP/Golden Gate and the involvement of national breast cancer activists,[13] negotiations finally started between the company and the activists.

These dragged on until August 1995, when activists publicised the story of two women who had died from breast cancer, having been denied access to Herceptin by Genentech. The headlines in the local press were particularly harsh on the company, and 'Once the darling of San Francisco for its pioneering role in the biotechnology industry, Genentech was now being portrayed as heartless and, through its actions, a contributor to the deaths of two women' (Bazell 1998: 129). Ironically, the company had already decided to add a 'parallel track' to its phase III trial, and was quietly sorting out the details when the press coverage left them teetering 'on the edge of a public-relations free fall' (Bazell 1998: 129).

---

[13] For further discussion of the relationship between national and local (particularly Bay area) breast cancer activists, see Klawiter 2000.

Instead of making the drug available to women who did not qualify for the trial (compassionate use), adding a parallel track to the clinical trial meant that a limited number of extra patients were enrolled in the trial and gained access to the new drug. In return, the parallel track provided extra information on safety and efficacy for clinical researchers (Anglin 1997: 1408). 'While this development was not equivalent to the establishment of a company policy on compassionate use, it was considered a victory by breast cancer activists' (Anglin 1997: 1409). Since Genentech could only spare twenty-five doses of Herceptin per quarter, a random lottery was felt to be the fairest way to distribute the drug, without claims of favouritism being raised.

Thus during the development of Herceptin, Genentech was extremely resistant to expanded access programmes, finally agreeing to the parallel track only after significant political pressure had been brought to bear by activists. The role of such expanded access in the introduction of Herceptin in the UK tells a very different story. Perhaps because the drug had already been developed, or because it had had more experience of marketing drugs, Roche was far less antagonistic towards an expanded access programme:

> We started this back in January 2000 . . . initially we thought they were going to give 150 patients in the UK free of charge drug Herceptin until disease progression . . . and we eventually put in . . . between January and August . . . we put in 168 patients from the UK into this programme; free of charge Herceptin. And we still have 19 patients ongoing, which is quite remarkable because this is two and half years more and . . . We also did make Herceptin available from December 1999 . . . a programme where hospitals could purchase Herceptin before licence, so it was special licence sales, and that went on from the end of December 1999 through till September 2000.
>
> *(Company 1)*

From Roche's perspective, such a programme made a great deal of sense. While NICE was running through its approval procedure, the company could get the drug out into the clinical community and get it used; by the time the drug was approved, clinicians would be in the 'habit' of prescribing Herceptin. One of the clinicians I spoke to 'sort of helped organise an expanded access programme in the UK which is a kind of glorified name for a marketing ploy which allows the company to get the drug out there and used in the community' (CR 4). Thus, clinicians are aware of the 'ulterior motive' behind expanded access programmes. One of my other interviewees spoke about the marketing of a different drug by another company in another country. In that case, 'the company did what's called expanded access programme, and they gave it to all these people and then totally unethically, they abandoned them once they got their licence'. With the drug approved by the authorities in the country concerned, the company ceased supplying the drug to patients on the expanded access programme, forcing either the local health providers to pick up the bill or 'patients ended up remortgaging their houses'. For this interviewee, such a programme is 'a form of back-door marketing: have a new drug, get as many people on it as you can, get the licence, abandon them, then you know you've got a ready market that you've created already' (CR 13). This was *not* the case in the Herceptin expanded access programme. The clinicians involved in helping set it up 'made sure that we got an agreement that if patients were started they would continue free of charge beyond licensing, and the company went along with that and ethically that was the only acceptable thing to do'. As a result of this compromise, 'they actually stumped up the loot, or stumped up the drug for over 160 patients treated in the UK free of charge, and actually beyond the licence' (CR 4). For clinicians, while expanded access programmes might be a form of 'glorified marketing', at the same time they provide access to new drugs for people who would otherwise not get them because of either cost or the time delays involved in getting Herceptin approved.

In the case of Herceptin, Roche's attempt to break the chicken and egg cycle went beyond the expanded access programme. A regular feature of debates around HER2 and Herceptin is how HER2 overexpression occurs in more than just metastatic breast cancer. Such a severe condition was chosen to test the drug because of a lack of alternative treatments. This in turn ensured that with few competitors, approval from the FDA and other licensing bodies was easier to obtain than it might have been had Herceptin been licensed for less severe forms of cancer. Yet as already mentioned, even as Herceptin was making its way through the clinical trials, Genentech was planning an expansion of its use beyond metastatic disease.

The major move for Herceptin is from its current position, as the last drug of choice for women with metastatic breast cancer, to a normal part of adjuvant (post-operative) breast cancer therapy. HER2 overexpressing tumours do not start out as metastatic cancers, and initially they are treated like any other breast cancer: with surgery to remove diseased breast tissue, with radiotherapy and with adjuvant chemotherapy to ensure the cancer has been killed off and to prevent its spread. In the US, two trials have been running since early 2000, testing Herceptin as an adjuvant treatment (Perez & Hortobagyi 2000; Hortobagyi & Perez 2001). In the rest of the world, Roche, in partnership with the Breast International Group (BIG), are running the Herceptin Adjuvant, or HERA, trial,[14] which aims to enlist around 3,000 women to test the use of

[14] BIG is a network of breast cancer specialist groups across the world which aims to allow discussion and cooperation in clinical trials, reducing 'doubling up' and speeding the spread of

Herceptin as an adjuvant therapy in conjunction with a range of chemotherapy regimens. As far as Roche is concerned, the HERA trial is currently going very well:

> we've got sixty-seven sites in the UK taking part in HERA and it will be . . . certainly Roche's biggest ever study undertaking of any drugs that we have currently, and it probably will be the biggest ever study undertaken in breast disease because we will have to screen up to about 32,000 patients in order to take in 3,196 . . . – it's competitive recruitment and I think that we've got a huge opportunity in the UK to try and get as many patients into the study as possible. But I do honestly believe that it will be less than four years before they close the books.
>
> *(Company 1)*

The majority of the clinicians I spoke to are enrolled in the HERA trial, and its logic is, for them, quite clear: 'obviously if it improves outcome in the advanced disease setting, it's like any good drug, you've got to bring it forward into the adjuvant setting because metastatic disease is all very well, we want newer treatments, but you don't survive metastatic breast cancer whereas if you save more lives in the adjuvant setting, it's got to be better' (CR 13). But not all my interviewees have found it easy to participate in this trial. The risk of cardiac problems associated with Herceptin, particularly when it is used with anthracyclines, are an obvious obstacle to safe adjuvant clinical trials (Horto-bagyi & Perez 2001). As mentioned, there are some cardiologists who regard the expansion of Herceptin treatment into non-metastatic cancers as unwise, because of the risk of heart failure. The HERA trial is obviously designed with these problems in mind, yet as a result of the close cardiological input required

> Our biggest, practical coalface problem has been the cardiological assessment, and that is also going to be a problem for us in terms of safe introduction of Herceptin, because with more data showing that there may be some cardiac problems, to provide excellent care for patients we're going to have to do that, and I've just spent a couple of hours this morning trying to work out that issue with the cardiologist.
>
> *(CR 16)*

In addition, questions were raised over the HERA trial's status: was it an academic or a commercial trial? For example, Clinician Researcher 20 pointed out that as a result of this blurred status, 'We had a bit of trouble getting it accepted into the NHS' (CR 20). Soon after the HERA trial started, new regulations came into place relating to the National Cancer Research Network (NCRN), which coordinates cancer clinical trials in the UK. Under these new regulations, 'whether or not a trial is academic now matters, because if it's in the NCRN

information to clinicians: see http://www.breastinternationalgroup.org/. The HERA trial has its own website at http://www.heratrial.com/index.htm.

portfolio, it has access to staff on the ground in the NHS, and if it's not, it doesn't . . . there's also the implication for NHS R&D for the treatment costs, which follow naturally in an NCRN trial and not in a commercial trial' (CR 20). In essence, academic trials get NHS staff time and resources for free. But one main way of differentiating academic trials from commercial trials is who owns the data, and 'in the contract for the HERA trial, the adjuvant trial, it says the data is owned by Roche', which puts the trial 'in something of a grey area with the main parts of the ownership of the data, lying with the clinical investigators, but Roche technically own the data, so technically it wasn't eligible, and the Department of Health were flexible, and allowed us to indicate that it should be in the NCRN portfolio' (CR 20). Put simply, 'if you saw it as a commercial trial, Roche are putting in not quite enough money; if you look at it as an academic trial, then it's a very useful bonus and the truth I suppose is somewhere between the two' (CR 20).

The HERA trial is an example of how Herceptin and HER2 testing have moved outside their original boundaries of metastatic breast cancer, making it more likely that other forms of cancer will become possibilities for treatment. By moving Herceptin beyond metastatic breast cancer, Roche have done their best to break the cycle that allowed clinicians to resist the spread of HER2 testing and the use of Herceptin itself.

The potential use of Herceptin to treat other forms of cancer has been a focus of debate for some time. In 1983 the US enacted an Orphan Drug Law, the aim of which is to encourage companies to develop drugs for rare conditions, defined as where there are fewer than 200,000 sufferers in the US. The law offers tax credits and small grants to companies developing drugs for such conditions, as well as seven years' exclusive marketing rights for these products. Prior to the September 1998 approval by the FDA, Genentech tried to get orphan drug status for Herceptin, which at first glance seems rather cheeky, bearing in mind that breast cancer is 'the leading cause of death from malignant disease in Western women' (Stebbing, Copson & O'Reilly 2000: 287). But the case becomes stronger if we take into account the facts that there are approximately 165,000 *metastatic* breast cancer patients in the US, and that of these, perhaps 30 per cent, 49,500 people, will have HER2 overexpressing tumours. Seen from this point of view, Herceptin looks like a good candidate for orphan drug status. Except that it was refused (Fogarty 1998).

The exact reasons for this are unclear, but the section of the FDA that administers the orphan drug act, the Office of Orphan Products Development (OOPD), claims that the most common reasons for refusal lie in disagreement between companies and the OOPD over the make-up of claimed orphan populations. For the OOPD, the target population for a drug is not those people a company deems eligible for clinical trials, but rather the total expected treatment population; in the case of Herceptin, there is no obvious reason why the target population should be limited to metastatic breast cancer patients, or even to breast cancer itself. As activist Sharon Batt puts it, 'Genentech never intended that this drug be reserved for dying women. Cancer drugs are always tested on the terminally ill' (Batt 2000: 14), and news reports from 1998 that discussed the success of the Herceptin clinical trials clearly suggest that the drug could be used on other forms of cancer (McNeil 1998: 883).

Since Herceptin targets HER2 overexpression, a large number of other possible cancers, including bladder, pancreatic, ovarian, colorectal and prostate cancers (Lohrisch & Piccart 2001), the possible market for Herceptin, could be far wider than the original licence specified. It is also worth noting that Gleevec, the other example of licensed pharmacogenetics that oncologists mentioned to me, is already undergoing a similar expansion:

> I think it's in the public domain that Novartis many, many times almost came close to stopping the Gleevec project, purely because it didn't really stack up in terms of the search for the billion dollar molecule. But what has in fact happened is that the drug is so effective in subset patients and now it happens to be active in these chest tumours, it could actually become quite a large success.
>
> *(R 1)*

Conclusion

While chapter 5 showed how a pharmaceutical company might block the development of a pharmacogenetic test, this chapter has explored industry's more constructive side. In this case, we can see how much time, effort and frankly, money, has to go into overcoming clinical resistance to a genetic test. Of course, the very existence of Herceptin means there is another, perhaps more clinically useful, reason to carry out a HER2 test, rather than prognosis. Yet Roche still felt the need to encourage clinicians' use of the HER2 test, and overcame clinical resistance, not by adopting a knowledge deficit perspective but by making HER2 testing relevant to clinical concerns.

That Roche had to put in this kind of effort in the UK, but not elsewhere in Europe or in the US, raises important issues for the way in which a pharmacogenetic test/drug might roll out across different markets. It is not enough for companies to assume that all they have to do is develop a product and get it licensed and there will be an even uptake across different countries. While industry may well expect to have to work hard at getting a drug through licensing procedures, most commentators' expectations about personalised medicine do not seem to include the idea that different clinicians in different countries might have different cultures when it comes to testing. Of course with Herceptin, the test concerned was relatively unproblematic in ethical terms, since it does not carry information about patients' families. A more conventional pharmacogenetic test, along the lines of APOE–Tacrine, might well produce significant variation between different countries in terms of clinical resistance.

In parallel with Roche's management of Herceptin's clinical reception in the UK, the company also faced a more formal hurdle to widespread uptake of the new drug: the National Institute of Clinical Excellence, and its requirement that drugs funded by the NHS be clinically tested and cost effective. Chapter 7 explores the role of healthcare funding and cost effectiveness in the movement of pharmacogenetics into the clinic.

7

The fourth hurdle – cost-effectiveness and the funding of pharmacogenetics

I've got plenty to say about NICE. It's the most unpopular organisation that has ever been created in healthcare in this country.

Clinician Researcher 6

While Roche set out to overcome the informal resistance presented to Herceptin and HER2 testing by clinicians, a separate struggle was taking place on a more formal footing. Herceptin was being considered by the National Institute for Clinical Excellence (NICE), to see whether it was suitable for funding by the NHS. While acceptance (or not) by clinicians matters, whether a new treatment gets funding or not is, in a system like the NHS, obviously the most important factor in determining whether it gets taken up in the clinic. Many clinicians felt that the only way they would get to prescribe Herceptin on a regular basis was if NICE decided that it was both clinically and cost effective. This situation is not unique to the UK of course, even private insurance schemes have their limits and a list of techniques and treatment that they do not cover. But more specifically, it is also important to note that NICE's influence spreads beyond just the UK's National Health Service. In the past few years a number of different countries have put in place organisations to carry out the same sort of assessments, and even a number of US-managed care organisations are introducing health technology assessment (Paul & Trueman 2001: 433). Although it was not the first organisation of its kind, the relative transparency of its decision-making has made NICE 'arguably the most influential of all the health care technology assessment agencies around the world . . . perceived as being at the cutting edge of health technology assessment' (Paul & Trueman 2001: 433–4; see also Hutton & Maynard 2000). Thus any analysis of the way in which NICE has assessed pharmacogenetic treatments may well tell us about more than just the UK.

Surprisingly perhaps, despite the growing literature on the social and ethical impact of pharmacogenetics, very little has been written about the possible effect personalised medicine may have on healthcare expenditure. Of course there are the claims made by commentators, that pharmacogenetics will reduce the cost of adverse drug reactions and lead to better prescribing, thus reducing expenditure on drugs (e.g. Housman & Ledley 1998; Anderson, Fitzgerald & Manasco 1999; Murphy 2000; Roses 2000; Akhtar 2001). Yet however important these statements are in constructing expectations about pharmacogenetics, they are rarely based on anything that might be called an economic assessment. A large part of the problem is the lack of actual examples of pharmacogenetics in the clinic, which might provide a basis for such calculations. As Wedlund and de Leon point out, 'If pharmacogenomic testing had been proven to save money by now, it would already be a routine clinical tool' (2001: 171). One of the few attempts to provide an economic framework for the assessment of pharmacogenetic tests concludes that instead of making sweeping statements about how this technology will reshape healthcare provision, 'pharmacogenomics likely will be cost-effective only for certain combinations of disease, drug, gene, and test characteristics, and that the cost-effectiveness of pharmacogenomic-based therapies needs to be evaluated on a case-by-case basis' (Veenstra & Higashi 2000: 8).

Herceptin is just such a case study. For the NHS at least, Herceptin use is in certain circumstances cost-effective. This chapter explores how that decision was reached, the political nature of the assessment, and the way in which this fits into broader debates around personalised medicine. Thus this is not a piece of health economics, but rather a study of how the economic assessment of one particular example of pharmacogenetics fits into the broader culture of the UK's National Health Service. The central reason why economic factors may prove more important in the case of pharmacogenetics than other new drugs is simply that

> drug companies are going to be developing drugs for smaller and smaller numbers of people. And because their sales are going to be less because of the smaller number of people . . . the profits are going to be less and therefore the drug's going to be more expensive. And with something like cancer, of course, people want . . . you know it's a life-threatening disease, a very emotive disease, and I think the drug companies realise that they are likely to be able to recoup the cost.
>
> *(CR 5)*

Yet at the same time, although a pharmacogenetic drug may be more expensive, the fact that it will not be given to a whole disease population is psychologically attractive to healthcare providers: 'pharmacogenetics is likely, I think, to be quite useful from a budgetary negotiation point of view because people are much more comfortable if you can rule out groups of patients who won't benefit from the treatment . . . in the case of Herceptin we can rule out 70 to 80 per cent of patients . . . [Prescribing] . . . suddenly becomes a somewhat more attractive proposition' (Pharmacist 2).

The structure of the NHS

The British National Health Service is a singular organisation: continually under review, forever undergoing change, its 'popularity as an institution has remained almost undiminished even while criticism of its performance has increased' (Klein 2001: vii). If we are to understand the way in which Herceptin was deemed to be economically suitable for prescription within the NHS, we need a rough outline of the structures that accommodate this new technology.

New Labour came to power in 1997 and sought to honour its manifesto pledge to sweep away the last major Conservative reform of 1991, which had introduced an 'internal market' to healthcare provision. Yet in keeping with their immediate predecessors, their plans emphasised the importance of primary care in the new NHS. The core of the system were to be groupings of GPs and primary care providers called first, Primary Care Groups and later, Primary Care Trusts, or PCTs, within which all the UK-based clinicians I spoke to were situated (Klein 2001: 205). A second relevant change introduced by the New Labour administration was the creation of NICE, the National Institute for Clinical Excellence.

Opening for business on the inauspicious 1st April 1999, NICE 'is a UK government-funded body that responds to requests by the Department for Health for guidance on the use of selected new and established technologies in the NHS in England and Wales' (Birch & Gafni 2002: 185). More colloquially, NICE is a 'fourth hurdle' to drug regulation. After the traditional three hurdles of safety, efficacy and quality of manufacture comes the fourth hurdle of clinical and cost effectiveness (Paul & Trueman 2001). Underpinning this move was an awareness that since the early 1990s rationing in the health service had become a headline issue. Of course there was nothing new about making decisions about the allocation of scarce resources: 'It was built into the very design of the NHS: rather than demands (professional and public) driving the budget, a fixed budget made it necessary to choose among the competing demands for treatment' (Klein 2001: 200). By the 1990s, however, complaints centred around the idea of 'post-code rationing', that different regions had access to different services and treatments. The idea that people in another part of the country, or even in the next street, could get access to drugs denied you by your local health provider 'offended against the equity principle' at the core of the NHS (Klein 2001: 200–1). Yet at the same time government ministers were understandably reluctant to take control of deciding what treatments should be available. Such a change would have 'implied that they would have to accept direct responsibility for the consequences of their budgetary policies rather than sheltering behind clinical judgements' (Klein 2001: 201).

New Labour thus found themselves on the horns of a dilemma when they came to power. The need to respect the equity at the heart of the NHS required that some sort of standards be set over what could and could not be prescribed, yet how

> could such common standards be achieved without ministers determining who should get what, thus abandoning the strategy of blame diffusion? Would they not inevitably be drawn into defining the criteria of eligibility for treatment and determining what should be available to whom, so in effect taking responsibility for rationing even while repudiating the notion? Enter the National Institute for Clinical Excellence (NICE).
>
> *(Klein 2001: 214)*

Rather than claiming to leave it up to clinicians as to how to use resources, ministers could impose some sort of national standard on prescribing practice, while being able to hide behind 'evidence-based medicine', itself an inherently political concept (Harrison 1998; Rodwin 2001). In setting NICE at the heart of its plans for the NHS, New Labour also reasserted the need for equity in health-care decision-making: 'a bold reassertion of the NHS's founding principles' (Klein 2001: 208).

As I will show, for an organisation founded to reinforce equity within the NHS, NICE has been subject to some very bitter attacks, both from within the press and by many of the clinicians I spoke to, one of whom described it as 'the most unpopular organisation that has ever been created in healthcare in this country' (CR 6). But such reactions are common when economic considerations interact with healthcare provision in an obvious and transparent way. In the early 1980s the sociologists of science Malcolm Ashmore, Michael Mulkay and Trevor Pinch studied the emerging discipline of 'health economics', looking at the way in which academic researchers tried to get their ideas taken up by health service managers (Ashmore, Mulkay & Pinch 1989). Many of the issues they found controversial in the early 1980s have now become embedded in NHS practice, such as the use of Quality Adjusted Life Years, QALYs, to make rationing decisions; QALYs are a routine part of NICE's decision-making process.[1] In addition, many of the features of the academic health economic community they noted, such as the longing for more influence and the 'rationality' that would result, are still notable (e.g. Hurst 1998).

In their study, Ashmore, Mulkay and Pinch note that there are two registers or 'rhetorics' that health economists switch between, depending on the audience they are addressing and the message they want to get across. The 'strong-program' rhetoric 'draws on economic principle and carries the promise of radical change – change that can be tested and evaluated in an independent and scientific manner'. This is contrasted with 'a weak-program rhetoric that is sensitive to the complex social and political realities of organizational change, presents clinical budgeting [an example of a health economic tool] in a mild unthreatening way . . . and recognizes that technologies are evaluated in a practical and political context' (Pinch, Ashmore & Mulkay 1992: 285).

In the case of NICE, strong-programme rhetoric can be seen in the announcement by Frank Dobson, the then Secretary of State for Health, heralding the launch of the institute:

> NICE will command the respect of doctors, nurses and other clinical professionals and provide authoritative guidance on what treatments work best for patients. Its evidence-based guidelines will be used right across the country, so NICE will help end the unacceptable geographical variations in care that have grown up in recent years.
>
> *(Department of Health 1999)*

Here we can see claims to evidence and authority, as well as changes to deep-seated aspects of NHS provision, such as geographic variation – the infamous 'post-code lottery'. Similarly, when one looks at how health economists themselves see the role of NICE, one cannot help but notice the wistful tone of much of their writing. Having NICE is nice – it emphasises the value of health economics – but if only it was more, well, economic. For example, in their analysis of NICE's guidelines for technology appraisal, the economists Birch and Gafni ask whether 'the NICE guidelines provide the basis for the rigorous auditing process called for in order to make economic evaluations of health-care resource allocation respectable?' Their sad conclusion is that the NICE guidelines will lead to 'economics being "sidelined" in the decision-making

---

[1] QALYs were invented by the economist Alan Williams as a way of quantifying the value people place on different forms of medical intervention. Combining a classification of disability caused by different illness states, survey data on peoples' attitudes towards those states, and the cost of various treatments, the QALY provides a way of comparing different medical interventions in terms of economic benefit. See Ashmore, Mulkay and Pinch 1989 (86–114) for a sociological critique of QALYs.

process', because 'many aspects of the guidelines are not justified from . . . an economics perspective' (Birch & Gafni 2002: 185, 186, 190).

Yet NICE itself, like Ashmore, Mulkay and Pinch's 'insider' health economists (those who have worked inside the NHS rather than just in the academic community), takes a broader, more pragmatic (or 'irrational', depending on your perspective) view of its role. As one insider pointed out:

> much as politicians said 'NICE will end post-code prescribing' . . . we'll never do that on our own, we're like a tiny organisation . . . we think of our roles more around promoting the reduction of inequity, you know, at least there is an equitable system and people are clear . . . people should be clear, if they live in Birmingham, Brighton or Bolton, that this is what the NHS is going to do about Trastuzumab.
>
> *(Reg. 4)*

NICE's documents are full of 'stakeholders', including clinicians, patients and their carers, and the need to take their opinions into account. Put frankly, 'the final guidance issued by NICE always draws upon the value judgements inherent to each stakeholder group . . . although NICE's approach to decision-making is evidence-based, pure research evidence alone is not sufficient to make judgements' (Littlejohns, Barnett & Longson 2003: 244). As will be seen, it is this input from outside groups that opens NICE up to the criticism that its decision-making processes are too 'political'.

Robbing Peter: controlling healthcare expenditure

Important as NICE is to the story of how Herceptin made it into clinical practice in the UK, the external nature of the institute should not obscure the significant amount of decision-making around resources, rationing and cost-effectiveness that goes on in the clinic. Many commentators suggest that the kind of implicit rationing that typifies the NHS is most clearly seen at the level of clinical decision-making (Hughes & Griffiths 1997). On a day-to-day basis, clinicians' decisions are shaped by the financial context within which they operate, both in terms of large-scale institutional issues and individual clinicians' choices:

> in terms of the overall budget that a PCT has got to spend, at one level, you're interested in how big a chunk is going to disappear from that budget, which is partly the function of the cost per patient, and partly the function of how many patients it's going to be applicable to. But at another level, for all interventions, you should be thinking about them in terms of cost-effectiveness with regard to the amount of health gain that you get. And, on that level, Herceptin is expensive for sure. I wouldn't disagree about that.
>
> *(Policy-maker 1)*

But while this local healthcare policy-maker may find it relatively easy to set decision-making in the big picture, clinicians find it hard to look outside their individual position and set the cost impact of their clinical decisions in a broader context.

> But there is no central way of actually seeing that if you were to get this extra money, that somebody else is going to lose; are you robbing Peter to pay Paul? The budgets which these things come from are so vast, and so inaccessible to us, we don't know where they will have come from . . . we spend hundreds of thousands now on taxanes which five years ago we couldn't spend because we were told the money didn't exist for that. And we were told, if you have the money for taxanes somebody has to do without . . . What I don't know is, is there somebody somewhere who is . . . I mean have some beds been closed because of that? I don't know. So as an individual doctor it's very difficult to make a decision about are these treatments worthwhile for the community because you don't know where the money would come from and what else would you not do in order to do this.
>
> *(CR 3)*

Yet individual clinicians do have to make decisions about treatment, decisions that are governed, at least in part, by cost considerations. In effect, individual clinicians act as health rationers. When they confront the rationing aspects of deciding to use Herceptin, the drug's very usefulness as a treatment, its low toxicity and limited side effects, can make choices harder than they might be with a 'conventional' chemotherapy: 'the major issue with them is going to be cost, and I think that unlike conventional chemotherapy where you get a lot of side effects from the treatment, then it can limit their use by the toxicity and here you cannot use that. And the spectrum of ages you can use it in is wide' (CR 3). And it is to age that clinicians turn when they have to 'rule out' certain women from using Herceptin.

> I would definitely use age, myself, as a rationing tool . . . what can we do to really cut down the costs to a minimum and get the best for the biggest number of patients . . . and I don't have a big problem in saying that the 75-year-old with 20 Node positive, ER negative, grade three disease, needs anything, except lots of alcohol and morphine. I don't have a problem with that. Other people do, and particularly with drugs like Herceptin, where the major toxicity is the inconvenience of therapy, not the therapy itself.
>
> *(CR 16)*

Although this kind of decision is phrased in terms of 'clinical judgement', it is, explicitly, a rationing decision, a choice focused on the costs incurred rather than the clinical outcome for a specific patient. In emphasising this, the aim is not to criticise clinicians who make these kinds of decisions, but to highlight two important points. First, that funding issues permeate clinical decision-making around Herceptin; most obviously in clinicians' statements that if NICE does not 'approve' Herceptin, then they will not get to prescribe it. Yet even if Herceptin is approved for use within the NHS, there are still regular decisions to be made about which individuals should get this expensive drug. In the case of Herceptin, it is, ironically, the drug's celebrated low toxicity that generates dilemmas for clinicians: one cannot rule out treating an elderly patient with Herceptin on grounds of toxicity, as you could a chemotherapy. The clarity of the rules as to who can and cannot qualify for treatment is a function of Herceptin prescription being formally linked to HER2 testing. With a pharmacogenetic drug, the risk is that the test will be seen as the only 'barrier' to access, yet as has already been emphasised, Herceptin has more in common with current cancer treatments than is often suggested. If Herceptin is placed in the context of clinical practice, then it becomes barely surprising that normal clinical decision-making (i.e. around age) still applies.

And this is the second point. In making such decisions around age, breast cancer clinicians are not exceptional. Social scientists have explored clinical rationing on the basis of age in a number of other conditions, such as end-stage renal dialysis (Varekamp, Krol & Danse 1998) and myocardial infarction (Elder and Fox 1992). So ubiquitous are clinical rationing decisions based on age, that it is described as 'the factor most often invoked to deny treatment. It provides an automatic pilot for doctors, so simplifying the perplexities and avoiding the agonies, of choosing between different lives' (Klein, Day & Redmayne 1996: 87). Given the prevalence of age-related clinical rationing in the NHS, it would be strange if Herceptin was treated differently in the clinic, however ground-breaking and revolutionary its method of action.

Moving outwards from the individual clinicians, institutional structures also come into play to restrict access to Herceptin. Sometimes such restrictions appear to be the results of bureaucratic confusion, rather than a considered decision relating to new drugs. Prior to the NICE decision, Clinician Researcher 1 described the situation at his/her hospital where the Trust had taken the decision to fund the drug. Unfortunately, 'they haven't given us any funding for the HER2 testing . . . and so we're struggling at the moment to try and get some funding for our pathology department to go on to do the HER2 testing, which is not something that's being done routinely'. While the Roche-funded reference centres were still running at this stage, the expectation was that they would close down in the near future (they actually ran for the best part of another year), and thus this clinician and his/her colleagues thought they might 'find ourselves in a situation where we're going to have to pay to get the tests done elsewhere when we can just as well be doing it here, it's just that we haven't identified a specific funding stream to pay for that as a service development'. This situation was less to do with problems raised by new drugs and more

> because of the way that budgets have been devolved within hospitals, there is now no overarching view of these sorts of things so what happens in the pathology department is viewed separately from what happens in the pharmacy, and is different from what happens on the wards. Trying to get all the people involved to look at this globally is very difficult, so you end up with these silly situations where you've got money for the drug, but not for the testing to identify the patients who would benefit.
>
> *(CR 1)*

None of the other clinicians I spoke to mentioned this problem. Most felt that with the cost of IHC testing being so low, at least in comparison with a course of Herceptin, funding issues around the HER2 test are not the biggest stumbling block to access. But this is not to say that institutions do not place formal restrictions on which people get access to Herceptin, as a way of rationing the drug and keeping costs down.

At a level above the individual hospital, that of the cancer network,[2] one solution was to have a 'named prescriber' system, where only a limited number of clinicians are regarded as 'expert' enough to indicate HER2 testing. The need for this was highlighted by Clinician Researcher 6, who talked about running a clinic in another location, where 'there's somebody else up there who's . . . been sending people he thought were HER2 positive, sending samples for testing'. Such decisions would be based on severity of the disease, age of the patient and various other features of the cancer that would lead one to think that the tumour was HER2 overexpressing. But in this case, of the samples sent to the lab, 'he's had about a 15 per cent hit rate which goes to show that actually the prediction of who is positive and who is not positive is not that good on the basis of other histological features'. The implication is that working out which patients' samples to send for HER2 testing is a skilled job, and one not to be undertaken by just any oncologist. The solution was that 'Within the network, we've actually said that the only two people who should instigate prescribing are [CR 2] and [CR 6]. So, we're actually trying to control the initiation of Herceptin so that we make sure that people are actually FISH 3 positive, have been properly tested, have been through the other options' (Pharmacist 1). The

---

[2] The thirty-four cancer networks provide cancer services in England, and were put in place over a nine-month period in 2001 (James 2002). They consist of specialist cancer centres and local units. Financial responsibilities are blurred between the Health Authorities, the PCTs and the cancer networks, perhaps as an inevitable consequence of a system where 'Some networks have as many as three [District Health Authorities] . . . within their areas, and up to five primary care groups or trusts' (Kewell, Hawkins & Ferlie 2002: 310).

clear aim of this named prescriber system is to ensure that Herceptin is 'not being prescribed willy-nilly' (Policy-maker 2).

Members of this cancer network admit that this sort of approach is not an original innovation on their part. 'I think that a number of other cancer networks have it' and beyond that, such an approach fits with general trends towards specialisation within oncology: 'it's a logical progression down the road of subspecialisation in medical and clinical oncology. It's another tool to make sure that that subspecialisation happens and you don't get oncologists somewhere treating every cancer under the sun. And, sometimes doing it appropriately and sometimes not, because they are not absolutely up to date' (Policy-maker 2). Thus the named prescriber strategy is not purely an economic measure, but also ties into broader debates within oncology surrounding specialisation and expertise.

NICE

The rest of this chapter tells the story of the NICE appraisal of Herceptin, and its decision to issue the current guidance that allows the drug to be prescribed by the NHS under certain circumstances. The story is told from two different points of view, producing two different 'narratives' about the appraisal process. The 'narrative of evidence' is told by NICE itself, in the form of Regulator 4, who is a member of the institute's secretariat, and who was involved in shepherding Herceptin through the NICE appraisal process. As already noted, as an example of insider health economics, NICE has a pragmatic, complex view of how its decisions get made; it engages with the weak-programme rhetoric. Yet even within the weak programme, evidence must be analysed, procedures must be followed, decisions must be clear and above board. This is the narrative of evidence, which focuses on evaluation committee meetings, consultation documents, transparency and process. It can be summed up by Regulator 4's statement that 'the Institute's guidance is based on the evidence, absolutely based on the evidence and based on the evidence that the appraisal committee see and their recommendations to the Institute'.

This is contrasted with the 'narrative of politics' provided by the alliance of Roche, breast cancer charities, clinicians and the press, emphasising delay, missed opportunities, the death of identifiable, individual women and the input of non-evidentiary factors. As a representative of Roche puts it, 'first of all they didn't review the monotherapy data. When they did go back and review it, then the data was so strong that they found it very difficult then therefore to turn it down' (Company 1). On a broader scale is the view that NICE is primarily a way for politicians to avoid having to make politically sensitive decisions about healthcare rationing: 'NICE has nothing to do with safety, also it has very little to do with efficacy, it's totally price' (Company 4). While the focus for this discussion is on Herceptin, it should be noted that the view of NICE as an essentially political organisation is part of broader debates about the institute (Smith 2000; Lipman 2001; Walker 2001).

Both narratives have many points in common. They both start and finish with the same events; they both follow the same time line. Yet there are also events that appear in only one narrative. For example, it is ironic that it is only in the apolitical narrative of evidence that the most obvious example of political power, a general election, appears. What follows is not an attempt to decide which narrative is 'right', but rather an exploration of how two very different perspectives can build up over the role of politics in the economic assessment of a personalised medicine.

Roche did not choose to 'translate' health economics into the network supporting Herceptin. The decision to refer Herceptin to the National Institute for Clinical Excellence was made by the UK's Department of Health, and since NICE 'tr[ies] to time our appraisals wherever to coincide within the license indications' (Reg. 4), and 'Herceptin got the EU licence in the very end of August' (Company 1), the NICE appraisal process began in September 2000. NICE's approach is to 'identify a whole range of stakeholders who have a direct role in relation to the technology' (Reg. 4) who are then asked to make a submission to the institute. In the case of Roche, the company was 'very pleased' that Herceptin was to be appraised and they 'were requested to make [their] submission by the end of December 2000' (Company 1). Of course, other stakeholders such as patients, national patient groups, clinicians and other interested parties, including 'the Department of Health and the Welsh Assembly Government [who] are always consultees in appraisals, and . . . groups like primary care trusts, commentators . . . those sorts of things' (Reg. 4) are also asked to make submissions. Roche was 'told that a decision would be made and that the news would be made public around about April–May 2001' (Company 1).

Once submissions have been received, NICE asks the NHS's National Coordinating Centre for Health Technology Assessment 'to commission for us an independent review of the literature . . . a systematic review to an agreed protocol, within that review we ask them to look at the manufacturer's submissions against that protocol' (Reg. 4). At this point, 'The patient groups, the professional groups, get to nominate independent experts to write their own perspective on the technology that has been looked at and also to attend the appraisal committee meetings' (Reg. 4). The appraisal committee then meets to discuss an 'evaluation report', which includes 'the executive summary of manufacturers' submissions, the full submission to the patient and professional organisations and the assessment report, the independent assessment report produced by [the NHS National Coordinating Centre] . . . supported by the full manufacturers' submissions when people want to see them' (Reg. 4). Within the meeting, the 'committee will then deliberate . . . talk with the experts and come to a conclusion. They will produce an *initial* decision, which is called an "appraisal consultation document"' (Reg. 4). This is one of a number of differences between early NICE procedure and current practice. While presently the appraisal consultation document is circulated to all consultees and posted on the website, at the time of the Herceptin appraisal the consultation document, at the time called a 'provisional appraisal determination' or PAD, was regarded as commercially sensitive and was sent to consultees on the understanding that its contents would remain secret.

The reason for this is quite straightforward: 'when [NICE] first established the process, manufacturers approached us and said, this is stock market sensitive data; your initial decisions could impact . . . and we said, absolutely, but . . . from the outset we've always wanted to be as widely consultative as possible' (Reg. 4). It was when the PAD was released for comment by the evaluation committee after the April 2001 meeting that, from Roche's point of view, the problems began.

When Herceptin was originally chosen for appraisal, it was selected along with another Roche breast cancer drug, called Vinorelbine; it was decided to appraise both the drugs at the same time. But of course it was never necessarily going to be the case that appraisal of the two drugs, even if they both treat the same condition, was going to take the same time. For Roche, this was one of two problems for the appraisal, the second of which was the different kinds of data required for Herceptin effectiveness in combination with a chemotherapy (Paclitaxil) versus as a monotherapy.

When it came to the joint Vinorelbine–Herceptin appraisal, Roche 'suggested to them [NICE] in the very early days that they split the two [Vinorelbine and Herceptin], to which they refused initially and then they reviewed the . . . well the vast comments that we got back' (Company 1). The possibility of splitting the two appraisals became overt after the committee's May 2001 meeting, when NICE 'wrote to all the manufacturers and said, "tell us what additional clinical data you have", because none of it's published; its data is on file, we have to access it from them [i.e. the companies]' (Reg. 4). In addition, NICE commissioned an extra review of data from the University of York (via the National Coordination Centre for HTA). 'As a consequence, York revealed a large body of non-randomised clinical trial data for Vinorelbine and a smaller data set for Trastuzumab. As a consequence the Institute . . . decided to separate the appraisals so hence we didn't want to hold up the Trastuzumab appraisal because there was a lot of data [to assess] for Vinorelbine' (Reg. 4).

As far as NICE is concerned, they were acting in a responsible manner, 'freeing up' Herceptin so that its appraisal would not be tied to the large body of new Vinorelbine data that needed to be assessed. For Roche, the added delay in commissioning a new data review was unnecessary; they had told NICE to split the appraisals early on, but had been rebuffed. For NICE, this process is an example of the way in which they listen to stakeholders, and allow them to include extra evidence throughout the appraisal process: 'We did a consultation, people came back and said actually we would love this data to be [included] . . . we listened to them and thought actually there may be some potentially useful information and said yes we'll extend [the timeframe for the appraisal] to include this data' (Reg. 4). From the institute's point of view, splitting the appraisals happened at the earliest time it could: 'we split the appraisal, so that came out at separate times. It continued along the line it could continue until it was clear that we weren't going to get information on Vinorelbine [analysed in time] and then they were split' (Reg. 4).

The information that produced the Vinorelbine–Herceptin split also contributed to the debate over the second source of friction between the two narratives: combination–monotherapy data. 'What they did agree to do before Christmas was then to split from Vinorelbine and Herceptin, because once they'd agreed to go back and look at the data that we had on the monotherapy data, they then said that . . . Vinorelbine had 20, 30 studies that they needed to look at . . . So they did eventually agree to split [Herceptin] from Vinorelbine' (Company 1). For Roche, when the PAD was issued for consultation, 'they had reviewed . . . Herceptin in combination with Paclitaxol, and they had given their comments on that, which we were quite satisfied with, but they hadn't reviewed the monotherapy data, and the reason they gave for not reviewing that was because they felt there were no randomised controlled trials' (Company 1). NICE sees things differently, suggesting that 'one of the things that manufacturers fed back on their first consideration of the PAD was that the assessment report had not considered observational data they would have wished it to do, so we extended the appraisal so that further assessment of this observational data could be conducted' (Reg. 4). While both informants are basically saying the same thing (following the PAD, Roche asked for different data regarding monotherapy to be taken into account), the emphasis is different. The company's perspective revolves around NICE being obstructive by requiring RCTs where none had been carried out, while NICE's point is that they were prepared to accept observational data, despite that fact that it was not part of a randomised clinical trial.

Roche's reason for not running RCTs on the Herceptin monotherapy was that 'the data for Herceptin was so strong in the early stage that you could not then deny a patient who was HER2 positive Herceptin, which is why there were no randomised controlled trials' (Company 1). While NICE evaluated the monotherapy data, Roche suggested that since they seem[ed] reasonably satisfied with the combination data, then let's split the two, so let's release [the combination data] . . . And then if you want to take longer . . . reviewing the data that we had on the monotherapy' at least patients could begin to get Herceptin in combination. Although 'after a bit of toing and froing they did agree to do that [look at the new monotherapy data] . . . they didn't agree to split the two because they wanted to keep them together and we felt that women in the meantime, were being denied Herceptin because of funding issues . . . a lot of doctors wanted to use Herceptin but weren't able to because of financial pressure' (Company 1).

Meanwhile, from outside this process, the view of clinicians was of the political nature of the process.

> I haven't heard anything for a while other than it keeps getting held up by appeals but the initial rumours were that maybe they would approve it as combination therapy where there is randomised trial evidence and that they were bouncing it for single agent use where there is no randomised trial evidence, and I think everybody involved in the management of breast cancer is a little bit frustrated by that because we all recognise that there never will be any randomised trials, you just won't be able to randomise patients in that predicament to treatment versus no treatment, which is essentially the sort of evidence they are looking for. So I think that whatever evidence there is, is the best that's ever going to be available, so we've got to make a judgement based on that.
>
> *(CR 1)*

While Roche and NICE were negotiating over splitting Vinorelbine from Herceptin, and monotherapy from combination treatment, media interest was beginning to build over the apparent delays that were taking place. Newspaper reports tended to follow a particular pattern, with individual cancer sufferers being introduced, followed by an explanation that they were not receiving Herceptin, although eligible, because of decisions made by local health providers. One woman was 'forced to use her mother's savings' to buy Herceptin privately, since she was 'caught up in a post-code lottery'. Officials at her local health authority 'argue that Herceptin has yet to be approved by the government's medicines rationing watchdog, the National Institute for Clinical Excellence', but cancer charities claimed this was an excuse to 'avoid paying for costly new drugs which are accepted as the gold standard treatment in other countries and suggest that "This is the human face of the NICE process . . . They are just too slow"' (Marsh 2001). The headline of another story suggests that 'Post-code lottery has condemned me to death', and that 'after more than a year [NICE is] yet to make a decision on Herceptin even though many cancer specialists are convinced of its value' (Tozer 2001). Such articles suggest that it is ironic that NICE, 'which was actually set up to end the post-code lottery, is putting cost before patients' and that its 'deliberations, which can take up to two years, are causing needless suffering and even death' (Johnston 2001).

In place of the old post-code lottery, where rationing decisions were made on a local basis for a variety of different reasons, the NHS was now subject to 'NICE blight', where health providers refused to fund treatments undergoing NICE appraisal, on the grounds that their clinical and cost effectiveness were still being determined (Tiner 2003). It is not that while Herceptin was being considered by NICE, no health providers were allowing it to be prescribed: 'a number of my colleagues in other major centres around the country . . . somehow they persuaded their purchasers to pay for it, the money has been found for it, and that has not happened in [here]. I would estimate that probably about 50 per cent of the country are like us and unable to fund it – prior to NICE guidance' (CR 16). This guesstimate of around 50 per cent access to Herceptin is supported by Clinician Researcher 2, who suggested that 'There's a huge discrepancy up and down the country between the health authorities in relation to whether they will let a new drug through pre-NICE or post-NICE . . . you'll find that for Herceptin for example, probably half the patients up and down the country who've got access to it' (CR 2). For Clinician Researcher 8, based in one of the health authorities which chose to wait until NICE issued its guidance before funding Herceptin, the realities of NICE blight were that she/he was 'seen to be as good as I possibly can be by our Trust people, by not using drugs in advance of NICE approval when they're expensive drugs, but I know that I'm flying in the face of the increasing body of evidence because I can read the papers just as well as NICE can' (CR 8).

One of the factors influencing this pre-NICE provision of Herceptin was the size of the cancer unit concerned. While a number of interviewees suggested that bigger units, like those in London, tended to fund Herceptin, this is contradicted by one clinician who said 'because of our size, that's just not possible here [to prescribe Herceptin], because once you approve it for one person . . . I mean eight or nine consultants treat breast cancer here so there is no limit to it' (CR 3). Yet such funding variations happened even within the same health service structure. And even though the situation has changed in the wake of NICE's approval of Herceptin, at the time

we came down and decided that we felt it was justified to use Herceptin for a
limited number of people and probably by a limited number of prescribers to limit
the prescribing of it, and what's happened is that within our own cancer network,
patients who lived within [one health authority] can get it, the ones in [another
health authority] can't. So we've got post-code prescribing within our own network

(CR 2)

When funding prior to NICE guidance was agreed, therefore, the limited nature
of such monies impacts upon clinical decision-making: 'we have actually used
quite a bit of Herceptin in advance of NICE, using some funding that we've
got, but it does mean that it's kind of when we think of perhaps using it for the
patient rather than systematically looking at every patient who might be eligible
for Herceptin, so we're not doing that' (C 1).

The theme of women dying while NICE took its time to make up its mind, so
prominent in news reports at this time, is one that is repeated in interviews with
those involved in the narrative of politics, such as people from breast cancer
charities: 'in the time that NICE took to review its guidance, a number of women
who we'd been working with died and would have been alive today, quite
possibly, had they had Herceptin earlier. So it was quite a tough time for patient
organisations because these were women who we knew were HER2 positive'
(Charity 1). From the company's perspective, 'we said, this isn't acceptable
because we had women writing in to us, women were dying because they were
being denied treatment, so we felt that this was quite a crucial one to get through
as quickly as possible' (Company 1).

One result of the length of time it took for the NICE guidance to be issued
was the impact on clinicians' 'morale' with regard to the chances of Herceptin
getting funded. I spoke to most of my interviewees in the wake of the NICE
decision, but those few I interviewed before 15 March 2002 had a pessimistic
outlook. Asked whether they thought that the NICE guidance would support
Herceptin, Clinician Researcher 2 said: 'I don't think it will . . . I don't think
they're going to, unfortunately. Ask me in about a month' (i.e. after the guidance
is issued). An equally pessimistic Clinician Researcher 3 'expect[ed] it to be
turned down. I was surprised to hear that is likely to happen, but it's not a very
reliable source so I don't know.' Prior to the guidance being released, the only
clinicians who thought that NICE *would* support some Herceptin use were those
like Clinician 1 who somehow, informally, gained early access to the guidance:

Well I can't say too much, I'm not involved with NICE at all, but they have actually
issued the guidance. It's highly confidential at the moment . . . and it will be
released [to the public] in about two weeks, so I'm not supposed to say anything.
But all I can say is that previously I had one opinion and now it's completely
changed, so you'll have to work out what's happening [laughs].

Interestingly, it is via NICE that 'proper', that is party political, issues have become enrolled in the Herceptin story. On 8 May 2001, Tony Blair called a general election for 7 June. This had a direct impact on NICE's release of information about Herceptin, since

> when you are an NHS organisation and there is a major national election as there was . . . you go into purdah . . . you have to put in place arrangements to avoid initiatives which may have the effect of competing with parliamentary candidates for the attention of the public, and it specifically says you are not allowed to issue major consultation documents. As a result, any of the documents that would result from the meeting on 22nd May wouldn't be available until the 8th June. Now people made a great deal out of that and actually that wasn't a long time period, but it meant that the documents couldn't come out on the date we said they would . . . I remember at the time people saying, oh this is the government influencing . . . no, no NHS organisation is allowed to put a document out that has a major impact because that's the process.
>
> *(Reg. 4)*

During this enforced silence

> the committee met, they looked at the documentation, looked at the appraisal, looked at all the responses from the consultees and said, actually we need to analyse this observational data and we want it involved and engaged. So we wrote to [Roche] saying we were going to delay this and then we also said in that, as soon as we have details of expected dates we will contact you as well. So Roche knew every step of the way.
>
> *(Reg. 4)*

For Roche, the main problem with NICE was not about being informed of the committee's decisions. It was more about the consistency of the information:

> then they said that they would definitely have a final decision . . . by November that year, 2001. Then it was pushed to December 2001 and there were several parliamentary questions asked at the time to say, this is denying patients treatment, can we please have a decision on this? . . . the government came back and said it definitely will be reviewed and released before Christmas 2001 . . . We got to Christmas – still no news, still no review at all . . . [they then said] that they would then make Herceptin news available early 2002 and it finally came through on the 15th of March this year . . . it was an 18-month process.
>
> *(Company 1)*

As already noted, the narrative of evidence stresses the need to inform consultees in the process of what is going on. As one of the consultees,

> Roche will have been informed because they were stakeholders; they would have known exactly the time lines, exactly the same with the details . . . whilst clinicians arguably under the old system might have had a reason for that perspective because

they weren't in direct correspondence (their professional organisations were), Roche would have been informed every step of the way, and from memory I don't know whether one of the things was around reanalysis of data; I'd have to look, but Roche would have been involved in that.

(Reg. 4)

The politics of Herceptin appraisal

As told above, the story of the NICE appraisal process shows how the two discreet narratives, of evidence and of politics, are intertwined. While they may have events and topics in common, the tone and emphasis of the two positions is clearly different, with Regulator 4 stressing how Roche, as one of the consultees, had been kept informed of all developments and decisions regarding Herceptin. In contrast, Roche emphasised the continually changing timetable of the appraisal, the committee's belated acceptance of positions that the company had held for months, and difficulties over non-RCT data.

When NICE issued its guidance for the use of Herceptin on 15 March 2002, there was significant newspaper coverage of the conclusion of 'one of the most obvious and fiercely contested examples of post-code prescribing', the result of 'a bitter two-year campaign' (Day 2002). Writing in the *Sun*, a mass-circulation tabloid, Jacqui Thornton suggested that while 'a minority of forward-looking health authorities allowed doctors to prescribe' Herceptin prior to the NICE decision, other health authorities took advantage of the 'tortuously slow' NICE decision-making process, using the need for cost-effectiveness as an 'excuse to refuse to pay'. As ever in press reports, 'Hundreds of women have died needlessly early' (Kandohla 2002), a point made again by the breast cancer charities (e.g. Laurance 2002) and by industry (e.g. Cummins 2002). Summing up the view of NICE as a political 'lightning rod', the *Sun*, in its leader column, suggested that 'not for the first time, NICE seems nasty if you're a patient . . . What is NICE for? To help make life better for people suffering life-threatening diseases . . . Or to take the heat off the government by soaking up all the blame when penny-pinching makes patients suffer?' (Sun 2002).

Yet according to Regulator 4, the invective around the Herceptin decision made no difference to the institute's decision-making: 'That puts no pressure on NICE at all, absolutely not', for a number of reasons. Firstly, NICE 'get[s] it with every one' and because of the possibility of appeals, 'our decisions have to be defendable and clear, and supported to those who use them. So if we just changed our mind because we actually had . . . "God, the Daily Mail has been so rude about us" . . . you know, how can you defend that decision? You can't defend it; it's an indefensible approach' (Reg. 4). Secondly, even if the NICE secretariat were influenced, the appraisal committee are 'a group of independent individuals and academics, so they're professionals, patients, representatives from the ABPI; if at any stage they thought we [the NICE staff] were overly influencing their process, or influencing their process per se, they'd walk because their reputation is on the line' (Reg. 4). The third defence against politics is the organisation's sophistication: 'we're an acute enough organisation that we know how the media works and we understand editorial policy, we understand editorial positioning . . . We're not naïve about it, so there is no pressure on us' (Reg. 4). Thus the narrative of evidence is apparent even when NICE staff are quoted in the press:

> Anne-Toni Rodgers, of NICE, said that was because the appraisal had been delayed by a request from interested parties for extra evidence to be considered. She declined to say who had made the request . . . Ms Rodgers said: 'I am aware that concerns have been expressed that the institute extended the time lines for this piece of work. This decision is incredibly important for women and it was appropriate that we made the right decision based on the right evidence'.
>
> *(Hawkes 2002)*

Yet however clearly NICE articulates its point that evidence is the key, we can be under no illusion that NICE's decision is a site of contestation and dissensus, and is thus, in the terms of this book, highly political. The perception of those outside the appraisal process was of an inherently political decision-making process. Pharmacist 1:

> [I]suspect the NICE decision was more governed partly by politics than anything else. Had it been a less 'sexy' disease like . . . a consultant oncologist once moaned at me that actually more people die of bladder cancer than of breast cancer, but because it's a lower socioeconomic group, they're not as vociferous, there's an awful lot of money goes into breast cancer which doesn't go into bladder cancer. And I think that it was partly a political decision.

For Clinician Researcher 17, the perceived political nature of the Herceptin decision undermined NICE as an organisation: 'it's appropriate to have a body doing that [making clinical and cost effectiveness decisions] because in some other countries drugs are introduced too early and inappropriately and some-times it's not a good evidence base for their introduction' (CR 17). But this clinician's understanding 'albeit from a distance' was that

> NICE's initial decisions were not to approve the drug at all and the decision was made purely on political grounds because it didn't fulfil their financial criteria and so their decision was reversed right at the last minute. And so if NICE are going to be influenced by political decisions, then it really puts into question their role. So I think the Herceptin process has identified flaws in the NICE system that need to be thought out very clearly.

At the same, another interviewee who also regarded him/herself as outside the debate presented a less negative view of the NICE process:

> it was unremarkable, that actually for a really very expensive new treatment . . . The kind of level of the debate seemed to me to be fairly reasonable and unremarkable by European standards. That's probably not what you'll hear from the breast cancer community, and they will say it was all shock, horror and terrible, but my perspective is wider than this, because I see these things in other tumour types.
>
> *(CR 20)*

Despite this, even Regulator 4 accepts that changes to the appraisal process have resulted from NICE's experience with Herceptin. At least one result of the Herceptin process has been that NICE changed its policy keeping PADs confidential for commercial reasons:

> The original decision was taken because it was very early days and we had no idea of the impact, and was that manufacturers and professional patient organisations would honour a confidentiality around the PAD. The change came because it was absolutely clear that nobody honoured . . . some people obviously honoured the confidentiality, but what was happening was selective leaking. So selective leaking actually arguably has much more to do with the oncologists' perceptions of what the issues were than the reality.
>
> *(Reg. 4)*

When NICE went to the Financial Services Authority (FSA, the UK financial regulator) for advice, they were told 'actually you're more in danger of creating a false market using the process you're using, because as we consult we can consult with 150 people who might then consult with five people, so there's 500 people out there who have access to preliminary data' (Reg. 4). And it was quite explicitly the selective leaking of the Herceptin PAD that triggered this change in policy: 'if you look at our press release at the time, what we've said is, due to media speculation surrounding the institute's appraisal, the institute has decided to publish the provision of the appraisal determination on its website' (Reg. 4). The result now is that the NICE process is far more open: consultation documents are posted on the website, so clinicians gain direct access to the way NICE is thinking about a particular treatment.

As for Roche, they felt that 'NICE have certainly improved the processes since then and it's much more transparent now so you do know that each stage, whether they're thinking positive, negative, midway, which I think is a better way' (Company 1). Of course, while NICE accepts that its new practices increase its transparency for those parties, such as individual clinicians, who were not consulted during the Herceptin appraisal, Roche, as a consultee in that process, would have had as much information about the Herceptin appraisal as it would have about one carried out now: 'The information process was very clear and was available to anybody who wanted to look at it' (Reg. 4).

Beyond the Herceptin appraisal's impact on NICE and its procedures, its most obvious effect was to make Herceptin available on the NHS. Put quite simply, 'NICE's pronouncement means that we have to consider it' (CR 8). Yet of course, the strict working of the NICE guidance provided a framework for decision-making within which clinicians could feel constrained.

> Post-NICE guidance, we find ourselves with purchasers and commissioners of care who are being advised by people who are reading the NICE guidance to the letter of the law, which is that you can only give it in combination with a taxane if you're going to use that taxane as your first line of metastatic therapy, because you've given other chemotherapies. And if that isn't the situation, you cannot give Herceptin until post three lines of metastatic chemotherapy which, from a clinical point of view, doesn't make sense.
>
> *(CR 16)*

And it is not just in terms of combination or monotherapy where the letter of the law is being firmly held to. For those centres without the in-house expertise, or money, to do FISH testing, metastatic breast cancer patients who get a borderline score (called 2+) on IHC testing present something of a challenge. When FISH testing is available, then some 2+ patients turn out to be overexpressing to the same level as high-scoring 3+ patients. But

> we can't afford to do the FISH testing and the NICE guidance, anyway, says only 3+. And on the assumption that we're not going to disadvantage . . . too many people by leaving out those who are 2+ . . . we've had to compromise and say well, we can't develop it ourselves, it's not a category that NICE accepts for treatment anyway, so maybe we should just forget about it, and that's what we've done.
>
> *(CR 16)*

Clinician Researcher 8 was unconvinced by evidence suggesting that a few 2+ patients *might* benefit from Herceptin, but accepted that by keeping within the letter of the guidance, 'you're going to have patients who say, "Why are you not using it if you know I've got some evidence of the antigen and you're denying me appropriate treatment?"' (CR 8).

Once the NICE guidance was issued, NHS organisations were meant to make Herceptin available within three months, but 'one of the big problems is . . . you can do a lot of analysis, good, bad or whatever, come to a recommendation, which then the PCT, as commissioners and holder of finance say, sorry we just can't afford this, or, we like to afford it but it's not one of our priorities for this year' (Policy-maker 2). The practicalities of health service budgeting are such that 'if you have no testing, or you don't have enough nurses or . . . there's a variety of other reasons' (Reg. 4) why you might not be able to afford Herceptin,

NICE guidance or not. One result of this is that eighteen months after the NICE guidance, the failure of many healthcare providers to make Herceptin available to patients, and the subsequent continued post-code prescribing, was still an acute political issue (Marsh 2003; Boseley 2003; Frith 2003).

Funding personalised medicine

While it might be tempting to see the story of the NICE approval of Herceptin as a local issue, both in terms of regulatory impact (after all, NICE's remit does not even cover Scotland) and the nature of the drug involved, broader themes can be drawn out. Firstly, although some features of the debate around Herceptin are located firmly within cancer drug development (the lack of RCTs, for example), as was pointed out in chapter 2 above, cancer is where commentators claim personalised medicine will have its first, and biggest, impact. And if this is the case, and if cost-effectiveness is viewed as a major hurdle to moving new cancer drugs into the clinic, then clearly debates in this area are of crucial importance when thinking about how pharmacogenetics will develop.

Looking at the debates around the Herceptin NICE guidance, perhaps the most interesting thing is the lack of discussion, in economic terms, around testing, which is what is meant to give personalised medicine its distinctive nature. Of my clinical interviewees, only Clinician Researcher 17 focused on the way in which NICE had assessed the cost of HER2 testing in its appraisal process. For this clinician, the way in which NICE dealt with testing was far too limited and 'demonstrated a huge flaw in the process'. The problem seemed to be that NICE's calculation of the costs of testing were far too low. Although Clinician Researcher 17 and other pathologists had

> some input into [the process] through the [Royal] College [of Pathologists]
> . . . [NICE] only cherry-picked out one or two bits of things that we put in there,
> and then they introduced right at the last minute with no professional input, to my
> knowledge, a value judgement on the test cost which was flawed. They said that
> testing will cost £21 – that is the cost of the re-agents if you use the DAKO
> HercepTest kit to its full capacity. While this is an accurate estimate of the cost of
> the test materials, it doesn't take into account any second-line testing with FISH, it
> doesn't take into account any technical time, any equipment costs, any professional
> time for medical people reading the slides . . . And, of course, district health
> authorities are now picking up on that as the price of the test, which is complete
> nonsense.
>
> *(CR 17)*

As a consequence, funders' expectations about the cost of the test were unreasonably low. But no other clinicians complained about NICE appraisal of the cost of HER2 testing, though as should be clear, oncologists have a great number of complaints about NICE in general, and in terms of the Herceptin decision in particular.

This lack of debate around NICE's testing decision emphasises the point about Herceptin that reoccurs when talking to clinicians and researchers in this area: that rather than seeing it as a revolutionary break with previous cancer treatments, it has to be seen in the context of the history and practice of the cancer clinic, as an ordinary technology. While James is correct to note that in oncology 'Better drugs seems the most logical answer and the genome project is providing a revolutionary approach to their design', the important issues around these new tailored cancer therapies is not the revolutionary, personalised nature of the treatment:

> in the UK their uptake appears to many oncologists to be hampered by the deliberations of the National Institute for Clinical Excellence . . . Cost as well as effectiveness is evaluated by NICE and clinicians suspect that the Treasury may well be looking with anxiety over the Atlantic. In the United States of America . . . annual inflation on cancer drugs is running at 35% . . . A publicly funded health care system could only respond by a politically embarrassing increase in general taxation.
>
> *(James 2002: 300)*

Clearly this quote reinforces the 'narrative of politics' running through clinicians' discussions of the Herceptin appraisal process, but more than that, it emphasises that the focused, personalised element to these new treatments is less important than their cost. If we are looking for factors that might underpin resistance to the spread of personalised medicine, commentators perhaps need to look away from debates about educating the public, clinicians and policymakers as to the benefits of our bright genetic future, and towards ways of reducing the cost of pharmacogenetic products as and when they arrive.

Organisations such as NICE are less interested in the exciting new way in which such drugs are made, and more in how well they work and crucially, how much they cost: 'The Institute makes its decision not on, is it pharmacogenetic? [but] on what the evidence is that's available' (Reg. 4). But it is quite possible that an organisation such as the National Institute for Clinical Excellence would be rather amenable to an approach which selected smaller numbers of patients for particular treatments. After all,

> we've conducted 62 appraisals and 38 of them have been a selective recommendation, which means within but not all of the licensed indications. So 27 of the 41 drugs we've looked at are within a selective range of licensed indications. What that means is we've been able to target the drug at areas where they may be more clinically and cost effective. Arguably if this pharmacogenetic issue is true, then

yes, you could say the targeting has been done for you. However, of course, if they are incredible expensive, then the overall analysis would still mean they might be clinically effective but not cost effective in that debate.

(Reg. 4)

Yet not everyone I interviewed had such a positive view of the possible relationship between pharmacogenetics and organisations such as NICE. One industry interviewee, who was not involved in the Herceptin debates, felt that, certainly in the case of pharmacogenetic tests for drug safety, NICE would be presented with much harder decisions. If

> you can be tested, [and] it says, that you're a patient who can take this new drug because it's safe for you, but your country will only allow this old drug, which may or may not work, and from which you get an adverse effect. The problem is, you can't sue the government, but in the United States, you'd sue the arse off the doctor and he'll never make the same mistake again. And so the Tort system in the United States brings about . . . an accountability for safety that is not the concern of NICE. NICE is solely, solely about price, and anything else that they say about that has been proven by fact, to be wrong. Now, will NICE exist then? No. If you have a way of measuring safety, then the old drugs that are cheap ought to be looked at with the same measures as the new drugs, and as soon as you do that they're no longer cheap.

(Company 4)

Of course, such a position assumes that NICE would not calculate that the cost of ADRs associated with the old drug outweighs the costs of the newer product. And NICE would counter claims that they are 'solely about the price', by suggesting they are equally interested in how effective a drug is. In the unlikely event that a company produced a very cheap drug that was less clinically effective than current treatments, then it is not at all clear that NICE would approve it. But that said, even with a very clinically effective drug, how much it costs will be the deciding factor. When it comes to personalised medicines, however well they work, cost is the key. The bottom line is the bottom line.

Conclusion

However hard NICE's supporters might protest, this chapter has highlighted the intensely political nature of decisions about the cost-effectiveness of new drugs. As an organisation, NICE was set up to allow politicians to influence prescribing practice while at the same time shielding them from criticism about healthcare rationing. It explicitly adopts a methodology which gives voice to different, competing interest groups and which tries to come to a decision which will satisfy most, if not all, of them. Thus it should not be surprising that the predominant view from those enrolled in the network of support behind Herceptin was that the NICE decision was infused with politics. While NICE's narrative of evidence may well be convincing, it is told from an internal point of view, and ignores the broader context surrounding Herceptin. Given NICE's origins, given Herceptin's cost, given the disease that Herceptin treats, how could this decision be seen as anything other than political?

Yet little of this politics derives from Herceptin's status as the standard bearer for personalised medicine. If pharmacogenetic drugs are going to be controversial in terms of healthcare costs, then it may well be less to do with them being pharmacogenetic, and more to do with their expense. Earlier parts of this chapter showed how the cost of drugs shapes clinicians' actions and options. While this may be particularly acute in the NHS, there seems little reason to doubt that US Health Maintenance Organisations do not have similar decisions to make about treatments. With the expectation that, in the short to medium term at least, pharmacogenetic drugs are going to be expensive drugs (to recoup the costs of developing such revolutionary products), the major obstacle to their uptake would seem to be health providers' willingness to pay. Yet NICE did approve Herceptin, and it has made it into the clinic. Chapter 8 explores what has happened since it got there.

8

Disappointment and disclosure in the pharmacogenetic clinic

You've got to give people realistic knowledge so that you don't raise
expectations unnecessarily, and part of it is putting it in context for them,
letting them know.

Clinician Researcher 9

Pharmacogenetics in the clinic

The past two chapters have shown how Roche mobilised support behind
Herceptin and moved it into clinical practice in the UK. This chapter is about
what happened when it got there. Thus we have moved from broad issues about
how you get a pharmacogenetic drug into clinical practice, to the small-scale,
'micropolitics' of the clinical encounter (Waitzkin 1991). Within this context
the 'shape' the technology takes is influenced by the institutional and cultural
setting within which it comes to be used. We have seen how Herceptin is seen
by many in the media and outside oncology as a clear example of pharmacogenetics, the first drug of its kind to make it into clinical practice, and how Roche
managed to get Herceptin into the clinic by enrolling a variety of actors in a
network of support behind the new drug. This chapter starts by looking at how
clinicians see Herceptin in terms of its value as a treatment. It then moves on to
discuss the way in which HER2 testing and Herceptin are presented to patients:
what women are told about HER2 testing and their eligibility for Herceptin.
Finally, I explore the ethical issues raised by the clinical use of Herceptin and
HER2 testing, highlighting the tensions between a 'traditional' medical ethics
position and a more situated perspective.

Broadly speaking, my interviewees welcomed the arrival of Herceptin in the
clinic. In terms of ease of use, it was 'not too difficult, it's a once a week injection
now, but now there are protocols for using it once every three weeks, so that's not

particularly difficult' (CR 3). Although many clinicians' experience of using the drug was limited, Clinician Researcher 4, who of all my interviewees seemed to have used it the most, commented: 'So I guess we've used it in combination, we've used it as single agent here, on and off trial. Not in many patients because of course it only applies to a quarter or a third of the patients with breast cancer so I don't know, a total of twenty to thirty odd patients, something like that.'

NICE regulations state that Herceptin can be prescribed in combination with chemotherapies, or, in the case of women who have not responded to previous chemotherapy, as a monotherapy. At the time of interview, the numbers treated were small.

> [A]t the moment I've got two or three patients on monotherapy and I've actually run out of the other patients, so I think all the patients I've got on at the moment happen to be monotherapy, not with chemo. There are a couple who have just finished the chemo part and we're carrying on with Herceptin and now progressed, so we've taken them off the Herceptin.
>
> *(C 1)*

As already suggested, prior to NICE approval access to and experience with Herceptin was, for many clinicians, limited by financial constraints: 'We've used very, very little Herceptin, in fact, because of difficulties of funding . . . we had access to Herceptin during the expanded access programme and treated two patients at that point' (CR 6). Put quite bluntly, 'If it is approved by NICE we'll be using it, if it doesn't we're not using it' (CR 3).

When clinicians did get to use Herceptin, they generally accepted that

> there is efficacy I have no doubt about that, and it's not a . . . it doesn't allow women to live for years where they would have lived for months, it's not that kind of treatment, but it appears to prolong life in a number of . . . several months, which is a worthwhile benefit . . . Preparation is easy, it's not like conventional cytotoxics. Toxicity is very low. So if there was no issue of funding we would be using it in a large number of patients. So it's a pure funding issue for us.
>
> *(CR 3)*

This kind of positive yet cautious position was characteristic of many clinicians' attitudes towards the drug: 'It's another therapy that we can use, it's not replacing anything, it's in addition to, so that's helpful' (CR 10). Clearly this is hardly the kind of reaction one might expect to a revolutionary, groundbreaking new product, and much of this caution to Herceptin stems from the gap between those people who overexpress HER2, and those of them who actually respond to the drug.

Herceptin is a perfectly good drug if you can identify the patients who will benefit. The difficulty has always been identifying the patients who benefit and if you're paying two thousand pounds a month for a drug to which roughly one in five of your eligible patients . . . make it one in four of your eligible patients, will actually benefit . . . then that's not value for money.

(CR 6)

We can thus see how financial concerns about Herceptin have coloured clinicians' attitudes towards it. For these people, Herceptin has to be seen in the context within which they will use it: the nature of this pharmacogenetic drug is not independent of the financial and institutional environment within which it is used.

While the use of the three Roche reference centres may have closed down debate over HER2 testing per se, when one looks at different response rates within HER2 overexpressers, the issue of what counts as a 'proper' overexpresser comes to the fore again, specifically the difference between those who are classed as 2+ and 3+ on the IHC scoring system: 'I think the view is that it is a 3+ expression that is associated with a higher response rate and I think I'm right in saying that you're approaching a 40 per cent response rate in that group, and they tend to be the FISH positive ones. There's a strong case [for Herceptin use] only in that group' (CR 8). The NICE appraisal requires that only those scoring 3+ on an IHC test can receive Herceptin, but even so 'the HER2 test isn't a good test because it does not give you a good prediction of who is going to respond, and you actually need to develop more sophisticated tests than the simple HER2 test' (CR 6). These variations in response rate within the broad group of HER2 overexpressers blur the true level of response to the drug: 'It's a good drug and when you talk about 20 per cent of 20 per cent [i.e. HER2 overexpressers], what you look at is in the survival curve of those pivotal studies, there was a small group, which is about 10 to 15 per cent of that 20 per cent who have a very, very, very long-term survival who go on and on and on' (CR 13).

But clinical experience is about more than just broad numbers. At its core is the individual, and in this context, cases of long-term survival came up frequently in the interviews.

[W]hen you see women who've had quite hefty amounts of disease in the liver and they're still alive two and a half years later you begin to think, hang on a minute, maybe this is slightly different. And the survival benefit is there. Relatively small measured in months, but to establish any survival benefit in metastatic breast cancer is pretty impressive, and for an agent which is relatively low toxicity it is even more impressive.

(CR 4)

Another interviewee, Clinician Researcher 13, claimed:

> We've got one lady who's had ninety-six cycles of Herceptin here, so that's weekly, and she had visceral disease, lymphangitis. So there is a small group who seem to do incredibly well. The average time for progression is in the order of seven, eight, nine months but there is a smaller group who do really rather well. Visceral disease can be controlled over the long term whereas it's normally only controlled for a short time, so 15 per cent of the 20 per cent are the ones who have this very long survival tail on the survival curve. And prolonged remission of their disease. It's an interesting group, I don't know what identifies them but it's interesting.
>
> *(CR 13)*

But even in those people who do respond to Herceptin, there are some limitations to the drug that cannot be avoided.

> In our series we saw a very high incidence of cerebral metastases. This is a very small series, but it does show that the incidence of metastases with Herceptin-treated patients is significantly higher than the background incidences of cerebral metatheses in our patients, and that makes perfect sense because a great big antibody molecule is not going to cross over a blood brain barrier.
>
> *(CR 8)*

As a result, even if the metastatic cancer in the rest of the body is controlled by Herceptin, brain metastases are resistant, simply because the drug cannot get to them. This problem is also mentioned by Clinician Researcher 19, who encapsulates the complex range of opinions on Herceptin present in the clinical community.

> I think that Herceptin is one of those rare instances where you introduce a new therapeutic intervention in a clinic and you can tell if it's making a difference. Many therapeutic interventions make a difference but you can only demonstrate that they're making a difference in thousands of patients, where you get small statistically significant differences in outcome measured in terms of a relatively small number of months, but with HER2 I think it was clear really quite early on that here was a drug that did seem to make a difference to the way in which the disease was behaving. We've all got patients who are alive and well much longer than you would expect them to have been and there's a whole raft of new complications arising in patients who are treated with Herceptin, like a much higher incidence of brain metastases.
>
> *(CR 19)*

Yet even with its limitations, Herceptin was seen as exciting because of its role as one of the first anti-cancer drugs targeted at a specific molecular difference: 'In general terms, I think it's exciting because it is proof of principle, i.e. that you can start off with looking at a cancer cell, finding some fundamental abnormality, and developing a treatment that works as a result' (Pharmacist 2). Yet even in a discussion of Herceptin as 'proof of principle' there was a lack of revolutionary fervour on the part of my interviewees. With Herceptin, 'what excites people about it is its novel sort of mode of action, rather than what it has been demonstrated to do so far' (C 2).

What we see here is a smaller-scale production of the expectations that are constructed around pharmacogenetics and personalised medicine as explored in chapter 2. For many of my interviewees, Herceptin was 'exciting' but mainly because 'it's got lots of potential' (CR 9). Some of this potential depends upon better identifying responders among breast cancer patients, but Herceptin's long-term value has extended beyond its clinical role: 'I find it hard to believe that in several years' time we will still be using Herceptin, I think other things will be used' (CR 3). Thus, for most of my interviewees, when it was introduced Herceptin was a moderately successful drug, with low toxicity and occasionally very impressive effect, interesting as a 'proof of principle' for future drug development.

Only one of my interviewees was openly sceptical about Herceptin, describing it as 'not very good. It's not as good as probably the worst form of chemotherapy we have' and 'a pretty weak agent' (CR 5). This interviewee then went on to talk about 'an old drug called Navelbine or Vinorelbine that's been around for twenty years and it's actually recently been shown to be effective. And that is three times or four times more effective.' Yet the reason this drug has a lower profile is 'because there's not a vast expense behind it' (CR 5).[1] And it is interesting to note that even those people who were far more in favour of Herceptin also expressed misgivings about the role of industry in the possible 'overselling' of the drug: 'There's a tremendous amount of hype going on at the moment and the company are positively selling their drug by feeding stories to the press and generating demand, and this is what drug companies do all the time, and they currently are doing it with Herceptin' (CR 9).

As was seen in chapter 5, some drugs companies are not overly keen on allowing independent clinical trials of their products, yet 'it's very important to have an independent ability, to be independent and to assess the data and to assess which patients are likely to benefit from it' (CR 9). The cost of drugs like Herceptin is such that there is a pressing need for companies to begin to recoup their expenditure.

---

[1] Although Navelbine (compound name Vinorelbine) has only recently been tested as a combination chemotherapy for Herceptin (Miles 2001: 382), initial reports on it were published in the early 1980s. It was developed by Roche and appraised by NICE at the same time as Herceptin (see chapter 7).

> [E]ach drug company only has a limited number of products in oncology and they will promote those. And I think they will ensure that every clinician is aware of it. So irrespective of any other kind of meeting that people will go to, the drug companies will ensure that people are aware of these new treatments, much more so than say twenty years ago.
>
> *(CR 3)*

Of course, the reverse is also true, so that 'If you are using a treatment which has been around for a long time and is not particularly an expensive treatment, then dissemination is slower', whereas a clinician using an expensive drug like Herceptin, finds that 'most people's information comes from the drug company as opposed to from independent sources' (CR 3).

One result of the industry dissemination of information is that 'there's no forum . . . for people to be critical. Or there's no forum with a large audience for the other side' (CR 3). This is not active stifling of dissent on the part of companies, 'You never "fail to get a job" kind of thing', it is just that even though

> you command respect amongst your peers in a way by being critical . . . you are not going to get opportunities to disseminate that kind of criticism. Partly because I think in order to be able to be critical you've got to be at a very senior level really. At the junior level . . . you tend to be invited to give a pro kind of argument, not against . . . But if you're senior enough you could do, but those senior people have many opportunities of travelling the world and speaking about the drug *for* as opposed to *against*.
>
> *(CR 3)*

For a number of my interviewees, there were concerns about where information and education about new drugs comes from.

> [T]he real truth of it is, who is educating us, who is telling us about all these things and keeping us up to date at the moment. It ain't the NHS, it's the drug companies . . . [they] are the ones that put on these meetings at vast expense and get all the clinicians there and teach them. Some say brainwash but I mean that's the reality.
>
> *(C 1; see Relman & Angell 2002)*

While those outside the system might hope that the NHS provides a bulwark against the impact of industry,

> the health service in Britain is a reactive service, it always has been . . . that's the problem. The idea was when it was set up that of course it would just implement best practice, and it was up to the doctors and the nurses to tell the service what the best practice was . . . But a lot of that stuff [i.e. best practice] . . . is actually driven by the large companies. So the possibility of distortion according to their priorities . . . well possibility, we're all worried about that, it's a major problem.
>
> *(C 1)*

Thus, following its introduction, there was a high degree of professional uncertainty around Herceptin. On the whole, clinicians have welcomed it as a new drug in the anti-breast cancer armoury, but in the same way opinion varies over whether Herceptin is an example of pharmacogenetics, there was clinical uncertainty over its long-term use, its value (given the poor prediction of response) and its role as 'proof of principle'. This ties into wider uncertainty about the role of the pharmaceutical industry in shaping expectations around new drugs and the education of professionals. Yet despite this uncertainty, Herceptin is used in the clinic and it is this day-to-day usage that the rest of this chapter explores.

Once in the clinic, Herceptin became subject to the rules of the doctor–patient encounter, the most obvious of which is informed consent, enshrined in both academic writing and international agreements on medical research, as the core of ethical medical treatment (Beauchamp & Childress 1993; World Medical Association 2000). Patients and research subjects ought to be given enough information to make a free, autonomous decision about their treatment (or participation in research). Yet while this sounds an obvious and straightforward requirement, a considerable body of empirical research has accrued over the years which highlights just how complex and 'messy' a concept like informed consent can be when applied in the real world (Zussman 1992; Anspach 1993).

Yet, quite rightly, complexity should not be seen as a barrier to ethical behaviour in the clinic: 'The fact that the issues surrounding autonomy are complex does not alter the fact that a mature rational woman who has been diagnosed with breast cancer should have the facts of her case explained to her in the amount of detail she requests and should . . . share in any decisions regarding her future treatment' (Maslin & Powles 1999: 27). And it is the role of information in facilitating an autonomous decision that is the focus of this chapter, for 'Unless a woman has access to relevant and accurate information about her disease, treatment, and prognosis, how can she exercise her autonomy and give consent to treatment in any meaningful way?' (Maslin & Powles 1999: 30).

Everyday testing

When a women is first diagnosed with breast cancer, her clinician will send her for a minor operation, a biopsy, to sample some of the breast tissue, and then arrange treatment, probably involving surgery and adjuvant chemotherapy. A number of different tests are done on the tissue in the pathology lab, one of which could be a HER2 test. Some of the tumour sample is then 'fixed' and embedded in paraffin wax, which allows long-term storage. Whether a particular tumour sample is HER2 tested depends on a variety of factors. The rules governing the prescription of Herceptin on the NHS state that the drug can only be given:

- in combination with a chemotherapy (paclitaxel) in patients who have not received chemotherapy for their metastatic breast cancer
- on its own, to women who have received at least two courses of chemotherapy, without effect

(National Institute for Clinical Excellence 2002: 1)

Following a relapse and presentation with metastatic cancer, a clinician can recall a patient's tumour sample from storage and ask that a HER2 test be run on it; 'even if it's two years down the line . . . you can go back to the original specimen and test it' (CR 2). While the ability to retrieve and test such samples years after they were taken allows HER2 testing to be delayed until a patient relapses and Herceptin becomes an option, there are clear practical difficulties with this:

> the nightmare that I have if I get patients referred from elsewhere is then chasing down the primary material, trying to extract it from the pathologist locally, getting it back here and getting it tested . . . Getting it tested is a piece of cake, I mean that can be done in twenty-four hours. Extracting it from some distant hospital that may have dealt with the patient three to four years ago is really difficult.
>
> *(CR 4)*

Seen from the point of view of those people handing over such samples to other hospitals, 'They want the blocks. They've got the patients to sign these things saying, yes, blocks can go. So I'm sort of, I have to agree and just give them the blocks, which screws my research up here, which isn't ideal. So that's a slight difficulty' (CR 15). This obviously raises interesting tensions between responsibilities in the research setting and the clinical setting over the ownership and control of these blocks.[2]

Added to these difficulties are the general problems raised by an under-funded pathology service, which, in terms of 'Both consultant pathologists and technical staff and secretarial staff it's a disaster all over' (CR 15). Clinicians, pathologists and local health policy makers all seemed to agree that 'pathology departments are working on a shoestring' (CR 7) and that lack of staff, both medical and technical, is hampering the speed and availability of laboratory services, including histopathological tests. One policy-maker, who was generally

---

[2] On 3 December 2003 the British government announced their Human Tissue Bill (http://www.parliament.the-stationery-office.co.uk/pa/cm200304/cmbills/009/2004009.htm), setting up an authority to regulate the taking and use of tissue samples and organs from live and dead bodies.

sceptical about claims of underfunding in oncology accepted that 'I don't think the pathologists were over-egging it. It happens in this part of the world we're relatively well off in the pathology department, but in the rest of the sector there are some huge gaps' (Policy-maker 1). Obviously, while Roche's funding of the reference centres temporarily took some pressure off local pathology labs, there are longer-term issues that may hamper the spread of HER2 testing and support for other pharmacogenetic tests. This has been tacitly accepted by the government. The October 2003 progress report on the National Cancer Plan noted that numbers of trained staff had fallen so low that there were around two hundred vacant posts nationally (Department of Health 2003: 55). That said, many people I spoke to felt that in comparison with the cost of Herceptin, IHC testing, at least, is financially insignificant and a technique that all pathology labs would be familiar with.

Perhaps because of the problems in getting hold of tumour samples held at other sites, because of pressure on pathology labs or the effects of Roche's efforts to change the UK testing culture, clinicians were considering moving HER2 testing 'forward' in the clinical encounter: 'Probably the best time of testing is at diagnosis, because you've got the tissue and you can do the testing there and then' (CR 4). In some areas clinicians were 'increasingly making it part of the standard bank of tests', though obviously they were 'experiencing a little bit of reluctance on behalf of the pathology department to test literally everyone for it at the beginning, because obviously there are financial aspects attached to that' (C 2).

For some clinicians, 'the minute somebody gets metastatic disease, my inclination is to back-test their original tumour for HER2' (CR 2), a standard policy for a number of my interviewees: 'Now it's automatic [for metastatic cases] . . . In our routine, we've been doing it for the last eighteen months or so, so everybody gets it now . . . The pathologist takes the tumour, they do everything else they need: size, grade, all the receptor status and HER2 status. It just all gets done' (CR 10). There are clear arguments in favour of such 'blanket' testing of metastatic patients. The alternative, of waiting to test until a patient exactly conforms to the rules for prescribing Herceptin (in terms of having undergone the required two courses of chemotherapy, for example) means that 'you've got to do the test and get the results before you can even get into the treatment and you may cause a treatment delay at that point . . . you've got to go back, get the block out, test it and find it' (CR 2). Clearly there are a variety of procedures when it comes to putting patients forward for HER2 testing. The strict rules for the use of Herceptin do not seem to necessarily discourage clinicians from applying the HER2 test earlier than needed, at least to get around problems in the pathology service.

The effect of the HERA trial may also be to move HER2 testing even further forward, making widespread screening a normal part of breast cancer treatment: 'if Herceptin moves into the adjuvant situation, i.e. you give it immediately after surgery, to high-risk patients to try and stop getting secondaries, then we have to test everybody' (CR 2). The costs of such a programme might not be as high as one might think, with economies of scale coming into play.

> Overall it might be ultimately cheaper to do it as a routine test on all new primary breast cancer patients because . . . a number are going to relapse, and . . . then this sort of treatment should be considered. It does mean . . . there's a volume effect and you could actually . . . it's cheaper to do ten than to do one, actually . . . because once you've used the antibody, you've used it. So I think, yes, I think that's right, I think there is an argument to do it up front on all patients.
>
> *(C 1)*

In addition, the lack of 'economies of scale' in current practice, where tumour samples are tested when women relapse, means that 'because he [the pathologist] has to batch them up every two or three weeks, there are often uncomfortable delays before the information is available to assist clinical decision-taking' (CR 20). Since the pathology lab has to wait until it has enough samples to justify running the IHC test (which uses the same amount of reagent, regardless of the number of samples being tested), some women have to wait weeks until enough other samples need to be tested. In contrast to the situation prior to Roche's attempt to transform the UK clinical culture, HER2 testing is now a regular part of clinical practice, with clinicians requiring HER2 testing earlier and earlier, to get patients on Herceptin as soon as possible.

Informing patients

What is clear from talking to clinicians is that, for the most part, oncologists restrict the information they give patients about the possibility of receiving Herceptin, about their breast tumour being tested for HER2 overexpression and about the genetic aspects of the HER2 test. It is not that patients are *never* informed about these things, but rather that clinicians act to control the flow of information and the timing of its release. This relates to a deep-seated feature of the clinical situation, that medical

> encounters are structured such that knowledge will be shared – only at the appropriate time. The 'appropriateness' is not simply a matter of externally imposed formal constraints on the interactions; it is constitutive of the role that the oncologist has as gatekeeper and as such instantiates his or her expertise in the

setting. Doctors present themselves as experts by displaying access to information and by controlling the flow of that information.

(Roberts 1999: 107)

Although as gatekeepers controlling the flow of information, clinicians can be seen as reinforcing professional roles and reifying medical power, as will become clear from the rest of this chapter, clinicians' motives for their control of information stem from concern for their patients, as well as the now familiar influence of funding concerns and the epistemological status of the HER2 test. For at least one interviewee, whether they told a patient about HER2 testing depended on the context in which the conversation took place.

> I think that would depend on the clinical situation a bit. If somebody's got metastatic breast cancer and they haven't had their HER2 status assayed, then I would tell them that I was arranging it. Somebody with newly diagnosed breast cancer who was having their tumour 'worked up' in the pathology department would not particularly be told that was being done, anymore than they would be told they were having hormone receptor or a histological grade done of the tumour, it would just be a part of the standard work-up, and we would tell them the results of it if it was relevant later on.
>
> *(CR 19)*

When asked if explicit consent for HER2 testing was sought from patients, Clinician Researcher 3 claimed: 'No that's not an issue really . . . you don't even need to discuss with the patient that kind of thing.' At the time, prior to the NICE approval, this clinician's experience of Herceptin was mainly through the expanded access programme, where she/he had treated half a dozen patients. Because the drug was free, they could test every metastatic patient: 'I wasn't informing patients that they were being tested, we just went ahead and did it, and if they overexpressed HER2, we discussed possible treatment' (CR 3). But with the end of the expanded access programme the use of HER2 testing wound down. When patients knew about Herceptin, this interviewee 'just tell[s] them that the drug is not funded. And incredibly they accept it. I mean I find it hard to believe that in too many developed countries the population would accept that a treatment is given somewhere else but not here because of cost' (CR 3). In many ways, Herceptin's targeted nature made this painful process easier to go through: 'because you know that 80 per cent of them will be negative and it makes it easy for those 80 per cent. The other 20 per cent obviously it's more of an issue for them in that they know they overexpress something which they're suitable for the treatment, but which is not funded' (CR 3).

But beyond the perennial issue of funding, one main reason clinicians do not tell their patients that their tumour samples are going to be tested for HER2 status relates to UK oncologists' resistance to HER2 testing at the cultural level:

HER2 status does not tell the clinician anything they do not already know in terms of prognosis. When a patient presents with breast cancer, the tumour itself is sampled and classified in a number of different ways, with each cancer stage graded according to tumour size, the involvement of lymph nodes, the presence of cancer spread (metastases) and extent of 'differentiation', which is determined by histopathological testing. For my interviewees, HER2 testing did not provide particularly useful prognostic information: 'it's not like the difference between being node-negative and node-positive, or having a grade 3 rather than a grade 1 tumour' (CR 6). To introduce the topic of HER2 testing into the clinical encounter, when a patient has just presented, is 'a needless complication of managing people who are already overloaded with information. Information overloading in cancer patients is beginning to be a big issue, I think' (CR 6).

Even if HER2 testing is not the powerful prognostic tool that many in the literature would claim, even if it is just on a par with, say, lymph node status, this does not explain why patients were not informed of their HER2 test, unless of course 'You don't get a patient's permission to look into the lymph nodes' (CR 7). Tissue was sampled from patients, who were told that 'tests' would be run on it, and it was dispatched to the histopathology lab at which point 'The current procedures are that if you've got a tumour, the pathologist can do what he wants to it, no one ever suggests that he should ask the patient for permission to do it' (CR 12). Of course, it is worth remembering that in the case of many women with metastatic breast cancer, their tissue sample might have been taken many months or even years before they become eligible for HER2 testing.

> They don't need another biopsy. In most cases we can use the previous stored tumour sample so it's just a matter of accessing the paraffin block: a routine pathology sample is embedded in paraffin wax and then sectioned, and then what doesn't get used gets stored in the path lab so we can go back and get that out and do the testing without having to do another biopsy.
>
> *(CR 1)*

But this makes it less likely that patients would be asked for consent to HER2 testing. Clinician Researcher 4 accepted that 'In this day and age it's difficult not to [ask for consent]', but rather than the issue being about the possible prognostic value of the HER2 test, she/he thought patients' concerns revolved around new legal moves, arising out of a series of scandals within the NHS concerning organ and tissue retention (Woodman 2000) and the requirement that 'now we have to consent patients to retain material' (CR 4). For this clinician, consent was not even about HER2 testing as opposed to the other tests that might be run on the tumour material, but about the retention of human tissue and the problems that can arise when people refuse: 'I'm still gobsmacked that some patients refuse and then you've got the problem that if that patient ever relapsed and a targeted treatment became available and you wanted to test tissue then you wouldn't have any [samples] and you might have to go and biopsy . . . which is a not inconsiderable undertaking' (CR 4).

What also became clear from talking to these clinicians was the difference in consent issues between treating a patient clinically and dealing with patients enrolled in research studies. For example, Clinician Researcher 7, who was not a huge user of Herceptin in the clinic but who had tested its effectiveness against other forms of cancer, suggested: 'What we did in the [other cancer] study because it was a research study, we had to get consent for the testing and then consent for the trial'. The difference between the clinical setting and the research setting was made even clearer by Clinician 1:

> Well you see there's even things like consent, I mean we don't have to . . . we don't tell patients well not that we don't particularly want to tell them, but it's just a question of time we don't necessarily tell them we're doing a HER2 test. Because if we're doing it for the possibility we might give them a treatment later, then it's on the basis of clinical rounds, not a research project or anything . . . currently you don't have to tell them anything really unless it's a research project.

Thus it seems quite possible to take part in the HERA clinical trials, researching Herceptin as an adjuvant treatment and requiring participants to give their informed consent for HER2 testing, while at the same time treating other patients with metastatic breast cancer and not even telling them their tumour tissue is being tested for HER2 status.

Even in research projects where patients are informed of HER2 testing, the exact nature of the information given to them is restricted: 'In all the studies that we do, we have to ask consent to even do the test, but I don't think we ever described it as a genetic test, certainly not in the information sheets' (CR 10). In the light of Herceptin's status as the first clinically applicable example of pharmacogenetics, it might seem odd that HER2 testing was not referred to as 'genetic testing', but in many ways this ties into the ambiguity over whether Herceptin is a 'proper' case of pharmacogenetics at all. Some of my interviewees had had experience of the issues surrounding BRCA1 and 2 testing, and all seemed to accept the 'conventional wisdom' that genetic testing is somehow special and involves important ethical issues: 'if you're in a situation where you're going to test a patient for an inherited genetic defect, almost everyone would accept that you had to get proper, informed consent' (CR 12). Yet HER2 testing was explicitly not seen in terms of traditional genetics: 'I guess in this sort of situation, we tend not to talk so much about the gene as the product of the gene, so we talk about the growth factor receptor which is a product of the gene even though when we do FISH testing for example, we're looking at gene amplification' (CR 1).

And any difference that did exist was not presented as a feature of the person, but of the tumour itself: 'the other aspect is that patients tend to think of their tumour as an enemy, it's not part of them, it's some alien being . . . And in my experience patient's genetic testing is to do with them as a normal person, their own personal genes, and they tend to regard the tumour as a totally alien thing' (C 1). One result of patients' separation from their tumour was, in the clinicians' minds at least, a reduced danger of confusion.

> [W]hen I'm talking to patients, I'm talking about characteristics of their tumour rather than saying this is specifically a genetic abnormality related to their tumour. I think patients get confused if you start talking about genetic abnormalities, that they often then do think it's something that's inherited and they get worried they might be passing it on to their children, so it makes sense to avoid that sort of confusion, it's better to talk about characteristics of the cancer cells.
>
> *(CR 1)*

As Clinician Researcher 16 said, 'It's called the genetic test, because you look at overexpression of gene, but as you say, it's somatic. And we don't know, we get confused sometimes . . . we don't mention the word *genetic*, because of the inherent dangers of saying that word to people'. What these clinicians expressed concern about is 'genetic exceptionalism', the idea that genetic information is somehow special, perhaps more risky than other medical data, and needs to be treated accordingly. In their report on the ethical issues surrounding pharmacogenetics, the Nuffield Council on Bioethics was sceptical about claims that pharmacogenetic data is morally problematic by virtue of its genetic origins (Nuffield Council on Bioethics 2003: 6). And my interviewees tend to agree; concerns about how patients will see the genetic elements of the HER2 test make them disguise its nature. Thus, instead of HER2 testing being seen as a prognostic genetic test, with all the implications that has for genetic counselling and privacy, clinicians rather see HER2 testing as a test with little or no prognostic value, which cannot be described as genetic in any serious sense. Those outside of the clinic seem to have a different point of view. For example, Klaus Lindpaintner, who works for Roche after all, accepts that Herceptin may raise important confidentiality issues: 'as soon as a patient with breast cancer submits her trastuzamab [Herceptin] prescription, the pharmacist and the cashier, as well as the data entry clerk, the claims adjuster, and any number of additional personnel involved in health care administration and reimbursement will by inference, know that patient's HER2-expressor status' (Lindpaintner *et al.* 2001: 81).

Similarly, the two pharmacists I spoke to, both of whom knew about Herceptin but who did not treat patients as clinicians, felt that HER2 testing and Herceptin raised important ethical issues.

> Do you tell a woman that she's HER2 positive at the start when you do the lumpectomy and they know they are going to have a worse prognosis? So it does raise quite a lot of ethical issues. When do you HER2 test? Do you HER2 test at the point of having had their surgery, when they're having adjuvant chemotherapy, or do you have it when they relapse with advanced disease? So it raises quite a lot of ethical issues in terms of what you tell your patient.
>
> *(Pharmacist 1)*

Pharmacist 2 also raised the issue of what happens when testing is broadened out beyond metastatic patients:

> It means that you are ultimately going to have to test everybody so it reduces your testing costs, but I think perhaps the more important one is do you want to burden your patient with the knowledge that they have a particularly bad prognosis disease and are probably going to be dead within eighteen months, when maybe you don't need to?
>
> *(Pharmacist 2)*

Both pharmacists seemed to accept that HER2 testing would expand to the adjuvant setting, and that this will raise ethical problems in terms of informing patients of what they are being tested for and the implications of this in terms of prognosis. Yet as has already been seen, if clinicians have their way, Herceptin's move to the adjuvant setting is unlikely to change current practice. Although most HER2 testing is done 'retrospectively' on tumour samples stored for months or years, in the expanded access programme there seemed to be a tendency to test women as and when they presented (since the testing and the drug were free). There is clearly a difference in perspective between those people who deal with patients face to face and those with less contact with clinical practice.

The HER2 test's status as a genetic (i.e. somatic) test but not a *genetic* (i.e. inherited) test reminds us that Herceptin does *not* raise many of the 'traditional' ethical issues associated with genetics (compare APOE and Alzheimer's). If Herceptin is an example of pharmacogenetics, this supports the claims of those commentators such as Allen Roses, who suggest that pharmacogenetics raises separate, simpler ethical issues compared to testing for genetic diseases.

Disappointment

At the centre of clinicians' attitudes towards the HER2 test and the kind of information given to patients about Herceptin is the question of why clinicians restrict patients' access to this information. Both clinical and non-clinical medical staff have access to the information on the prognostic and predictive value of HER2 testing; what clearly comes out of these interviews is clinicians' desire to avoid causing emotional and psychological harm – phrased as disappointment – to their patients. Clinicians' experience of being involved in the Herceptin clinical trials is that when patients know that they are being HER2 tested to check for eligibility for treatment with Herceptin, finding out that they do not overexpress the protein is disappointing: 'I've had patients when we were doing this as part of the study, we sent the HER2 for testing and the tests came back essentially negative, and this patient with advanced breast cancer was disappointed because we were not going to use this nice new treatment' (CR 9).

This experience is not new; as has already been pointed out, there are considerable similarities between HER2 testing and oestrogen receptor (ER) testing for eligibility for Tamoxifen. The issue of patient disappointment has already been experienced in the area of ER testing: 'certainly patients are interested in the oestrogen receptor and whether they are positive or negative, and they all know really it's bound to be negative and it's better to be positive . . . But they are interested in that and of course they get very disappointed if they're HER2 negative because they want to have Herceptin . . . again I think it's a disappointment' (C 1). In this context, clinicians' reaction to Herceptin is shaped by its role as an ordinary technology, as similar to Tamoxifen/ER testing. Whatever the revolutionary rhetoric, when it comes to the clinic, the core ethical theme in Herceptin use is that of protecting the patient from disappointment.

Of course there is an apparent contradiction here. HER2 overexpressing cancers are more dangerous, are more likely to reoccur and have a worse prognosis. Surely finding out that you are not in this group should be a source of comfort rather than disappointment.

> Yes, well that's one way I suppose of looking at it, but when you've already got that disease and you're metastatic then you want to be able to have a treatment. So my impression at the moment is that patients . . . they're looking at it in purely practical terms at the moment, that this is a cancer which they don't really want . . . and they will take all the good treatments they can get.
>
> *(C 1)*

In a similar vein, Clinician Researcher 9 suggested that the serious nature of metastatic breast cancer colours patients' views of HER2 testing: 'For the patients that we do HER2 testing on later on, they have metastatic disease therefore, and they know that their days are numbered effectively, they don't know how many there are going to be though, and they know that we're doing the testing to help find treatment. I think it is viewed as being a positive thing' (CR 9). Whether this apparently contradictory position – wanting to overexpress HER2 – will hold with patients who have not developed metastatic breast cancer, those involved in the HERA trial for example, is not clear.

One of the clinicians I spoke to who did tell their patients about HER2 testing and the possibility of Herceptin outlined the dilemmas she/he faced.

> So I guess we do discuss it with the patients, which is probably the right thing to do. It is a two-edged sword though because if it transpires that they're negative for a certain marker that you're looking for then there's clearly a degree of disappointment on their behalf that they are not then eligible for treatment X that you were aiming to target. In some ways with HER2 you can kind of turn the conversation around that when patients, if they are negative, and say well at least from what we know of HER2 expression then perhaps your disease is not quite as aggressive . . . as the person whose disease does overexpress HER2. So that's the kind of sop that we keep in our back pocket.
>
> *(CR 4)*

Given the choice between offering the 'sop' of low HER2 expression in the face of disappointment, and not informing patients of what their tumour is being tested for, many clinicians seemed to opt for the latter. Such an approach was accepted as 'paternalistic' by Clinician 1, and quite possibly not a long-term option:

> We don't tell them because it's actually kinder in a way because if they're negative, if they don't bring up the question of Herceptin . . . Sometimes they'll say, 'Can I have Herceptin?', you say, 'Well we'll do the test', and then you say, 'I'm sorry, it's negative, it's not going to work.' But if I am thinking of it ahead of them then I'll just do the test and I'll only mention the drug if they're positive, to avoid disappointment. But that's a paternalistic approach that we currently do, and it probably won't last long, because they'll all ask for Herceptin.

And it is clear that change is being driven from two different directions: proactive patients and the broadening range of people who can be prescribed Herceptin. In the same way that the children of Alzheimer's patients could use the Internet to unearth the prognostic value of a parent's APOE test, breast cancer patients can easily find out about Herceptin and the need for a HER2 test.

> You've got to give people realistic knowledge so that you don't raise expectations unnecessarily, and part of it is putting it in context for them, letting them know. I get lots of people asking me whether they can have Herceptin for their ovary cancer or their bowel cancer because as far as the general public is concerned, it's cancer, and 'here's a new treatment so why can't I have it?'
>
> *(CR 8)*

What come out of these interviews are the different degrees of knowledge that patients can access and the different ways in which they can do this.

> [T]here are patients who very carefully download everything off the Internet and therefore have got all that information and will ask you, you know, is Herceptin possible for me? Has my status been looked at, etc., etc. So there is a demand for it and that will increase, I think. Because I think, particularly in breast cancer, there obviously is a very active patient lobby, as it were. And therefore there are lots of sorts of bits of information which are available. Most hospitals do have breast support groups where sufferers go along and chat. And certainly one of the things that they chat about is of course, the new developments and so on. So if someone has the ability to get access to that information, everyone will equally have access to it.
>
> *(C 2)*[3]

This theme of 'realistic knowledge' is closely related to clinicians' concerns about disappointment at a negative HER2 test result, and ties into their micro-political role as experts, privileged dispensers of knowledge. Even when patients qualify for Herceptin there are still, from a medical point of view, unrealistic expectations about the chances of response.

> [T]hey've read all about it [Herceptin] and most of them don't actually believe that they won't respond to it because it's so new and so wonderful that frankly, if they don't respond to it, they're kind of taken aback. You know, here is the latest thing, hot off the press, we are not responding to it. Whereas a more sanguine look at the literature, would of course indicate that that's actually the anticipated response rather than the other way around.
>
> *(C 2)*

An obvious major source of information for patients is the mass media, particularly newspapers (Carlsson 2000), but this is not always appreciated by clinicians.

> [T]hey see the stories, great new cancer cure, Roche's shares go up, and we cop it in the clinic next week, saying, 'Why can't I have the new wonder drug?'
>
> Question: Does it increase demand?
>
> Oh yes, every week. The drug companies aren't allowed to sell directly to the public like they are in America now, so they do it through the journalists. You ask who pays the journalists? It's the companies who give them the data.
>
> *(CR 9)*[4]

---

[3] This 'grapevine' aspect of breast cancer information also played an important part in mobilising interest in the original Herceptin clinical trials, putting pressure of Genentech to increase access to Herceptin while it was still an experimental drug (Bazell 1998).

[4] Of the UK newspapers, it is the middle-brow tabloid the *Daily Mail* that most incurs the wrath of my interviewees: 'The media's reprehensible; the *Daily Mail* takes the prize' (CR 13); 'the whole way that the public get information at the moment, and it's often out of the *Daily Mail*, and as you know it's not very accurate usually' (C 1).

Even in the UK, without direct to consumer advertising for pharmaceutical products, companies can generate demand for their drugs via the well-placed newspaper story. Clinicians deal with these demands by telling patients that

> either it's not appropriate to have at this moment in time in terms of your pathway of disease, or yes, we're thinking about that but you don't need it at the moment, or actually we introduce it and say, this is something that might be helpful for you and what we need to do is to go back and test your tumour for this.
>
> *(CR 10)*

Bearing in mind the way and the reasons behind clinicians' control of the flow of information to patients about HER2, the kinds of requests stirred up by newspaper reports are bound to generate significant opposition among professionals. This may have an important impact on the doctor–patient relationship since there is some research that suggests that patients who request a particular treatment, and who are refused it by a doctor, generally report lower satisfaction with their doctors (Bell, Wilkes & Kravitz 1999). While in this study patients got their information direct from consumer advertising, it is not inconceivable that a similar reaction might result in the case of information gained from newspaper articles.

The approach to HER2 testing outlined here, with clinicians controlling the information patients get and focusing the use of HER2 testing on Herceptin treatment, is under pressure. But not just from patients. As noted above, the other possible source of change for HER2 testing is the expansion of Herceptin use beyond metastatic breast cancer, as demonstrated by the on-going HERA trial. Clinician Researcher 8 accepts that current practice around patient consent to HER2 testing will change if Herceptin moves into the adjuvant setting.

> It is going to be especially important if the HERA trial comes out to say that Herceptin is of value in the adjuvant setting. If that happens and we're saying why we're going to offer you Herceptin as part of this package of treatment following the operation, patients will then go through knowing that bit more detail about their prognosis while knowing the HER2 result in that context. For most patients, of course, it's going to be a case of your tumour is HER2 negative and that's a relatively good prognostic indicator.

The HERA trial still has some time to run, and it is too early to say whether Herceptin will move into the adjuvant setting and thus become the treatment of choice for many more women. Clearly, many of these patients will access information about HER2 testing and Herceptin from the internet, newspapers, support groups and other women with breast cancer.

While there are important issues concerning the tensions between expert and non-expert conceptions of scientific knowledge, it is not clear exactly how these debates relate to the case of HER2 testing and Herceptin in current clinical practice, constrained as it is by a number of formal regulations, such as the NICE guidance. And although the internet, patient groups and oncologists' favourite hate figures, the *Daily Mail* and other tabloid newspapers, may make patients *aware* of Herceptin, patient knowledge is not in a position to mediate medical expertise. A clinician may *want* to prescribe Herceptin to a 2+ overexpresser, or to a woman who has only had one course of chemotherapy for metastatic breast cancer, but if their health provider sticks to the letter of the NICE guidance, they will not be able to do this. A patient may be more knowledgeable than an oncologist about their own condition and the mechanisms relating HER2 overexpression to breast cancer, but they will not be able to debate or change clinical practice, since the clinician is so tightly constrained.

Ethical issues in Herceptin use

A number of different ethical themes emerge from the discussion of the way in which HER2 testing and Herceptin are used in the clinic. Issues familiar to medical ethicists come to the fore, in terms of informed consent, differences between clinical and research use, and the over-protective, paternalistic attitude of clinicians towards their patients. The aim of this chapter, in keeping with other social-science-based research into medical encounters, is to highlight the complexity and ambiguity that characterises such ethical issues when they arise in the clinical context, as opposed to theoretical discussion (Fox & Swazey 1984; Bosk 1992; Rapp 2000).

At the broadest level, clinicians' tales about the use of this new drug should alert us to a very simple state of affairs: if a hospital or healthcare funder does not allow the prescription of Herceptin, then the ethical issues surrounding HER2 testing are rather limited. Add to this UK oncologists' attitudes towards the value of HER2 testing when there is no access to Herceptin, and we have a messy picture of how funding issues intersect with ethical decision-making. In their consideration of the ethical issues involved in the clinical use of pharmacogenetics, the Nuffield Council on Bioethics suggests that problems may arise for clinicians since 'Pharmacogenetic tests based on genetic variation between individuals are unlikely, in general, to allocate patients to exclusive categories of those who respond to a medicine and those who do not' (2003: 60). The trouble with this claim is that it assumes a separation between a test and the decision to use it or not. But the way in which Herceptin is constituted as a technology, within a particular setting, with specific rules and restrictions, means that there is no option for the clinician to offer Herceptin to those women who do not fit the healthcare provider's conditions (probably the same as the NICE recommendations). Nuffield note that 'Where a pharmacogenetic test is part of the licence conditions of a medicine, it is unlikely that a health professional would wish to prescribe the medicine without the test', yet where in the picture painted by clinicians does the option of such off-label prescription for Herceptin come? It is not that these authors are unrealistic. They admit that 'bodies such as NICE may provide guidance about the circumstances in which medicines may be provided, and this may include reference to the results of a pharmacogenetic test, as in the case of Herceptin'. But they imply that 'Although not formally binding on health professionals . . . physicians may feel obligated to restrict prescription to those individuals who . . . meet the necessary criteria . . . and indeed, health providers may impose such requirements' (Nuffield Council on Bioethics 2003: 66). To some extent, an ethical review of a new technology has to contain an element of abstraction, which is where empirically based studies can add to the picture. The Nuffield Council may be right that there is no legal requirement for clinicians to stick to the NICE recommendations, but it should be clear by now that, in the case of Herceptin at least, most of the people I spoke to had little option. Ethical decision-making comes in how individuals and groups of clinicians try to get round such restrictions, how they adapt their behaviour to get as many women treated as possible, within the terms of the drug's licence.

While the evidence presented in this book has focused on the situation in the UK, the general influence of the NICE approach within US health maintenance organisations suggests that these issues are not limited to British-based oncologists. The US-based Consortium on Pharmacogenetics meditates on just these kinds of problems.

> Suppose that a managed care organization, or Medicare, or for that matter a national health system, adopts a rational drug use policy that includes the rule that a very expensive cancer drug will only be covered for those who are classified as 'high-responders' according to a reliable PGx test. The justification for this rule is that given the high costs of the drug and the severity of the side effects, and given a limited budget from which care for many individuals must be provided, responsible stewardship of resources requires providing this drug only to those who are most likely to benefit significantly from it.
>
> *(Buchanan et al. 2002: 31)*

This scenario (except the severity of the side effects) is essentially the challenge Herceptin presents healthcare providers. The Consortium correctly notes that the tension this situation produces, between the needs of the individual (a less than high responder, say) and those of the group (needing to rationalise expenditure), 'is not in any way peculiar to PGx, and in fact has nothing to do with the methodology itself' (Buchanan *et al.* 2002: 31). Yet this simply reinforces the position of Herceptin, and other examples of pharmacogenetics, as ordinary technologies. It is not clear that supporters of personalised medicine are right to claim that pharmacogenetics is going to reduce healthcare budgets. As Rothstein and Epps note: "pharmacogenomic-based drugs will be expensive, because of . . . the need to recoup the cost of investment in new technologies" (Rothstein & Epps 2001: 228). Whether or not Herceptin and other examples of personalised medicine are considered revolutionary or ordinary technologies, it needs to be acknowledged that in the context of a modern healthcare system, ethical responsibility for their use has largely been taken out of clinicians' hands. Indeed, ethical decisions about the use of these technologies are taken at the political, economic and structural levels, and it is these areas to which ethicists might more profitably pay attention.

If we focus on the choices made by individual clinicians, we can see more clearly the socially constituted structure around ethical decision-making. Clinicians tended to stick to the letter of the regulations, for example only putting the strongest, 3+, expressers forward for treatment, even if they suspected that some of the weaker expressers might also benefit. The testing culture among UK oncologists has been such that if HER2 testing in the absence of Herceptin was seen as useful, there would be less of a dilemma (since testing would serve some purpose).[5] In the US and elsewhere in Europe, where the attitude towards the prognostic and predictive value of HER2 testing is more forgiving, the ethical issues in testing do not revolve around the availability of Herceptin.

The point is the rather obvious one that ethics depends upon epistemology, a well-worn debate within medical ethics over, for example, conditions required for clinical equipoise to pertain (Freedman 1987; Ashcroft 1999). But since HER2 tests are epistemologically different in different places (in the US they are prognostic; in the UK they are only of value in deciding on eligibility for Herceptin), the ethical issues involved in HER2 testing differ according to where the testing is offered. While what results from this is relativism, it is deeper than the kind of moral relativism that mainstream bioethics is inclined to combat (e.g. Macklin 1999). Clinicians on both sides of the Atlantic (or indeed the Channel) might have the same ethical values with regard to who gets access to tests, what one tells patients about tests and informed consent. Yet there would still be a difference in how they saw the HER2 test, since the epistemological status of the test would be different.

---

[5] I accept that in such a situation, where HER2 testing was used for prognostic purposes but where NHS staff were not allowed to prescribe Herceptin, there would be considerable disquiet on the part of clinicians. However the issue would not be one of whether to use the HER2 test or not, but only about access to Herceptin.

It is a truism that differences in treatment practice between the US and the UK are often the result of the different ways in which healthcare is funded in the two countries. In the US, with private health insurance footing the bill for most people's healthcare, medical staff are far more willing to use 'heroic measures' to treat individual patients, since they are not denying treatment to anyone else:

> In contrast to the 'closed system' of British medicine, which operates within fixed budgets . . . American physicians operate within an 'open system' in which they have no assurance that savings incurred on one patient will remain within the health care system at all. Accustomed to concerning themselves with that which they can control, physicians concentrate on the individual case while neglecting collective consequences.
>
> *(Zussman 1997: 182)*

In the UK, the more money one spends on one person, the less there theoretically is for anyone else.[6] But as chapter 7 has shown, however socially minded UK clinicians are, it is very difficult for individuals to get to grips with the kinds of money involved. How many hospital beds has the NHS lost as a result of Herceptin being made available?

Thus the attitude towards treatments, tests and interventions on the part of UK oncologists is a pragmatic balance between being part of a socialised healthcare system and a need to do the best for individual patients. If NHS funds are going to be spent on HER2 testing, then it ought to be useful. Since for these clinicians, HER2 testing *on its own* serves little diagnostic, prognostic or predictive purpose, in the UK, not providing a HER2 test, in the absence of the availability of Herceptin, is a responsible approach to take. Of course, what counts as 'responsible' is a complex web of social, ethical and economic factors which make up a particular group's opinion of a specific test. In other countries, changes in those factors may mean a change in what responsible use of HER testing means.

One obvious ethical criticism of the current use of Herceptin in the clinic revolves around informed consent and what patients get told about HER2 testing. The Nuffield Council on Bioethics report notes that 'written consent forms are not used when patients have samples taken to test for overexpression of HER2', and that this is probably because the test is only used for Herceptin eligibility and the limited nature of the genetic information revealed

---

[6] Richard Ashcroft has pointed out to me that this attitude is a 'typically American myth about British medicine', and that British clinicians are just as willing to treat people as individuals on the assumption that the financial details will somehow sort themselves out (personal communication). While this may often be the case, it is still a theme in discussions about socialised systems, that 'decisions to treat one patient . . . may mean that others are denied care' (Newdick 1995: 21).

(2003: 61).[7] A result of this is that 'it is not clear that pharmacogenetic information is different from that which routinely has to be communicated by their physicians following non-genetic tests'. From this they conclude that rather than a blanket requirement for written consent for pharmacogenetic tests, we need to assess tests on an individual basis (Nuffield Council on Bioethics 2003: 61).

An alternative take on this would be concerned about the paternalistic attitude of clinicians towards their patients, and the way in which they restrict access to information about possible treatments. Such a position is supported by considerable work looking at women's preferences in cancer care, suggesting that as well as women preferring to be informed of a diagnosis of cancer, many women would like more information in the clinical setting as a rule (Graydon *et al.* 1997; Benbassat, Pilpel & Tidhar 1998; Maslin & Powles 1999, Sainio & Lauri 2003). Although most of this research discusses information in broad terms and most of these 'studies have generally failed to differentiate between preferences for diagnostic, treatment and prognostic information needs' (Hack, Degner & Dyck 1994: 278), it is clear that among certain groups of breast cancer patient, there is a desire to be told about the procedures that might be possible. Seen from this viewpoint, there are a number of interlinked ethical problems with the way in which clinicians currently use Herceptin, namely: they tend not to inform patients of HER2 testing prior to their tumour sample being tested; when they do inform them of HER2 testing, they do not tell patients about the genetic aspects of the HER2 test; and clinicians tend not to tell patients of the possibility of Herceptin prior to a positive HER2 result. Thus from the point of view of conventional medical ethics, many oncologists are involved in a serious restriction of informed consent.

Yet to assume that patients ought to be informed of HER2 testing when their tumour biopsy is carried out is presumably to assume that patients should also have explained to them the details of all the other pathological tests done at this time. Certainly, in the opinion of the UK oncological community, these other tests tell more about a patient's prognosis than the HER2 test does. Under the current NICE guidance, the results of the HER2 test only really become relevant when a woman relapses and develops metastatic breast cancer. At this stage, clinicians suggest that to protect them from 'disappointment' they do not tell patients about Herceptin until a HER2 test confirms that it is an option. When, because of a positive HER2 test, Herceptin becomes available, then

[7] On a reflexive note, the results of my research project fed into the early stages of the Council's deliberations about pharmacogenetics in the summer of 2002, as well as the formal public consultation process between November 2002 and February 2003. Thus it may be that the Council's conclusions in this area are not independent of my own research.

clinicians inform patients and discuss it as a treatment. If patients' autonomy is being infringed by clinicians, it may well be that it is justified in terms of the clinicians' desire to protect patients from the psychological harm resulting from disappointment at a negative HER2 result.

Perhaps in the case of treatments such as Herceptin, we need to rethink the concept of informed consent. Rather than it being seen as an 'event', informed consent makes more sense as a process spread out over time. Of course, the idea of process is supposedly at the core of informed consent, and complaints that process is more than just 'signing a form' are not new (Berg *et al.* 2001; Kuczewski & Marshall 2002), but the implications of such an approach need to be thought out more fully than is perhaps currently the case. It is not just that at different stages of an illness, different interventions may become available, and new consent required at each point. More than this, 'consent as a process' sees clinicians restricting information (about possible future treatments, for example) until it becomes relevant, as a way of caring for their patients. Such a view of consent conflicts with both the dominant tone of contemporary medical ethics and the patient-centred perspective, which has come to the fore in cancer care. Yet in terms of actual clinical practice, it is a far better description of what goes on. It is also more compatible with the empirical literature, which suggests that although some women are proactive and do want more information, many women do not, and that it is very difficult to predict an individual patient's information needs prior to treatment (Benbassat, Pilpel & Tidhar 1998; Bruera *et al.* 2002). In making this point, I am simply adding to the growing body of literature that challenges conventional conceptions of informed consent from an empirical perspective (see Sugarman *et al.* 1999 for an extensive bibliography). If pharmacogenetics, of whatever kind, becomes a commonplace piece of clinical technology, then we need the regulations controlling informed consent, and the ethical concepts underpinning them, to adapt to the lived reality of these technologies.

Of course, the situation concerning informed consent to HER2 testing is changing, both because patients are becoming better informed about possible treatments and because of Herceptin's possible move to the adjuvant setting, should the HERA trial produce the expected results. This merely reinforces the need for a re-evaluation of what we expect from informed consent, what it is for and how to achieve that.

The final point concerns the difference between the requirements for informed consent in trials as opposed to standard clinical practice. As Charles Bosk has noted, the problems of informed consent are 'exacerbated by a social organization of research that blurs the distinction between clinician and researcher, patient and subject as well as by a rhetoric that justifies risky research by confusing therapeutics and experimentation' (Bosk 2002: V64). Clinician Researcher 19 puts it simply: 'outside clinical trials I wouldn't formally be seeking written consent from the patients to go back to do a test . . . [but] with big clinical trials there is an issue about getting written consent'. In terms of physical interventions, of course consent is sought for the taking of a biopsy, otherwise the clinician could be accused of assault. It is just that in the clinic, the tests such a biopsy undergoes are not explicitly outlined to the patient, whereas in a research setting, the participant is made aware of the kinds of tests their tissue will undergo.

Thus there is the slightly odd situation that the same clinician may operate two very different consent regimens, with the same drug, depending on whether the patient is being treated as part of the HERA trial or in ordinary clinical practice. The HERA trial is not testing an experimental drug to see whether it is safe or not, rather it is testing the efficacy of a product already deemed to be safe, in new circumstances. There does not seem to be any significant difference between the two situations. In neither case is actual treatment being given without consent, but in a clinical trial, it is important to gain consent for a test which in the clinic is just one of a batch of regular tests run on tumour samples.

That clinical treatment requires a lower level of informed consent than research is nothing new. It is generally felt that while 'Clinical practice is oriented towards providing patients with individualized care . . . clinical research is oriented toward developing knowledge to help future patients' (Chen, Miller & Rosenstein 2003: 669). Yet once again, the trouble with this position is that it is based more on theoretical concerns about ethical theory than it is on clinicians' lived experience. For example, Clinician Researcher 8 gives the lie to the idea of clinical treatment and research being distinct.

> With the new drugs, it's a lot harder [to get access]. My approach is to put patients into clinical trials wherever possible and we think we do that very effectively at this hospital, if you look at the league tables of entry into clinical trials we don't appear too badly in that. When you're doing that, of course, you do make a contract with the patient about the use of drugs, so that in the FOCUS trial in bowel cancer, for example, the standard they specify which is the control arm for the whole study, is 5FU and folinic acid followed by Irinotecan where you want a second-line treatment, and since the contract with the patient is that if you do not enter the study, you'll be treated on the same basis as if you did, then you're saying that that's how we're going to treat you, and the Trust accepts that, that there is a commitment to use Irinotecan there and that's how we applied it. Of course, that has been formalised because NICE has said that's the right thing to do and so it's a NICE recommendation.

This is not a case of the 'therapeutic misconception', where patients think that experimental treatments must be more effective than the base-line care. Rather, this interviewee is suggesting clinical trials as a way of getting patients treated with a drug known to be effective (Irinotecan), that at the time had not been approved for use by NICE. Whether the same process is taking place in the HERA trial is not clear, although it is worth noting clinicians' extreme eagerness to sign patients up for HERA. Roche are delighted, since

> we're due to have a four-year recruitment period, but the rate that recruitment is going at the moment, it won't be four years – it's competitive recruitment and I think that we've got a huge opportunity in the UK to try and get as many patients into the study as possible. But I do honestly believe that it will be less than four years before they close the books.
>
> *(Company 1)*

In a healthcare system where access to new drugs is restricted, either through formal regulations (such as NICE recommendations) or local funding priorities, putting patients in trials, especially for drugs that are known to be safe, is a way for clinicians to act ethically, a way for them to get patients the best treatment possible. I am not claiming that such an approach is widespread even within oncology, let alone in other medical specialties (though see Epstein 1996 for similar cases). But the point is that this elision between clinical treatment and clinical trial underlines the peculiarities present in an ethical system which claims that these two contexts have different requirements in terms of informed consent. Kathryn Taylor has noted how, since the rise of the randomised clinical trial in the 1960s and 1970s, the roles of clinician and researcher have become increasingly blurred, with the reward systems and professional interaction of these two very different approaches running together (Taylor 1992). Herceptin is merely a recent example of this phenomenon.

Conclusion

While more theoretical analyses of technologies may raise interesting questions about possible ethical dilemmas and conflicts, one can only truly come to terms with the implications a new technology has for society when one has seen how it works in context – in this case, a clinical context. And in the clinical context, Herceptin is seen as less of a revolutionary example of pharmacogenetics and more as an ordinary technology – a useful form of treatment but like all treatments, subject to structural restrictions. The use of this example of personalised medicine has less to do with the ethical decisions made by individual clinicians and more to do with those choices made by various other actors – Genentech for deciding to license the drug for metastatic breast cancer, NICE for imposing certain requirements on how the drug is used, health authorities and hospital Trusts for making money available prior to the NICE decision – which provide the environment within which the clinician gets to make his or her decision. This is not to say that there are not issues that fit into a more conventional ethical analysis, but even these, such as the blurring of the distinction between clinician and researcher and the subsequent consent issues, only make sense in the context of the broader social and economic structures within which Herceptin is prescribed.

Thus future assessments of the ethics of pharmacogenetics need to take into account the economic, social and structural issues that play such an important part in shaping the use of new technologies. Describing a pharmacogenetic test in terms of 'genetic testing' needs to be done with an eye on exactly what 'genetic' means in a particular context. Describing a test as prognostic and/or predictive, without being aware of the other kinds of tests routinely run on tumour tissues, and their predictive value, is to abstract a technology from its clinical setting. Such an approach, of course, means that the kinds of claims one can make about pharmacogenetics are rather limited. Not all examples of personalised medicine are going to be like Herceptin, or for that matter, like APOE–Tacrine; pharmacogenetics is a heterogeneous technology. We need to be cautious about what conclusions we draw from only two cases, however in depth we look at them. Yet at the same time we can still comment on the kinds of claims being made and the expectations being created around personalised medicine.

9

The personalised is political

Ordinary coalface knowledge

This book has followed two high-profile examples of pharmacogenetics, unpacking assumptions, beliefs and contexts along the way. I have shown both how to, and how not to, get an example of personalised medicine into clinical practice, and have explored the messy intersection between industry, health service funders and clinicians. This chapter draws together ideas around pharmacogenetics by returning to the three dichotomies introduced in chapter 1: coalface–expectations, knowledge–resistance and ordinary–revolutionary technology.

Having just explored the ordinariness of Herceptin, it is to this dichotomy that I first turn. In both case studies, I have shown how pharmacogenetic tests do not arise out of nowhere, but rather, how they are enmeshed in their technical, social and ethical context and can only be understood in those terms. Whatever the claims of commentators, APOE testing for Alzheimer's pharmacogenetics does raise some of the same ethical issues as 'ordinary' susceptibility gene testing. And however revolutionary Herceptin seems when it is discussed on the financial pages, once it enters the clinic it becomes an ordinary cancer treatment, subject to the same institutional stresses and strains, with clinicians' attitudes towards and understating of it shaped by their experience of other, older treatments, for example Tamoxifen. If, when they arrive, pharmacogenetic tests are better thought of as ordinary, as opposed to revolutionary, then this should alert us to the importance of the context within which such tests are used. The role of the clinical context is key in shaping the final form of a pharmacogenetic technology, and since clinical context in turn is formed by social, cultural and most of all economic factors, it is these that we should pay attention to when considering the broader aspects of personalised medicine.

Working our way back along the list, the next opposition is between knowledge and clinical resistance to personalised medicine. However counterintuitive it may seem to supporters of pharmacogenetics, clinical resistance to this technology is not a function of clinicians' knowledge (or lack of it) about the disease, genetics or a particular drug. It is socioethical factors that make or break clinicians' acceptance of new technology. In Alzheimer's, clinicians helped block the clinical use of APOE-based pharmacogenetics, not because they lacked knowledge about APOE4, but because they worked in an area where socioethically based resistance to clinical APOE testing was a feature of the clinical culture. Breast cancer clinicians were sceptical about the use of HER2 testing for prognosis and diagnosis, not because they did not *know* about research supporting this claim, but because of a belief, partly derived from financial pressure, that such a test was not clinically useful. Simply educating clinicians about the benefits of personalised medicine, trying to fill a deficit that does not exist, will not lead to greater uptake of these new technologies. Rather than thinking in terms of the general benefits that pharmacogenetics brings to the clinic, supporters need to tailor their claims to specific conditions and specific diseases. To tell Alzheimer's professionals that pharmacogenetics does not raise the same ethical problems for them as disease-gene testing is as misleading as telling breast cancer specialists that personalised medicine *does* raise the same issues. Pharmacogenetics is a heterogeneous technology, and those who wish to promote its use need to acknowledge this. It seems suitable that those who claim that pharmacogenetics will do away with 'one size fits all' prescribing should avoid similarly monolithic claims about personalised medicine.

At the beginning of this book I described pharmacogenetics, or rather personalised medicine, as a promissory science that exists mainly in the expectations about how it will develop being created in editorials, commentaries, reviews and press articles. I suggested that rather than dismissing such expectations as 'hype', it is more productive to view them as a point of focus for sociological analysis. Throughout this book there has been a contrast between the views of professionals at the 'coalface' (as they evocatively describe it) and other experts, pharmacologists, pharmacists, geneticists, within and without industry, who are busy constructing expectations about personalised medicine. This dichotomy has helped highlight how particular research papers (for example, linking APOE4 to reduced effectiveness of Tacrine) serve as political resources for supporters of these new technologies. That a particular scientific fact is seen differently by another group of scientists should not surprise us. Such a disparity simply echoes much of what Donald MacKenzie has shown in his exploration of a quite different technology (nuclear missile guidance systems), that those scientists and engineers involved in the creation of facts are far more uncertain about their work than those further from the lab bench, who use these results and for whom such facts are stable and uncontested (MacKenzie 1990). The picture of Herceptin painted by those who actually use it in the clinic is significantly different from its position as the 'poster boy' for personalised medicine that industry's expectations would have one believe.

And of course resistance to such expectations is not the sole preserve of clinicians involved in using pharmacogenetics. There are sceptics about pharmacogenetics, about whom little has been said so far. They include organisations such as the pressure group GeneWatch, who, in a response to the UK White Paper on Genetics, question how useful genetic tests will be in the prediction of ADRs, claiming that 'Genetic testing is unlikely to remove the need for monitoring . . . Relying on genetic tests alone could do more harm than good if it means that signs of a dangerous drug reaction are ignored' (GeneWatch 2003: 3). There are also those within the scientific establishment, such as Andrew Coats, editor-in-chief of the *International Journal of Cardiology*, who asks: 'What then . . . [is] . . . the prospect for an SNP pattern being accepted in all countries of the world, being tested prospectively in an adequately powered trial and being utilised to determine who should, and perhaps more importantly who should not, receive treatment from a new block-buster drug [?]' (Coats 2000: 2). He suggests that he 'cannot be the only person who believes this is fantasy and hype rather than realistic expectation' (Coats 2000: 3). Then there are those who raise questions about individual personalised medicines, such as Sharon Batt, who questions Herceptin's usefulness for the majority of women with breast cancer, both on the grounds of cost and of the drug's specific mechanism (Batt 2000).

Rather than assuming that these sceptics have privileged access to the future, we can view their claims as simply another form of expectation about pharmacogenetics, no less rhetorical and purpose-driven than the claims of industry and other supporters. For the rest of this chapter I wish to suggest how such an even-handed approach to the kinds of claims being made about personalised medicine can have very real, practical use in terms of thinking about how to deal with pharmacogenetics, if it does arrive in the clinic on a large scale.

Promises and realities

The most important starting point is one of 'symmetry' with regard to the different claims being made about how pharmacogenetics will develop. That those at the clinical coalface have quite different views about particular tests from the industry executives and academic scientists, for whom there is a need to construct expectations about the development and use of pharmacogenetics, is not a source of criticism for either group. For these commentators, there is little uncertainty about the cases they cite. Both APOE–Tacrine and HER2–Herceptin are good examples of pharmacogenetics, pointing us in the direction that personalised medicine will go. To criticise these people for their use of examples which others regard as misnomers or even just plain false, is to miss the point somewhat. For the commentators, the rightness or wrongness of a particular example is less important than the rhetorical, persuasive role it plays in constructing credible expectations about the future of personalised medicine. Judging those involved in the construction of expectations by the professional standards of the coalface is to insist on comparing two very different social worlds.

Donald MacKenzie suggests that the contrast in attitude between bench scientists and commentators, 'technological decision-makers and senior managers' in his terms, should alert us to a possible problem, that confident sounding but highly speculative statements may generate undue confidence about a particular technology (MacKenzie 1998). In a survey of public attitudes about pharmacogenetics, Rothstein and Horung reveal 'a public generally interested in genetics, optimistic about the prospects of genetic research to develop improved medication, and willingness to participate in genetic research' (Rothstein & Hornung 2003: 25). How much of that interest, optimism and willingness derives from the expectations that are being created about personalised medicine it is hard to say, yet should these expectations not come to pass, or the uncertainty at the core of them 'surface', then the public may well show how temporary such positive attitudes towards a particular technology can be.

The nature of expectations are such that it is probably unreasonable to expect the scientists and industry representatives involved in their construction to moderate their claims. As noted in chapter 2, a great deal of money is tied into specific visions of how pharmacogenetics will develop (e.g. the ADR versus the disease-gene perspectives). Business plans cannot be chopped and changed at will. So it is up to the rest of us, social scientists, journalists, health policy makers, politicians, unallied scientists and members of the public to adopt a perspective that allows us see such speculation for what it is; not irresponsible hype to be dismissed, but an attempt to shape the social, political and economic environment so that it is more supportive towards the final form these technologies take.

Thus, taking expectations about pharmacogenetics seriously requires us to start with its heterogeneity. There are a number of different approaches to pharmacogenetics that can be thought of as complementary, but which can also appear incompatible. Viewing pharmacogenetics as being about ADRs does not necessarily fit with the idea that pharmacogenetics reveals the genetic component underlying different common diseases. And the concept that pharmacogenetics includes drugs that act on *tumour* genomes, rather than on the inherited genetics of individuals, is another twist (though it may fit better with broader definitions of pharmacogenomics). Neither policy-makers nor any others of us that we might describe as 'interested outsiders' should feel the need to choose any of these forms of pharmacogenetics: the end result may well be that all three approaches make some inroads into clinical practice.

Rather, the need is for those discussing the broader issues around personalised medicine to be aware of this heterogeneity, and to appreciate that companies that have invested considerable sums of money in a single interpretation of what the word *pharmacogenetics* 'really' means, may have reason to promote a particular vision. People arguing for regulations structured around a single approach to pharmacogenetics are engaged in an important part of constructing expectations. This does not mean that they should be taken at face value.

A second point that we interested outsiders might take from these case studies is that while we understand the rhetorical power of presenting pharmacogenetics as a revolutionary approach to healthcare, so useful in injecting urgency into one's expectations, seeing personalised medicine as an ordinary technology implies certain approaches to future research. If we are to get to grips with pharmacogenetics' implications, then we need to see it, and research it, as a 'technology-in-practice' (Timmermans & Berg 2003: 103). One consequence of this resolutely empirical approach to the assessment of a technology is the limits it places on what we can claim to know about personalised medicine as a whole. Thus regulations need to remain flexible if they are to respond to pharmacogenetics' impact on clinical practice, rather than on what we think such an impact might be.

A side effect of seeing personalised medicine as an ordinary technology is the attention it focuses on the broader structures of healthcare provision. Pharmacogenetics' role in reducing healthcare expenditure is an attractive element to the expectations being created, usually helping industry to portray these developments as a win–win situation for both the company and the healthcare provider. But this needs to be balanced with an understanding of how current funding structures impact on access to and use of new technology. In the NHS, a significant limiting factor to clinicians' uptake of HER2 testing is the underfunding of histopathology services. This form of personalised medicine depends less upon high-tech screening centres and regional genetic services, and more on the staffing and financing of small, local departments not normally associated with personalised medicine.

Of course the expectations being constructed around personalised medicine could be expanded to include a debate over the levels of cost-effectiveness that might be required for particular healthcare providers to fund access to particular drugs. It may well be in industry's interests to stimulate discussion in this area, perhaps by modifying the kinds of futures being talked about. It is not clear that companies benefit greatly from the kind of high-profile wrangling that accompanied the NICE assessment of Herceptin. Industry cannot always rely on healthcare providers to pay high prices for new drugs.

When we consider what we know about the expectations being created around personalised medicine, it is clear that if there is a knowledge deficit, then it lies on the side of those trying to promote the technology. It does not matter if specialists in the treatment of particular diseases do not know about pharmacogenetics as a whole. They simply need to know about how a specific treatment works in the case of a specific disease, and in this way, there is very little difference between pharmacogenetics and other treatments. But if you are constructing expectations about personalised medicine, then you take a much broader view and are forced to discuss examples from diseases you may know little or nothing about. You might make sweeping generalisations about ethical problems without the sort of discipline-centred, localised knowledge required. This is not a criticism of the supporters of pharmacogenetics; it is a necessary evil of what they are trying to do that, in the process of constructing expectations, an individual's knowledge base will be stretched. It is just that the side effects of this stretching may be unwelcome. When commentators confidently cite a study (APOE and S12024) that Alzheimer's experts regard as spurious, the battle has already been lost. In the same way, clinicians' experience with Tamoxifen means that they have already used personalised medicine in the clinic, and are thus more knowledgeable about this technology than many of those promoting it.

Thus there is a need for those of us outside the expectation-generation process to ask questions of commentators' authority, to suggest that they might benefit from discussing their ideas with specialists in particular disease areas, to root their claims in clinical practice. At the very least, it would allow them to make a more persuasive case, to carry more professionals along with them as they create their expectations – which is after all the point.

At the heart of the creation of expectations are the pharmaceutical and biotechnology industries. It is companies that have the most to gain from particular expectations coming to pass, but also most to lose. It is they that have put their money where the commentators' mouths are, either in the form of business plans for biotech start-ups, or as the R&D cost of a large pharmaceutical company, or in the alliance between companies. It is industry that actually invests in expectations; if they cannot shape either the regulatory environment or the social environment in such a way that it supports their pharmacogenetic product when it arrives, then the expectation has failed in its performative role as a persuasive device.

Given this context, it is understandable that companies played such important roles in both of the case studies covered in this book. Industry is central in deciding whether personalised medicine gets into the clinic at all. A company may obstruct the use of a pharmacogenetic test, as seems to be the case in Alzheimer's, or it may invest a great deal of time and money in gathering support for a particular product, and shape clinical cultures to get it into the clinic, as in the case of Herceptin. Yet in many expectations, commentators suggest that in the short to medium term at least, the main public health benefit from pharmacogenetics may arise from more accurate use of current medicinal products, rather than the development of new drugs. While this might occur in the case of adverse drug reactions, it seems unlikely that large pharmaceutical companies will allow the development and marketing of tests that threaten current market share. Commentators may need to revise their expectations, but more crucially, this may be a central point of interest for those preparing healthcare systems for the impact of personalised medicine, as well as those people involved in discussing the future regulation of pharmacogenetics. Whether we are talking about the UK's NHS or about US-based private health insurers, it seems unlikely that health funders will happily pay for treatments that they suspect they could use far more efficiently, if only industry would release the required information and allow the marketing of a pharmacogenetic test.

By seeing the claims made by supporters of pharmacogenetics as expectations rather than hype, we can see that the future is not fixed, that the development of particular technologies is not inevitable, that there is still time before expectation(s) become(s) reality. We do not have to accept the future that is being constructed around personalised medicine, in part because that future is still in flux, is still undecided: there are still too many competing expectations. In this environment, those outside the expectation production process, we interested outsiders, can still influence what happens. We can highlight alternative views and expert opinions, keep regulations flexible to allow and challenge companies to develop technologies that genuinely serve the interests of public health.

Bibliography

Abate, T. 2001a. 'Genentech can widen drug's use', *San Francisco Chronicle*,15 May, p. B1.

Abate, T. 2001b. 'Researchers ready to move to next genome discoveries; drug developers to see new tools at Trade Show', *San Francisco Chronicle*, 5 March, p. C1.

Abraham, J. 1995. *Science, Politics and the Pharmaceutical Industry: Controversy and Bias in Drug Regulation*. London: University College London/St Martins Press.

Aerssens, J. 2002. 'Pharmacogenomic approaches in Alzheimer's disease drug development', *Drug Development Research* 56: 67–73.

AGS Ethics Committee 2001. 'Genetic testing for late-onset Alzheimer's disease', *Journal of the American Geriatric Society* 49: 225–6.

Akhtar, S. 2002. 'Pharmacogenomics: are pharmacists ready for genotyped prescribing?', *Pharmaceutical Journal* 268: 296–9.

Almkvist, O, Jelic, V., Amberla, K., Hellstrom-Lindhal, E., Meuling, L. and Nordberg, A. 2001. 'Responder characteristics to a single oral dose of cholinesterase inhibitor: a double-blind placebo-controlled study with tacrine in Alzheimer patients', *Dementia and Geriatric Cognitive Disorders* 12(1): 22–32.

Altman, L. K. 2000. 'Reading the book of life: the doctor's world; genomic chief has high hopes, and great fears, for genetic testing', *New York Times*, 27 June, section F, p. 6.

Altman, R. 1996. *Waking Up/Fighting Back: The Politics of Breast Cancer*. Boston: Little, Brown.

Álvarez, X. A., Mouzo, R., Pichel, V., Perez, P., Laredo, M., Fernandez-Novoa, L., Corzo, L., Zas, R., Alcaraz, M., Secades, J. J., Lozano, R. and Cacabelos, R. 1999. 'Double-blind placebo-controlled study with citicoline in APOE genotyped Alzheimer's disease patients. Effects on cognitive performance, brain bioelectrical activity and cerebral perfusion', *Methods and findings in Experimental and Clinical Pharmacology* 21(9): 633–44.

Anderson, D. C., Gomez-Mancilla, B., Spear, B. B., Barnes, D. M., Cheeseman, K., Shaw, P. M., Friedman, J., McCarthy, A., Brazell, C., Ray, S. C., McHale, D., Hashimoto, L., Sandbrink, R., Watson, M. L., Salerno, R. A., Cohen, N. and Lister, C. E. on behalf of the Pharmacogenetics Working Group 2002. 'Elements of informed consent for pharmacogenetic research; perspective of the Pharmacogenetics Working Group', *Pharmacogenomics Journal* 2(5): 284–92.

Anderson, W. H., Fitzgerald, C. G. and Manasco, P. K. 1999. 'Current and future applications of pharmacogenomics', *New Horizons: Science and Practice of Acute Medicine* 7(2): 262–9.

Anglin, M. K. 1997. 'Working from the inside out: implications of breast cancer activism for biomedical policies and practices', *Social Science and Medicine* 44(9): 1403–15.

Anon. 1998. 'Editorial: pharmacogenomics at work', *Nature Biotechnology* 16(10): 885.

Anspach, R. 1993. *Deciding who Lives: Fateful Choices in the Intensive-Care Nursery.* Berkeley: University of California Press.

Ashcroft, R. 1999. 'Equipoise, knowledge and ethics in clinical research and practice', *Bioethics* 13(3–4): 314–26.

Ashmore, M., Mulkay, M. and Pinch, T. 1989. *Health and Efficiency: A Sociology of Health Economics.* Milton Keynes: Open University Press.

Bailey, D. S., Bondar, A. and Furness, L. M. 1998. 'Pharmacogenomics – it's not just pharmacogenetics', *Current Opinion in Biotechnology* 9: 595–601.

Barry, A. 2001. *Political Machines: Governing a Technological Society.* London and New York: Athlone.

Barton, G. 2000. *Genetic Services in the NHS: An Institute of Healthcare Management Discussion Paper.* London: HMSO.

Baselga, J. 2001. 'Clinical trials of Herceptin® (trastuzumab)', *European Journal of Cancer* 37: S18–S24.

Bast, R. C., Ravdin, P., Hayes, D. F., Bates, S., Fritsche, H., Jessup, J. M., Kemeny, N., Locker, G. Y., Mennel, R. G. and Somerfield, M. R. 2001. '2000 update of recommendations for the use of tumor markers in breast and colorectal cancer: clinical practice guidelines of the American Society of Clinical Oncology', *Journal of Clinical Oncology* 19(6): 1865–78.

Batt, S. 1994. *Patient no More: The Politics of Breast Cancer.* London: Scarlet.

Batt, S. 2000. 'The new genetic therapies: the case of herceptin for breast cancer', in *The Gender of Genetic Futures: The Canadian Biotechnology Strategy. Women and Health Proceedings of the National Strategic Workshop*, NNEWH Working Paper Series. Toronto: York University Press, pp. 9–17.

Bazell, R. 1998. *Her2: The Making of Herceptin, a Revolutionary Treatment for Breast Cancer.* New York: Random House.

Beauchamp, T. L. and Childress, J. F. 1993. *Principles of Biomedical Ethics.* 4th edn. Oxford: Oxford University Press.

Bell, R. A., Wilkes, M. S. and Kravitz, R. L. 1999. 'Advertisement-induced prescription drug requests: patient's anticipated reactions to a physician who refuses', *Journal of Family Practice* 48(6): 446–52.

Benbassat, J., Pilpel, D. and Tidhar, M. 1998. 'Patient's preferences for participation in clinical decision making: a review of published surveys', *Behavioral Medicine* 24(2): 81–8.

Berg, J. W., Appelbaum, P. S., Lidz, C. W. and Parker, L. S. 2001. *Informed Consent: Legal Theory and Clinical Practice.* 2nd edn. Oxford: Oxford University Press.

Bijker, W., Hughes, T. and Pinch, T. (eds.) 1987. *The Social Construction of Technological Systems*. Cambridge, MA: MIT Press.

Bijker, W. E. and Law, J. (eds.) 1992. *Shaping Technology-Building Society: Studies in Sociotechnical Change*. Cambridge, MA: MIT Press.

Binstock, R. H. and Murray, T. H. 1998. 'Genetics and long-term-care insurance: ethical and policy issues', in S. G. Post and P. J. Whitehouse (eds.), *Genetic Testing for Alzheimer's Disease: Ethical and Clinical Issues*. Baltimore: Johns Hopkins University Press, pp. 155–76.

Birch, S. and Gafni, A. 2002. 'On being NICE in the UK: guidelines for technology appraisal for the NHS in England and Wales', *Health Economics* 11: 185–91.

Bird, T. 1995a. 'Apolipoprotein E genotyping in diagnosis of Alzheimer's disease: a cautionary view', *Annals of Neurology* 38(1): 2–3.

Bird, T. 1995b. 'Reply', *Annals of Neurology* 38(6): 967.

Birner, P. 2002. 'Is fluorescence in situ hybridization really superior to Hercept Test?' *Journal of Clinical Oncology* 20(23): 4607.

Bogdanovic, S. and Langlands, B. 1999. *Pharmacogenomics Players*. London: Financial Times.

Bonnor, J. 1998. 'Designer drugs', *Guardian*, 5 February, p. 14.

Booth, B., Glassman, R. and Ma, P. 2003. 'Oncology's trials', *Nature Reviews Drug Discovery* 2(8): 609–10.

Borroni, B., Colciaghi, F., Pastorino, L., Archetti, S., Corsini, P., Cattabeni, F., Di Luca, M. and Padovani, A. 2002. 'ApoE genotype influences the biological effect of donepezil on APP metabolism in Alzheimer disease: evidence from a peripheral model', *European Neuropsychopharmacology* 12: 195–200.

Boseley, S. 2003. 'Cancer fund urged to end postcode lottery', *Guardian*, 29 October, p. 11.

Bosk, C. L. 1992. *All God's Mistakes: Genetic Counselling in a Pediatric Hospital*. Chicago: University of Chicago Press.

Bosk, C. L. 2002. 'Obtaining voluntary consent for research in desperately ill patients', *Medical Care* 40(9): V64–8.

Bowe, C. and Pilling, D. 2001. 'Abbott labs links with Millennium', *Financial Times*, 13 March, p. 17.

Bracco, L. 2002. 'Pharmacogenomics and personalised medicine', *Pharmacogenomics* 3(2): 166–71.

Branca, M. 2002. 'Gambling on pharmacogenomics: a Q&A with Klaus Lindpaintner', *Bio IT World*, 9 October, http://www_bio-itworld.com/archive/100902/path_sidebar_1303.htm.

Brill-Edwards, M. 1999. 'Canada's Health Protection Branch: whose health, what protection?', in M. L. Barer, K. M. McGrail, K. Cardiff, L. Wood and C. J. Green (eds.), *Tales from the Other Drug Wars: Papers from the 12th Annual Health Policy Conference* (held in Vancouver, BC, 26 November 1999). Vancouver: University of British Columbia, Centre for Health Services and Policy Research, http://www.chspr.ubc.ca/misc/drugwars2.pdf.

Brodaty, H., Conneally, M., Gauthier, S., Jennings, C., Lennox, A., Lovestone, S., Koczyn, A., Mangone, C., Rossor, M. and Whitehouse, P. 1995. 'Consensus statement on predictive testing for Alzheimer Disease', *Alzheimer Disease and Associated Disorders* 9(4): 182–7.

Brower, V. 1997. 'Allen Roses: rebel with a cause', *Nature Biotechnology* 15: 1310.

Brown, H. 2003. 'Does hope match the hype for targeted drugs?', *Lancet Oncology* 4(8): 452.

Brown, L. 1998. 'The evolution of managed care in the US', *Pharmacoeconomics* 14(1): 37–43.

Brown, N., Rappert, B. and Webster, A. (eds.) 2000. *Contested Futures: A Sociology of Prospective Science and Technology.* Aldershot: Ashgate.

Bruera, E., Willey, J. S., Palmer, J. L. and Rosales, M. 2002. 'Treatment decisions for breast carcinoma-patient preferences and physician perceptions', *Cancer* 94(7): 2076–80.

Buchanan, A., Califano, A., Kahn, J., McPherson, E., Robertson, J. and Brody, B. 2002. *Pharmacogenetics: Ethical and Regulatory Issues in Research and Clinical Practice. Report of the Consortium on Pharmacogenetics. Findings and Recommendations.* http://www.bioethics.umn.edu/News/pharm_report.pdf.

Bullock, R. 2002. 'New drugs for Alzheimer's disease and other dementias', *British Journal of Psychiatry* 180: 135–9.

Butler, R. N. 1994. 'ApoE: new risk factor for Alzheimer's', *Geriatrics* 49(8): 10–11.

Cacabelos, R., Alvarez, A., Lombardi, A., Fernandez-Novoa, L., Corzo, L., Perez, P., Laredo, M., Pichel, V., Hernandez, A., Varela, M., Figueroa, J., Prous, J., Windisch, M. and Vigo, C. 2000. 'Pharmacological treatment of Alzheimer's disease: from psychotropic drugs and cholinesterase inhibitors to pharmacogenomics', *Drugs of Today* 36(7): 415–99.

Cambrosio, A. and Keating, P. 1995. *Exquisite Specificity. The Monoclonal Antibody Revolution.* Oxford: Oxford University Press.

Carlsson, M. 2000. 'Cancer patients seeking information from sources outside the health care system', *Supportive Care in Cancer* 8(6): 453–7.

Casamayou, M. H. 2001. *The Politics of Breast Cancer.* Washington, DC: Georgetown University Press.

Chadwick, R. 1999. 'Criteria for genetic screening: the impact of pharmaceutical research', *Monash Bioethics Review* 18(1): 22–6.

Chamberlain, J. C. and Joubert, P. H. 2001. 'Opportunities and strategies for introducing pharmacogenetics into early drug development', *Drug Discovery Today* 6(11): 569–74.

Chen, D. T., Miller, F. G. and Rosenstein, D. L. 2003. 'Clinical research and the physician–patient relationship', *Annals of Internal Medicine* 138(8): 669–72.

Clarke, A., English, V., Harris, H. and Wells, F. 2001. 'Report on ethical Considerations', *International Journal of Pharmaceutical Medicine* 15: 89–94.

Coats, A. 2000. 'Pharmacogenomics: hope or hype?', *International Journal of Cardiology* 76: 1–3.

Cockett, M., Dracopoli, N. and Sigal, E. 2000. 'Applied genomics: integration of the technology within pharmaceutical research and development', *Current Opinion in Biotechnology* 11: 602–9.

Collins, H. 1985. *Changing Order: Replication and Induction in Scientific Practice.* London: Sage.

Collins, H. 1999. 'Tantalus and the aliens: publications, audiences and the search for gravitational waves', *Social Studies of Science* 29(2): 163–97.

Connor, S. 1999. 'Genetic blueprint to predict illness', *Independent*, 15 April, p. 10.

Connor, S. 2003a. 'Glaxo chief: Our drugs do not work on most patients'. *Independent*, 8 December, p. 1.

Connor, S. 2003b. 'Demolished: the myth that allows drugs giants to sell more'. *Independent*, 8 December, p. 8.

Cook-Deegan, R. 1998. 'Some questions arising in the commercial development of genetic tests for Alzheimer's disease', in S. Post and P. Whitehouse (eds.), *Genetic Testing for Alzheimer Disease: Ethical and Clinical Issues*. Baltimore: Johns Hopkins University Press, pp. 84–100.

Cookson, C. 1999. 'Future cancer research may emphasise control not cure', *Financial Times*, 18 September, p. 7.

Corrigan, O. 2002. 'A risky business: the detection of adverse drug reactions in clinical trials and post-marketing exercises', *Social Science and Medicine* 55(3): pp. 497–507.

Cronin, M. T., Pho, M., Dutta, D., Frueh, F., Schwarcz, L. and Brennan, T. 2001. 'Utilization of new technologies in drug trial and discovery', *Drug Metabolism and Disposition* 29(4 part 2): 586–90.

Cummings, J. L. 2003. 'Use of cholinesterase inhibitors in clinical practice', *American Journal of Geriatric Psychiatry* 11(2): 131–45.

Cummins, F. 2002. 'Breast cancer NHS pill', *Mirror*, 16 March, p. 8.

Cunning, A. M. and Robertson, F. W. 1984. 'Polymorphism at the apolipoprotein E locus in relation to risk of coronary disease', *Clinical Genetics* 25: 310–13.

Czaban, J. N. 2001. 'Pharmacogenomics: the uncertain path to decoding the regulatory genome', *Food and Drug Law Institute Update* 3: 33.

Day, M. 2002. 'Women to win cancer drug fight', *Express*, 15 March, p. 23.

Department of Health 1999. 'NICE proposals launched today: patients get faster access to modern treatment', press release, 3 February.

Department of Health 2003. *Our Inheritance, Our Future. Realising the Potential of Genetics in the NHS*. London: HMSO.

Department of Health 2003. *The NHS Cancer Plan. Three Year Progress Report. Maintaining the Momentum*. London: HMSO.

Diederich, F. 2002. 'Nanotechnology – separating hype from reality', *Chemical Engineer* Dec.: 26.

DiMasi, J. A., Hansen, R. W., Grabowski, H. G. and Lasagna, L. 1991. 'Cost of innovation in the pharmaceutical industry', *Journal of Health Economics* 10: 107–42.

DiMasi, J. A., Hansen, R. W. and Grabowski, H. G. 2003. 'The price of innovation: new estimates of drug development costs', *Journal of Health Economics* 22: 151–85.

Drazen, J. M., Yandava, C. N., Dube, L., Szczerback, N., Hippensteel, R., Pillari, A., Israel, E., Schork, N., Silverman, E. S., Katz, D. A. and Drajesk, J. 1999. 'Pharmacogenetic association between ALOX5 promoter genotype and the response to anti-asthma treatment', *Nature Genetics* 22: 168–70.

Economist 1997. 'Drug companies' target practice', *Economist*, 6 December, pp. 94–5.

Einsiedel, E. F. and Eastlick, D. L. 2000. 'Consensus conferences as deliberative democracy – a communications perspective', *Science Communication* 21(4): 323–43.

Elder, A. T. and Fox, K. A. A. 1992. 'Thrombolytic treatment for elderly patients', *British Medical Journal* 305: 846–7.

Ellis, I. O., Dowsett, M., Bartlett, J., Walker, R., Cooke, T., Gullick, W., Gusterson, B., Mallon, E. and Barrett Lee, P. 2000. 'Recommendations for HER2 testing in the UK', *Journal of Clinical Pathology* 53: 890–2.

EMEA 2000. *Report to the CPMP on the EMEA Seminar on the use of Pharmacogenetics in the Drug Development Process*. 5 June. London: EMEA.

Emery, J. and Hayflick, S. 2001. 'The challenge of integrating genetic medicine into primary care', *British Medical Journal* 322: 1027–30.

Emilien, G., Ponchon, M., Caldas, C., Isacson, O. and Maloteaux, J. M. 2000. 'Impact of genomics on drug discovery and clinical medicine', *Quarterly Journal of Medicine* 93(7): 391–423.

Ensom, M. H. H., Chang, T. H. K. and Patel, P. 2001. 'Pharmacogenetics: the therapeutic drug monitoring of the future', *Clinical Pharmacokinetics* 40(11): 783–802.

Epstein, S. 1996. *Impure Science: AIDS, Activism and the Politics of Knowledge*. Berkeley: University of California Press.

Evans, W. E. and Relling, M. 1999. 'Pharmacogenomics: translating functional genomics into rational therapeutics', *Science* 286: 487–91.

Evans, W. E. and Johnson, J. A. 2001. 'Pharmacogenomics: the inherited basis for interindividual differences in drug response', *Annual Review of Genomics and Human Genetics* 2: 9–39.

Evans, W. E. and McLeod, H. L. 2003. 'Pharmacogenomics – drug disposition, drug targets and side effects', *New England Journal of Medicine* 348(6): 538–49.

Farlow, M., Gracon, S., Hershey, L., Lewis, K., Sadowsky, C. and Dolanureno, J. 1992. 'A controlled trial of Tacrine in Alzheimer's disease', *Journal of the American Medical Association* 268(18): 2523–9.

Farlow, M., Lahiri, D. K., Poirier, J., Davignon, J. and Hui, S. 1996. 'Apolipoprotein E genotype and gender influence response to tacrine therapy', *Annals of the New York Academy of Science* 802: 101–10.

Farlow, M., Lahiri, D. K., Poirier, J., Davignon, J., Schneider, L. and Hui, S. L. 1998. 'Treatment outcome of tacrine therapy depends on apolipoprotein E genotype and gender of the subject with Alzheimer's disease', *Neurology* 50: 669–77.

Farrer, L. A., Brin, M. F., Elsas, L., Goate, A., Kennedy, J., Mayeux, R., Myers, R. H., Reilly, P. and Risch, N. J. 1995. 'Statement on use of apolipoprotein-E testing for Alzheimer-disease', *Journal of the American Medical Association* 274 (20): 1627–9.

FDA 1991. 'Tacrine as a treatment for Alzheimer's dementia: an interim report from the FDA', *New England Journal of Medicine* 324(5): 349–52.

Feldman, A. M., Lorell, B. H. and Reis, S. E. 2000. 'Trastuzumab in the treatment of metastatic breast cancer', *Circulation* 102: 272–4.

Feltham, C. 2002. 'Pioneer's bright vision for new age of medicine', *Daily Mail*, 10 October, p. 81.

Fentiman, I. S. 1998. *Detection and Treatment of Breast Cancer*. 1st edn. London: Martin Dunitz.

Ferentz, A. E. 2002. 'Integrating pharmacogenomics into drug development', *Pharmacogenomics* 3(4): 453–67.

Ferguson, J. H. 1996. 'The NIH consensus development program: the evolution of guidelines', *International Journal of Technology Assessment in Health Care* 12(3): 460–74.

Financial Times (FT) 1994. 'Alzheimer's drug hope for sufferers', *Financial Times*, 6 April, p. 9.

Financial Times (FT) 1997. 'FT guide to: Genetic engineering', *Financial Times*, 29 September, p. 10.

Financial Times (FT) 2001. 'Inside track', *Financial Times*, 12 July, p. 10.

Firn, D. 2000. 'EU gives approval for Roche cancer treatment', *Financial Times*, 31 August, p. 31.

Fogarty, M. 1998. 'Up for adoption: pharmacogenetics and the orphan drug law', *HMS Beagle* 44, http://news.bmn.com/hmsbeagle/44/people/op_ed.htm.

Fortun, M. 1998. 'Sixty-five roses, Pulmozyme. Steve Shak, Genentech Inc.', in G. E. Marcus, (ed.), *Late Edition 5: Corporate Futures*. Chicago: University of Chicago Press, pp. 209–42.

Fortun, M. 2001. 'Mediated speculations in the genomics futures markets', *New Genetics and Society* 20(2): 139–56.

Fox, R. C. and Swazey, J. P. 1984. 'Medical morality is not bioethics – medical ethics in China and the United States', *Perspective in Biology and Medicine* 27(3): 336–60.

Frank, R. G. 2003. 'Editorial: New estimates of drug development costs', *Journal of Health Economics* 22: 325–30.

Franz, S. and Smith, A. 2003. 'New drug approvals for 2002', *Nature Reviews Drug Discovery* 2: 95–6.

Freedman, B. 1987. 'Equipoise and the ethics of clinical research', *New England Journal of Medicine* 317(3): 141–5.

Freeman, C. and Soefe, L. 1997. *The Economics of Industrial Innovation*. 3rd edn. London: Cassell.

Frisoni, G. B. 2001. 'Treatment of Alzheimer's disease with acetylcholinesterase inhibitors: bridging the gap between evidence and practice', *Journal of Neurology* 248: 551–7.

Frith, M. 2003. 'Reid orders inquiry into postcode drug prescribing', *Independent*, 29 October, p. 6.

Frost, S., Myers, L. B. and Newman, S. P. 2001. 'Genetic screening for Alzheimer's disease: what factors predict intentions to take a test?', *Behavioral Medicine* 27(3): 101–9.

GeneWatch 2003. *Pharmacogenetics: Better, Safer Medicines?* Briefing number 23.

GenomeWeb 2001. 'Pharmacogenomics seen growing to $6B by 2005, report says', http://www.genomeweb.com/articles/view.asp? Article no. 20017355957.

Ginsburg, G. and McCarthy, J. 2001. 'Personalized medicine: revolutionizing drug discovery and patient care', *Trends in Biotechnology* 19(12): 491–9.

Glaser, V. 1998. 'Pharmacogenomics: laying the foundation for prescriptive medicine', *Genetic Engineering News*, 1 January, pp. 1, 9, 31 and 39.

Gonzalez, F. J., Skoda, R. C., Kimura, S., Umeno, M., Zanger, U. M., Nebert, D. W., Gelboin, H. Y., Hardwick, J. P. and Meyer, U. A. 1988. 'Characterization of the common genetic-defect in humans deficient in debrisoquine metabolism', *Nature* 331(6155): 442–6.

Goodman, J. and Walsh, V. 2001. *The Story of Taxol: Nature and Politics in the Pursuit of an Anti-Cancer Drug*. Cambridge: Cambridge University Press.

Gottlieb, S. 2000. 'Cancer drug may cause heart failure', *British Medical Journal* 321: 259.

Graydon, J., Galloway, S., Palmer Wickham, S., Harrison, D., Richvanbder Bij, L., West, P., Burlein Hall, S. and Evans Boyden, B. 1997. 'Information needs of women during early treatment for breast cancer', *Journal of Advanced Nursing* 26(1): 59–64.

Green, M. C., Murray, J. L. and Hortobagyi, G. N. 2000. 'Monoclonal antibody therapy for solid tumors', *Cancer Treatment Reviews* 26: 269–86.

Griffith, V. 2000. 'Mammoth task to untangle the genome: interpreting the genome', *Financial Times,* 15 November, Biotechnology supplement, p. 2.

Griffith, V. 2001. 'Tailored care for cancer patients genetics', *Financial Times*, 3 May, p. 10.

Griffith, V. 2003a. 'Breakthrough in tailor-made medicines. ASCO Conference', *Financial Times*, 2 June, p. 26.

Griffith, V. 2003b. 'Optimistic Genentech reports earnings increase', *Financial Times*, 16 January, p. 18.

Growden, J. H. 1998. 'Editorial: Apolipoprotein E and Alzheimer disease', *Archives of Neurology* 55: 1053–4.

Guardian, 2003. 'Roche's biggest sellers', *Guardian*, 27 February, p. 28.

Guice, J. 1999. 'Designing the future: the culture of new trends in science and technology', *Research Policy* 28: 81–98.

Guston, D. H. 1999. 'Evaluating the first US consensus conference: the impact of the citizens' panel on telecommunications and the future of democracy', *Science, Technology and Human Values* 24(4): 451–82.

Hack, T. F., Degner, L. F. and Dyck, D. G. 1994. 'Relationship between preferences for decisional control and illness information among women with breast cancer', *Social Science and Medicine* 39: 279–89.

Hall, C. 1995. 'Makers appeal for Alzheimer's drug licence', *Independent*, 22 March, p. 4.

Hamilton, A. and Piccart, M. 2000. 'The contribution of molecular markers to the prediction of response in the treatment of breast cancer: a review of the literature on HER-2, p53 and BCL-2', *Annals of Oncology* 11: 647–63.

Harrison, S. 1998. 'The politics of evidence-based medicine in the United Kingdom', *Policy and Politics* 26(1): 15–31.

Haseltine, W. 1998. 'Letter: Not quite pharmacogenomics', *Nature Biotechnology* 16(12): 1295.

Hawkes, N. 2002. '£15,500 breast cancer drug to be free on NHS' *The Times*, 16 March, p. 6.

Hedgecoe, A. 2003. 'Terminology and the construction of scientific disciplines: the case of pharmacogenomics', *Science, Technology and Human Values* 28(4): 513–37.

Hedgecoe, A. and Martin, P. 2003. 'The drugs don't work: expectations and the shaping of pharmacogenetics', *Social Studies of Science* 33(3): 327–64.

Herrman, N., Sadavoy, J. and Steingart, A. 1987. 'Letter', *New England Journal of Medicine* 316(25) 1603–4.

Highfield, R. 2001. 'Genetic scientists in commercial row over "Book of Life" ', *Daily Telegraph*, 13 February, p. 14.

Highfield, R. 2002. '500,000 to provide DNA samples for "biobank" ', *Daily Telegraph*, 29 April, p. 6.

Hoban, C. J. 2002. 'From the lab to the clinic: integration of pharmacogenetics into clinical practice', *Pharmacogenomics* 3(4): 429–36.

Hortobagyi, G. N. and Perez, E. A. 2001. 'Integration of Trastuzumab into adjuvant systemic therapy of breast cancer: ongoing and planned clinical trials', *Seminars in Oncology* 28(5), supplement 16: 41–6.

190   *Bibliography*

Houghton, J. and Tobias, J. S. 2001. 'Adjuvant radiotherapy in the management of early breast cancer', in J. S. Tobias, J. Houghton and I. C. Henderson (eds.), *Breast Cancer: New Horizons in Research and Treatment.* London: Edward Arnold. pp. 189–94.

Housman, D. and Ledley, F. 1998. 'Why pharmacogenomics? Why now?', *Nature Biotechnology* 16: 492–3.

Hughes, D. and Griffiths, L. 1997. ' "Ruling in" and "ruling out": two approaches to the micro-rationing of health care', *Social Science and Medicine* 44(5): 589–99.

Hughes, T. P. 1983. *Networks of Power: Electrification in Western Society 1880–1930.* Baltimore: Johns Hopkins University Press.

Hunt, L. 1996. 'Unravelling the tangles of dementia', *Independent on Sunday*, 28 April, Sunday Review, p. 42.

Hurst, J. 1998. 'The impact of health economics on health policy in England, and the impact of health policy on health economics 1972–1977', *Health Economics* 7: S47–S62.

Hutton, J. and Maynard, A. 2000. 'A NICE challenge for health economics', *Health Economics* 9: 89–93.

Hyman, B. T. and Wallace, R. B. 1997. 'Reply', *Annals of Neurology* 41(3): 415–16.

Independent 2000. 'Genome challenge', *Independent*, 28 June, p. 20.

Independent 2003. 'Leader: Multinational drug company: honest, decent, public-spirited?', *Independent*, 8 December, p. 16.

Ingelman-Sundberg, M. 2001. 'Pharmacogenetics: an opportunity for a safer and more efficient pharmacotherapy', *Journal of Internal Medicine* 250: 186–200.

Irwin, A. and Wynne, B. 1996. *Misunderstanding Science? The Public Reconstruction of Science and Technology.* Cambridge: Cambridge University Press.

Issa, A. M. 2000. 'Ethical considerations in clinical pharmacogenomics research', *Trends in Pharmacological Science* 21: 247–9.

Issa, A. M. 2002. 'Ethical perspectives on pharmacogenomic profiling in the drug development process', *Nature Reviews Drug Discovery* 1(4): 300–8.

Issa, A. M. and Kegserlingk, E. W. 2000. 'Apolipoprotein E genotyping for pharmacogenetic purposes in Alzheimer's disease: emerging ethical issues', *Canadian Journal of Psychiatry* 45: 917–2.

Jacoby, I. 1985. 'Editorial: The consensus development program of the National Institues of Health', *American Journal of Psychiatry* 142(4): 477–8.

James, R. J. 2002. 'Commentary on Kewell *et al.* (2002), Calman-Hine reassessed', *Journal of Evaluation in Clinical Practice* 8(3): 299–301.

Jazwinska, E. C. 2001. 'Exploiting human genetic variation in drug discovery and development', *Drug Discovery Today* 6(4): 198–205.

Jenkins, P. 2002. 'The future is made-to-measure: pharmacogenomics', *Financial Times*, 30 April, Survey section, p. 3.

Johnson, J. A. and Evans, W. E. 2002. 'Molecular diagnostics as a predictive tool: genetics of drug efficacy and toxicity', *Trends in Molecular Medicine* 8(6): 300–5.

Johnston, L. 2001. 'Scandal of the vital life-saving treatments that NHS won't buy', *Sunday Express*, 29 July, p. 11.

Jordan, K. and Lynch, M. 1998. 'The dissemination, standardization and routinization of a molecular biological technique', *Social Studies of Science* 28(5–6): 733–800.

Jordan, V. C. 2003. 'Tamoxifen: a most unlikely pioneering medicine', *Nature Reviews Drug Discovery* 2: 205–13.

Joss, S. and Bellucci, S. (eds.) 2002. *Participatory Technology Assessment. European Perspectives*. London: CSD and TA Swiss.

Kakulas, B. A. and van Bockxmeer, F. M. 1995. 'Apolipoprotein E genotyping in the diagnosis of Alzheimer's disease: a cautionary view', *Annals of Neurology* 38(6): 966–7.

Kalow, W. 1990. 'Pharmacogenetics: past and future', *Life Sciences* 47: 1385–97.

Kandohla, T. 2002. 'Deadly delay', *Sun*, 16 March, p. 29.

Kaptain, S., Tan, L. K. and Chen, B. 2001. 'Her-2/ *neu* and breast cancer', *Diagnostic Molecular Pathology* 10(3): 139–52.

Kendall, P. 2001. 'Tailor-made drugs to combat cancer', *Daily Mail*, 22 February, p. 39.

Kewell, B., Hawkins, C. and Ferlie, E. 2002. 'Calman–Hine reassessed: a survey of cancer network development in England, 1999–2000', *Journal of Evaluation in Clinical Practice* 8(3): 303–11.

Klawiter, M. 2000. 'Racing for the cure, walking women and toxic touring: mapping cultures of action within the Bay area terrain of breast cancer', in Potts L. K. (ed.) *Ideologies of Breast Cancer: Feminist Perspectives*. London: Macmillan, pp. 63–97.

Klein, R. 2001. *The New Politics of the National Health Service*. 4th edn. London: Prentice Hall.

Klein, R., Day, P. and Redmayne, S. 1996. *Managing Scarcity: Priority Setting and Rationing in the National Health Service*. Milton Keynes: Open University Press.

Kleyn, P. W. and Vesell, E. S. 1998. 'Genetic variation as a guide to drug development', *Science* 281: 1820–1.

Knopman, D. S., DeKosky, S. T., Cummings, J. L., Chui, H., Corey-Bloom, J., Relkin, N., Small, G. W., Miller, B. and Stevens, J. C. 2001. 'Practitioner parameter: diagnosis of dementia (an evidence based review). Report of the Quality Standards Subcommittee of the American Academy of Neurology', *Neurology* 56: 1143–53.

Koenig, P. 1991. 'Money and the medicine men', *Independent on Sunday*, 12 May, Review section, p. 2.

Koepp, R. and Miles, S. H. 1999. 'Meta-analysis of Tacrine for Alzheimer disease: the influence of industry sponsors', *Journal of the American Medical Association* 281(24) (June 23/30): 2287.

Kolata, G. 1999. 'Using gene tests to customize medical treatment', *New York Times*, 20 December, Section A, p. 1.

Koselleck, R. 1985. *Futures Past: On the Semantics of Historical Time*. Cambridge, MA: MIT Press.

Krall, W. J., Sramek, J. J. and Cutler, N. R. 1999. 'Cholinesterase inhibitors: a therapeutic strategy for Alzheimer's disease', *Annals of Pharmacology* 33: 441–50.

Kuczewski, M. G. and Marshall, P. 2002. 'The decision dynamics of clinical research: the context and process of informed consent', *Medical Care* 40(9) special supplement: 45–54.

Kuivenhoven, J., Jukema, W., Zwinderman, A., de Knijff, P., McPherson, R., Bruschke, A., Lie, K. and Kastelein, J. 1998. 'The role of a common variant of the CETP gene in the progression of coronary artherosclerosis', *New England Journal of Medicine* 338(2): 86–93.

192   *Bibliography*

Kumar, S. 1999. 'Resisting revolution: generalism and the new genetics', *Lancet* 354: 1992–3.

Kumar, S. and Gantley, M. 1999. 'Tensions between policy makers and general practitioners in implementing new genetics: grounded theory interview study', *British Medical Journal* 319: 1410–13.

Kurth, J. H. 2000. 'Pharmacogenomics: future promise of a tool for identifying patients at risk', *Drug Information Journal* 34: 223–7.

Lahiri, D. K., Farlow, M., Greig, N. H. and Sambamurti, K. 2002. 'Current drug targets for Alzheimer's disease treatment', *Drug Development Research* 56: 267–81.

Lanctôt, K. L., Hermann, N. and LouLou, M. M. 2003. 'Correlates of response to acetylcholinesterase inhibitor therapy in Alzheimer's disease', *Journal of Psychiatry and Neuroscience* 28(1): 13–26.

Lappin, T. 2001. 'The year in ideas: A to Z – Pharmacogenomics', *New York Times*, 9 December, section 6, p. 88.

Larkin, M. 1997. 'Allen Roses: "Enfant terrible" of Alzheimer's research', *Lancet* 349: 1302.

Latour, B. 1987. *Science in Action: How to Follow Scientists and Engineers Through Society*. Cambridge, MA: Harvard University Press.

Latour, B. 1988. *The Pasteurization of France*. Cambridge, MA: Harvard University Press.

Lau, K. and Sakul, H. 2000. 'Pharmacogenomics', in A. M. Doherty (ed.), *Annual Reports in Medicinal Chemistry*. London and San Diego: Academic Press, pp. 261–9.

Laurance, J. 2002. '£20,000-a-year cancer drug approved for NHS', *Independent*, 16 March, p. 4.

Lavori, P. W., Krause-Steinrauf, H., Brophy, M., Buxbaum, J., Cockroft, J., Cox, D. R., Fiore, L., Greely, H. T., Greenberg, H., Holmes, E. W., Nelson, L. M. and Sugarman, J. 2002. 'Principles, organization, and operation of a DNA bank for clinical trials: a Department of Veterans Affairs cooperative study', *Controlled Clinical Trials* 23(3): 222–39.

Law, J. 1987. 'Technology and heterogeneous engineering: the case of Portuguese expansion', in W. Bijker, T. Hughes and T. J. Pinch (eds.), *The Social Construction of Technological Systems: New Directions in the Sociology and History of Technology*. Cambridge, MA.: MIT Press, pp. 111–34.

Lazarou, J., Pomeranz, B. H. and Corey, P. N. 1998. 'Incidence of adverse drug reactions in hospitalized patients', *Journal of the American Medical Association* 279(15): 1200–5.

Lebeau, A., Deimling, D., Kaltz, C., Sendelhofert, A., Iff, A., Luthardt, B., Untch, M. and Lohrs, U. 2001. 'HER-2/neu analysis in archival tissue samples of human breast cancer: comparison of immunohistochemistry and fluorescence in situ hybridization', *Journal of Clinical Oncology* 19(2): 354–63.

Lehman Brothers. 2001. *The Fruits of Genomics*. New York: Lehman Brothers.

Lerner, B. H. 2001. *The Breast Cancer Wars: Hope, Fear and the Pursuit of a Cure in Twentieth-Century America*. Oxford: Oxford University Press.

Leyland-Jones, B. 2002. 'Trastuzumab: hopes and realities', *Lancet Oncology* 3: 137–44.

Liggett, S. B. 2001. 'Pharmacogenetic applications of the Human Genome Project', *Nature Medicine* 7(3): 281–3.

Lindpaintner, K. 1999. 'Genetics in drug discovery and development: challenge and promise of individualizing treatment in common complex disease', *British Medical Bulletin* 55(2): 471–91.

Lindpaintner, K. 2002. 'The importance of being modest – reflections on the pharmacogenetics of abacavir', *Pharmacogenomics* 3(6): 835–8.

Lindpaintner, K. 2003. 'Pharmacogenetics: a new – or not so new? – concept in healthcare', *Geneva Papers on Risk and Insurance* 28(2): 316–30.

Lindpaintner, K., Foot, E., Caulfield, M. and Hall, I. 2001. 'Pharmacogenetics: focus on pharmacodynamics', *International Journal of Pharmaceutical Medicine* 15: 74–82.

Lipman, T. 2001. 'Letter: NICE and evidence based medicine are not really compatible', *British Medical Journal* 322: 489–90.

Lipton, P. 2003. 'Pharmacogenetics: the ethical issues', *Pharmacogenomics Journal* 3: 14–16.

Littlejohns, P., Barnett, D. and Longson, C. 2003. 'The cancer technology appraisal programme of the UK's National Institute for Clinical Excellence', *Lancet Oncology* 4: 242–50.

Lohrisch, C. and Piccart, M. 2001. 'An overview of HER2', *Seminars in Oncology* 28(6): 3–11.

Lovestone, S. 1998. 'Letter: Genetics consortium can offer views facilitating best practice in Alzheimer's disease', *British Medical Journal* 317: 471.

Lovestone, S., Wilcock, G., Rosser, M., Cayton, H. and Ragan, I. 1996. 'Letter: apolipoprotein E genotyping in Alzheimer's disease', *Lancet* 347: 1775–6.

Lucotte, G., Oddoze, C. and Michel, B. F. 1995. 'Apolipoprotein E and response to tacrine in French Alzheimer's disease patients', abstract presented at the International Psychogeriatrics Association Conference, Apolipoprotein E et Maladie d'Alzheimer, 29 May, Paris.

MacGowan, S. H., Scott, M., Agg, M. and Wilcock, G. 1995. 'Influence of apolipotien E genotype on response to tacrine in male and female patients with Alzheimer's disease', abstract presented at the International Psychogeriatrics Association Conference, Apoilpoprotien E et Maladie d'Alzheimer, 29 May, Paris.

Macgowan, S. H., Wilcock, G. and Scott, M. 1998. 'Effect of gender and apolopoprotein E genotype on response to anticholinesterase therapy in Alzheimer's disease', *International Journal of Geriatric Psychiatry* 13: 625–30.

MacKenzie, D. 1990. *Inventing Accuracy: A Historical Sociology of Nuclear Missile Guidance*. Cambridge, MA: MIT Press.

MacKenzie, D. 1998. 'The certainty trough', in R. Williams, W. Faulkner and J. Fleck (eds.), *Exploring Expertise: Issues and Perspectives*. London: Macmillan, pp. 325–9.

MacKenzie, D. and Wajcman, J. (eds.) 1999. *The Social Shaping of Technology*. 2nd edn. Milton Keynes: Open University Press.

Macklin, R. 1999. *Against Relativism: Cultural Diversity and the Search for Ethical Universals in Medicine*. Oxford: Oxford University Press.

Maimone, D., Dominici, R. and Grimaldi, L. 2001. 'Pharmacogenomics of neurodegenerative diseases', *European Journal of Pharmacology* 413: 11–29.

Maitland-van der Zee, A. H., Boer, A. de and Leufkens, H. G. M. 2000. 'The interface between pharmacoepidemiology and pharmacogenetics', *European Journal of Pharmacology* 410: 121–30.

Mancinelli, L., Cronin, M. and Sadée, W. 2000. 'Pharmacogenomics: the promise of personalized medicine', *AAPS Pharmsci* 2(1) (7 March): article 4.

March, R. 2000. 'Pharmacogenomics: the genomics of drug response', *Yeast* 17: 16–21.

March, R., Cheeseman, K. and Doherty, M. 2001. 'Pharmacogenetics – legal, ethical and regulatory considerations', *Pharmacogenomics* 2(4): 317–27.

Margolese, R. G. 2001. 'Neoadjuvant systemic primary therapy – is surgery the true adjuvant?', in J. S. Tobias, J. Houghton and I. C. Henderson (eds.), *Breast Cancer: New Horizons in Research and Treatment*. London: Edward Arnold, pp. 177–87.

Marsh, B. 2001. 'Breast cancer victim uses mother's £20,000 savings as NHS refuses to buy drug; how cruel postcode lottery denies a wife her "last chance" of survival', *Daily Mail*, 27 December, p. 17.

Marsh, B. 2003. 'Thousands still dying in cancer postcode lottery', *Daily Mail*, 29 October, p. 10.

Marshall, A. 1997. 'Getting the right drug into the right patient', *Nature Biotechnology* 15: 1249–52.

Marshall, A. 1998. 'Laying the foundations for personalized medicines', *Nature Biotechnology* 16, supplement: 6–8.

Marshall, E. 1998. 'Allen Roses: from "street-fighter" to corporate insider', *Science* 280: 1001–4.

Martin, P. 1995. 'The American gene therapy industry and the social shaping of a new technology', *Genetic Engineer and Biotechnologist* 15(2–3): 155–67.

Martin, P. 1999. 'Genes as drugs: the social shaping of gene therapy and the reconstruction of genetic disease', *Sociology of Health and Illness* 21: 517–38.

Maroc, J. 1993. 'New Alzheimer's theory stirs controversy', *Science* 262: 1210–11.

Maslin, A. M. and Powles, T. 1999. *Breast Cancer: Sharing the Decision*. Oxford: Oxford University Press.

Mayeux, R., Saunders, A. M., Shea, S., Mirra, S., Evans, D., Roses, A. D., Hyman, B. T., Crain, B., Tang, M. X. and Phelps, C. H. 1998. 'Utility of the apolipoprotein E genotype in the diagnosis of Alzheimer's disease', *New England Journal of Medicine* 338(8): 506–11.

McConnell, L. M., Koenig, B. A., Greely, H. T. and Raffin, T. A. 1998. 'Genetic testing and alzheimer's disease: has the time come?', *Nature Medicine* 4: 757–9.

McConnell, L. M., Sanders, G. D. and Owens, D. K. 1999. 'Evaluation of genetic tests: APOE genotyping for the diagnosis of Alzheimer disease' *Genetic Testing* 3(1): 47–53.

McKie, R. 1999. 'Genetic key to personal medicines', *Observer*, 5 December, p. 9.

McLeod, H. L. and Evans, W. E. 2001. 'Pharmacogenomics: unlocking the human genome for better drug therapy', *Annual Review of Pharmacology and Toxicology* 41: 101–21.

McNeil, C. 1998. 'Herceptin raises its sights beyond advanced breast cancer', *Journal of the National Cancer Institute* 90(12): 882–3.

Medical Research Council 2003. 'MRC response to the MHRA consultation letter on the *Medicines for Human Use (Clinical Trials) Regulations* 2003 (MLX 287) and draft legislation'. London: Medical Research Council.

Merz, J. F., Cho, M. K. and Leonard, D. G. B. 1998. 'Letter: testing for Alzheimer's', *Science* 281: 1288–9.

Meyer, U. A. 1990. 'Molecular genetics and the future of pharmacogenetics', *Pharmacological Therapies* 46: 349–55.

Meyer, U. A. 2000 'Pharmacogenetics and adverse drug reactions', *Lancet* 356: 1667–71.

Miles, D. W. 2001. 'Update on HER-2 as a target for cancer therapy: herceptin in the clinical setting', *Breast Cancer Research* 3: 380–4.

Miller, S. and Gregory, J. 1998. *Science in Public: Communication, Culture and Credibility.* New York: Plenum.

Mitchell, M. S. and Press, M. F. 1999. 'The role of immunohistochemistry and fluorescence in situ hybridization for HER-2/*neu* in assessing the prognosis of breast cancer', *Seminars in Oncology* 26(4), supplement 12: 108–16.

Mokbel, K. and Hassanally, D. 2001. 'From HER2 to herceptin', *Current Medical Research and Opinions* 17(1): 51–9.

Møldrup, C. 2001. 'Ethical, social and legal implications of pharmacogenomics: a critical review', *Community Genetics* 4: 204–14.

Moore, W. 2001. 'Designer drugs: in less than a decade, tailor-made medication could make fatal side effects a thing of the past', *Observer*, 15 April, p. 47.

Moyses, C. 1999. 'Pharmacogenetics, genomics, proteomics: the new frontiers in drug development', *International Journal of Pharmaceutical Medicine* 13(4): 197–202.

Mudher, A. and Lovestone, S. 2002. 'Alzheimer's disease – do Tauists and Baptists finally shake hands?', *Trends in Neuroscience* 25(1): 22–6.

Mullan, F. and Jacoby, I. 1985. 'The town meeting for technology: the maturation of consensus conferences', *Journal of the American Medical Association* 254(8): 1068–72.

Murphy, M. P. 2000. 'Pharmacogenomics: a new paradigm for drug development', *Drug Discovery World* (fall): 1–7.

Murray, M. D. and Deardorff, F. W. 1998. 'Does managed care fuel pharmaceutical industry growth?', *Pharmacoeconomics* 14(4): 341–8.

Myers, G. 1990a. *Writing Biology: Texts in the Social Construction of Scientific Knowledge.* Madison, WI: University of Wisconsin Press.

Myers, G. 1990b. 'Making a discovery: narratives of split genes', in C. Nash (ed.), *Narrative in Culture. The Uses of Storytelling in the Sciences, Philosophy, and Literature.* London: Routledge, pp. 102–25.

Myers, G. 1991. 'Stories and styles in two molecular biology review articles', in C. Bazerman and J. Paradis (eds.), *Textual Dynamics of the Professions.* Madison, WI: University of Wisconsin Press, pp. 45–75.

National Institute for Clinical Excellence 2001. 'NICE issues guidance on drugs for Alzheimer's disease', press release, 19 January.

National Institute for Clinical Excellence 2002. *Guidance on the Use of Trastuzumab for the Treatment of Advanced Breast Cancer.* London: National Institute for Clinical Excellence.

Nebert, D. W. 1997. 'Pharmacogenetics: 65 candles on the cake', *Pharmacogenetics* 7: 435–40.

Neumann, P. J., Hammitt, J. K., Mueller, C., Fillit, H. M., Hill, J., Tetteh, N. A. and Kosik, K. S. 2001. 'Public attitudes about genetic testing for Alzheimer's disease', *Health Affairs* 20(5): 252–64.

Newdick, C. 1995. *Who Should We Treat?: Law, Patients and Resources in the NHS.* Oxford: Clarendon.

Nicoletto, M. O., Donach, M., De Nicolo, A., Artioli, G., Banna, G. and Monfardini, S. 2001. 'BRCA-1 and BRCA-2 mutations as prognostic factors in clinical practice and genetic counselling', *Cancer Treatment Reviews* 27: 295–304.

Norton, R. M. 2001. 'Clinical pharmacogenomics: applications in pharmaceutical R&D', *Drug Discovery Today* 6(4): 180–5.

Nuffield Council on Bioethics 2003. *Pharmacogenetics. Ethical Issues: Report of Working Party.* London: Nuffield Council on Bioethics.

O'Connell, S. 2001. 'Could medicines be made to measure?', *Independent*, 31 August, p. 8.

Oddoze, C., Michel, B. F., Berthezene, P., Clavel, C. and Lucotte, G. 1998. 'Apolipoprotein E epsilon 4 allele predicts a positive response to tacrine in Alzheimer's disease', *Alzheimer's Report* 1(1): 13–16.

Oddoze, C., Michel B. F. and Lucotte, G. 2000. 'Apolipoprotein E epsilon 4 allele predicts a better response to donepezil therapy in Alzheimer's disease', *Alzheimer's Report* 3(4): 213–16.

Oestreicher, P. 2001. '4th Annual Pharmacogenomics and Medicine Lecture: 3 April 2001, New Haven, Connecticut', *Pharmacogenomics* 2(3): 291–6.

Olson, J. S. 2002. *Bathsheba's Breast: Women, Cancer and History.* Baltimore: Johns Hopkins University Press.

Pang, T. and Weatherall, D. 2002. 'Genomics and global health: hype, reality, and a call for action in the developing and the developed world', *British Medical Journal* 324: 1051–2.

Pauletti, G., Dandekar, S., Rong, H. M., Ramos, L., Pong, H. J., Seshadri, R. and Slamon, D. J. 2000. 'Assessment of methods for tissue-based detection of the HER-2/neu alteration in human breast cancer: a direct comparison of fluorescence in situ hybridization and immunohistochemistry', *Journal of Clinical Oncology* 18(21): 3651–64.

Paul, J. E. and Trueman, P. 2001. 'Fourth hurdle reviews, NICE, and database applications', *Pharmacoepidemiology and Drug Safety* 10: 429–38.

Paulson, H. L. 2002. 'Diagnostic testing in neurogenetics. Principles, limitations, and ethical considerations', *Neurologic Clinics of North America* 20: 627–43.

Perez, E. A. and Hortobagyi, G. N. 2000. 'Ongoing and planned adjuvant trials with trastuzumab', *Seminars in Oncology* 27(6), Supplement 11: 26–32.

Perlman, D. 1999. 'Stubborn scientists, heroic women lead to a cancer breakthrough', *San Francisco Chronicle*, 17 January, Sunday Review, p. 5.

Perry, S. 1987. 'The NIH Consensus development program: a decade later', *New England Journal of Medicine* 317(8): 485–8.

Persing, B. F. and Cheek, D. J. 2000. 'Pharmacogenomics', *Nursing Clinics of North America* 35(4): 975–80.

Pfost, D. R., Boyce-Jacino, M. T. and Grant, D. M. 2000. 'A SNPshot: pharmacogenetics and the future of drug therapy', *Trends in Biotechnology* 18: 334–8.

Pharma Marketletter, 1993. 'HMO excludes Cognex from formulary', *Pharma Marketletter*, 4 October.

Pharma Marketletter, 1999. 'SB licences Memris to UK biotech Cerebrus', *Pharma Marketletter*, 1 June.

Pharmaceutical Business News 1994. 'Athena Neurosciences to acquire Genica Pharmaceuticals', *Pharmaceutical Business News*, 21 December.
Phillips, K., Veenstra, D., Oren, E., Lee, L. and Sadée, W. 2001. 'Potential role of pharmacogenomics in reducing adverse drug reactions: a systematic review', *Journal of the American Medical Association*, 286(18): 2270–9.
Piccart, M. and Kaufman, M. 2001. 'Introduction', *European Journal of Cancer* 37: S1–S2.
Pilling, D. 1999a. 'Drug group in drive for cancer breakthrough', *Financial Times*, 11 November, p. 14.
Pilling, D. 1999b. 'Smarter weapons to combat cancer', *Financial Times*, 12 November, Comment and Analysis section, p. 21.
Pilling, D. 2000. 'Uncertainty prefaces book of life', *Financial Times*, 18 December, Weekend section, p. 1.
Pinch, T. J. and Bijker, W. E. 1987. 'The social construction of facts and artefacts – or how the sociology of science and the sociology of technology might benefit each other', in Bijker, Hughes & Pinch 1987.
Pinch, T., Ashmore, M. and Mulkay, M. 1992. 'Technology, testing, text: clinical budgeting in the UK National Health Service', in W. Bijker and J. Law, (eds.), *Shaping Technology/Building Society: Studies in Sociotechnical Change*. Cambridge, MA: MIT Press, pp. 265–89.
Pirmohamed, M. and Park, B. K. 2001. 'Genetic susceptibility to adverse drug reactions', *Trends in Pharmacological Sciences* 22(6): 298–305.
Pirmohamed, M. and Park, B. K. 2003. 'Adverse drug reactions: back to the future', *British Journal of Clinical Pharmacology* 55(5): 486–92.
Poirier, J. 1999a. 'Apolipoprotein E: a pharmacogenetic target for the treatment of Alzheimer's disease', *Molecular Diagnosis* 4(4): 335–41.
Poirier, J. 1999b. 'Apolipoprotein E4, cholinergic integrity and the pharmacogenetics of Alzheimer's disease', *Journal of Psychiatry and Neuroscience* 24(2): 147–53.
Poirier, J., Delisle, M. C., Quirion, R., Aubert, I., Farlow, M., Lahiri, D., Hui, S., Bertrand, P., Nalbantoglu, J., Gilfix, B. M. and Gauthier, S. 1995. 'Apolipoprotein E allele as a predictor of cholinergic deficits and treatment outcome in Alzheimer disease', *Proceedings of the National Academy of Sciences* 92: 12260–4.
Pollack, A. 1999. 'In the works: drugs tailored to individual patients', *New York Times*, 20 December, Section C, p. 8.
Pollack, A. 2000. 'Talking biotechnology with: George Rathmann', *New York Times*, 18 December, Section C, p. 3.
Pollack, A. 2002. 'New era of consumer genetics raises hope and concerns', *New York Times*, 1 October, Section F, p. 5.
Post, S. G. 1996. 'On not jumping the gun: ethical aspects of APOE gene testing for Alzheimer's disease', in N. R. Relkin, Z. Khachaturian and S. Gandy, (eds.), *Apolipoprotein E Genotyping in Alzheimer's Disease: Annals of the New York Academy of Sciences*. vol. 802. New York: New York Academy of Science.
Post, S. G., Whitehouse, P. J., Binstock, R. H., Bird, T. D., Eckert, S. K., Farrer, L. A., Fleck, L. M., Gaines, A. D., Jeungst, E. T., Karlinsky, H., Miles, S., Murray, T. D., Quaid, K. A., Relkin, N. R., Roses, A. D., Georgehyslop, P. H. S., Sachs, G. A., Steinbock, B., Truschke, E. F. and Zinn, A. B. 1997. 'The clinical introduction

of genetic testing for alzheimer disease – an ethical perspective', *Journal of the American Medical Association* 277(10): 832–6.

Pricewaterhouse Coopers 1998. *Pharma 2005: An Industrial Revolution in R&D*, http://www.pwcglobal.com/gx/eng/about/ind/pharma/ industrial_revolution.pdf.

Qizilibash, N., Whitehead, A., Higgins, J., Wilcock, G., Schneider, L. and Farlow, M. 1998. 'Cholinesterase inhibition for Alzheimer disease: a meta-analysis of the Tacrine trials', *Journal of the American Medical Association* 280(20): 1777–82.

Radford, T. 2003. 'On the edge of a genetic revolution to map out medical future at birth', *Guardian*, 25 June, p. 3.

Rampaul, R. S., Pinder, S. E., Gullick, W. J., Robertson, J. F. R. and Ellis, I. O. 2002. 'HER-2 in breast cancer – methods of detection, clinical significance and future prospects for treatment', *Critical Reviews in Oncology/Hematology* 43: 231–44.

Rapp, R. 2000. *Testing Women, Testing the Fetus: The Social Impact of Amniocentesis in America*. New York: Routledge.

Raskind, M. A., Peskind, E. R., Wessel, T. and Yuan, W. 2000. 'Galantamine in AD: a 6-month randomized, placebo-controlled trial with a 6-month extension', *Neurology* 54: 2261–8.

Regalado, A. 1999. 'Inventing the pharmacogenomics business', *American Journal of Health-System Pharmacy* 56: 40–50.

Reichert, J. M. 2001. 'Monoclonal antibodies in the clinic', *Nature Biotechnology* 19: 819–22.

Reichert, J. M. 2003. 'Trends in development and approval times for new therapeutics in the United States', *Nature Reviews Drug Discovery* 2: 695–702.

Relkin, N. R., Kwon, Y. J., Tsai, J. and Gandy, S. 1996a. 'Consensus statement: apolipoprotein E genotyping in Alzheimer's disease', *Lancet* 347: 1091–5.

Relkin, N. R., Kwon, Y. J., Tsai, J. and Gandy, S. 1996b. 'The National Institute on Aging/Alzheimer's Association recommendations on the application of apolipoprotein E genotyping to Alzheimer's disease', *Annals of the New York Academy of Sciences* 802: 149–71.

Relman, A. S. and Angell, M. 2002. 'America's other drug problem: how the drug industry distorts medicine and politics', *New Republic*, 16 December: 27–41.

Rennie, D. 1981. 'Consensus statements', *New England Journal of Medicine* 304(11): 665–6.

Richard, F., Helbecque, N., Neuman, E., Guez, D., Levy, R. and Amouyel, P. 1997. 'APOE genotyping and response to drug treatment in Alzheimer's disease', *Lancet* 349: 539.

Richard, F. and Amouyel, P. 2001. 'Genetic susceptibility factors for Alzheimer's disease', *European Journal of Pharmacology* 412: 1–12.

Riekkinen, P. J., Koivisto, K. and Reinikaianen, K. J. *et al.* 1998. 'Can apo-4 subtype predict response to selegiline treatment in Alzheimer's disease?', in E. Giacobini, A. Nordberg, J-P. Michel, B. Winblad and R. Becker (eds.), *Proceedings of the 5th International Geneva/Springfield Symposium on Advances in Alzheimer's Therapy*. Springfields, IL: Southern Illinois University Press, p. 91.

Rigaud, A. S., Traykov, L., Caputo, L., Guelfi, M. C., Latour, F., Couderc, R., Moulin, F., de Rotrou, J., Forette, F. and Boller, F. 2000. 'The apolipoprotein E ε4 allele and the response to tacrine therapy in Alzheimer's disease', *European Journal of Neurology* 7: 255–8.

Rioux, P. 2000. 'Clinical trials in pharmacogenetics and pharmacogenomics: methods and applications', *American Journal of Health System Pharmacy* 57(9): 887–98.

Ritchie, K. and Lovestone, S. 2002. The dementias, *Lancet* 360(9347): 1759–66.

Roberts, F. D. 1999. *Talking about Treatment: Recommendations for Breast Cancer Adjuvant Therapy.* Oxford: Oxford University Press.

Roberts, J. S. 2000. 'Anticipating response to predictive testing for Alzheimer's disease: a survey of first-degree relatives', *Gerontologist* 40(1): 43–52.

Robertson, J. 2001. 'Consent and privacy in pharmacogenetic testing', *Nature Genetics* 28(3): 207–9.

Robertson, J. A., Brody, B., Buchanan, A., Kahn, J. and McPherson, E. 2002. 'Pharmacogenetic challenges for the health care system', *Health Affairs* 21(4): 155–67.

Roche, 2003. 'Roche Diagnostics launches the AmpliChip', press release, 25 June.

Roden, D. M. and George, A. L. 2002. 'The genetic basis of variability in drug responses', *Nature Reviews Drug Discovery* 1: 37–44.

Rodwin, M. A. 2001. 'The politics of evidence-based medicine', *Journal of Health Politics, Policy and Law* 26(2): 439–46.

Ronald and Nancy Reagan Research Institute of the Alzheimer's Association and the National Institute on Aging Working Group 1998. 'Consensus report of the Working Group on: "Molecular and Biochemical Maters of Alzheimer's Disease"', *Neurobiology of Aging* 19(2): 109–16.

Rose, S. 2003. 'Science, not fiction', *Guardian*, 15 November, Review section, p. 11.

Roses, A. D. 1994. 'Apolipoprotein affects the rate of Alzheimer's disease expression: ß-Amyloid burden is a secondary consequence dependent on APOE genotype and duration on disease', *Journal of Neuropathology and Experimental Neurology* 53(5): 429–37.

Roses, A. D. 1995a. 'Apolipoprotein E genotyping in the differential diagnosis, not prediction of Alzheimer's disease', *Annals of Neurology* 38(1): 6–14.

Roses, A. D. 1995b. 'Reply', *Annals of Neurology* 38(6): 969.

Roses, A. D. 1996a. 'Apolipoprotein E alleles as risk factors in Alzheimer's disease', *Annual Review of Medicine* 47: 387–400.

Roses, A. D. 1996b. 'Apolipoprotein E and Alzheimer's disease: a rapidly expanding field with medical and epidemiological consequences', in N. R. Relkin, Z. Khachaturian and S. Gandy (eds.), *Apolipoprotein E Genotyping in Alzheimer's Disease: Annals of the New York Academy of Sciences*, vol. 802: 50–7. New York: New York Academy of Sciences.

Roses, A. D. 1996c. 'Apolipoprotein E genotype: utility in clinical practice in Alzheimer's disease', *Journal of the American Geriatric Society* 44: 1479–81.

Roses, A. D. 1997a. 'APOE4 genotyping: in reply', *Journal of the American Geriatric Society* 45(9): 1155–6.

Roses, A. D. 1997b. 'Genetic testing for Alzheimer disease: practical and ethical issues', *Archives of Neurology* 54: 1226–9.

Roses, A. D. 1997c. 'Letter: Various views on anonymity', *Nature Medicine* 3(1): 2.

Roses, A. D. 1998a. 'A new paradigm for clinical evaluations of dementia: Alzheimer disease and apolipoprotein E genotypes', in S. Post and P. Whitehouse (eds.), *Genetic Testing for Alzheimer Disease: Ethical and Clinical Issues*. Baltimore: Johns Hopkins University Press, pp. 37–64.

Roses, A. D. 1998b. 'Letter: Patent income', *Science* 281, 18 September: 1805.

Roses, A. D. 2000a. 'Pharmacogenetics and future drug development and delivery', *Lancet* 355: 1358–61.

Roses, A. D. 2000b. 'Pharmacogenetics and the practice of medicine', *Nature* 405: 857–65.

Roses, A. D. 2002a. 'Genome-based pharmacogenetics and the pharmaceutical industry', *Nature Reviews Drug Discovery* 1: 541–9.

Roses, A. D. 2002b. 'Pharmacogenetics' place in modern medical science and practice', *Life sciences* 70: 1471–80.

Roses, A. D. 2002c. 'SNPs – where's the beef?', *Pharmacogenomics Journal* 2: 277–83.

Roses, A. D. and Saunders, A. M. 1996. 'Letter: evaluation of suspected dementia', *New England Journal of Medicine* 335(26): 1996.

Roses, A. D. and Saunders, A. M. 1997. 'Prediction for unimpaired subjects is different from diagnosis of demented patients', *Annals of Neurology* 41(3): 414–15.

Roses, A. D., Strittmatter, W., Periack-Vance, M. A., Corder, E. H., Saunders, A. M. and Schmechel, D. E. 1994. 'Letter: clinical application of apolipoprotein E genotyping to Alzheimer's disease', *Lancet*, 343: 1564–5.

Ross, J. S. and Fletcher, J. A. 1998. 'The HER-2/*neu* oncogene in breast cancer: prognostic factor, predictive factor, and target for therapy', *Stem Cells* 16: 413–28.

Rothenberg, M. L., Cabone, D. P. and Johnson, D. H. 2003. 'Improving the evaluation of new cancer treatments: challenges and opportunities', *Nature Reviews Cancer* 3: 303–9.

Rothman, B. K. 1998. *Genetic Maps and Human Imaginations: The Limits of Science in Understanding Who We Are.* New York: W. W. Norton.

Rothstein, M. A. (ed.) 2003. *Pharmacogenomics: Social, Ethical and Clinical Dimensions.* New York: John Wiley.

Rothstein, M. and Griffin Epps, P. 2001. 'Ethical and legal implications of pharmacogenomics', *Nature Reviews Genetics* 2: 228–31.

Rothstein, M. and Hornung, C. A. 2003. 'Public attitudes about pharmacogenomics', in Rothstein 2003.

Rusnak, J. M., Kisabeth, R. M., Herbert, D. P. and McNeil, D. M. 2001. 'Pharmacogenomics: a clinician's primer on emerging technologies for improved patient care', *Mayo Clinic Proceedings* 76: 299–309.

Sadée, W. 1999. 'Pharmacogenomics', *British Medical Journal* 319: 1286.

Sainio, C. and Lauri, S. 2003. 'Cancer patients' decision-making regarding treatment and nursing care', *Journal of Advanced Nursing* 41(3): 250–60.

Salter, B. G. 1998. *The Politics of Change in the Health Service.* London: Macmillan.

Saunders, A. M., Strittmatter, W. J., Schmechel, D., Georgehyslop, P. H. S., Periack-Vance, M. A., Joo, S. H., Rosi, B. L., Gusella, J. F., Crappermaclachlan, D. R., Alberts, M. J., Hulette, C., Crain, B., Goldgaber, D. and Roses, A. D. 1993. 'Association of apolipoprotein E allele ε4 with late-onset familial and sporadic Alzheimer's disease', *Neurology* 43: 1467–72.

Saunders, A. M., Trowers, M. K., Shimkets, R. A., Blakemore, S., Crowther, D. J., Mansfield, T. A., Wallace, D. M., Strittmatter, W. J. and Roses, A. D. 2000. 'The role of apolipoprotein E in Alzheimer's disease: pharmacogenomic target selection', *Biochimica et Biophysica Acta* 1502: 85–94.

Saunders, A. M., Hulette, C., Welsh-Bohmer, K. A., Schmechel, D. E., Crain, B., Burke, J. R., Alberts, M. J., Strittmatter, W. J., Breitner, J. C. S., Rosenberg, C., Scott, S. V.,

Gaskell, P. C., Periack-Vance, M. A. and Roses, A. D. 1996. 'Specificity, sensitivity, and predictive value of apolipoprotein-E genotyping for sporadic Alzheimer's disease', *Lancet* 348: 90–3.

Schappert, K., Sevigny, P. and Poirier, J. 2002. 'Apolipoprotein E as a marker in the treatment of Alzheimer's disease', in B. Lerer, (ed.), *Pharmacogenetics of Psychotropic Drugs*. Cambridge: Cambridge University Press, pp. 360–71.

Schmitz, G., Aslanidis, C. and Lackner, K. J. 2001.'Pharmacogenomics: implications for laboratory medicine', *Clinica Chimica Acta* 308: 43–53.

Schnitt, S. J. and Jacobs, T. W. 2001. 'Current status of HER2 testing: caught between a rock and a hard place', *American Journal of Clinical Pathology* 116: 806–10.

Shak, S. 1999. 'Overview of the Trastuzumab (Herceptin) Anti-HER2 Monoclonal antibody clinical program in HER2-overexpressing metastatic breast cancer', *Seminars in Oncology* 26(4), supplement 12: 71–7.

Shapiro, S. D. 2003. 'The post-genomic red journal charting the path from hope (not hype) to cure', *American Journal of Respiratory Cell and Molecular Biology* 29(4): 425–6.

Shi, M. M., Bleavins, M. R. and de la Iglesia, F. 2001. 'Pharmacogenetics application in drug development and clinical trials', *Drug Metabolism and Disposition* 29(4), part 2: 591–5.

Siest, G., Bertrand, P., Herbeth, B., Vincent-Viry, M., Schiele, F., Sass, C. and Visvikis, S. 2000. 'Apolipoprotein E polymorphisms and concentration in chronic disease and drug responses', *Clinical Chemistry and Laboratory Medicine* 38(9): 841–52.

Sinding, C. 1996. 'Literary genres and the construction of knowledge in biology: semantic shifts and scientific change', *Social Studies of Science* 26: 43–70.

Sjögren, M., Hesse, C., Basun, H., Köl, G., Thostrup, H., Kilander, L., Marcusson, J., Edman, A., Wallin, A., Karlsson, I., Troell, M., Wachtmaister, G., Ekdahl, A., Olofsson, H., Sandström, A., Andreasen, N., Minthon, L. and Blennow, K. 2001. 'Tacrine and rate of progression in Alzheimer's disease – relation to ApoE allele genotype', *Journal of Neural Transmission* 108: 451–8.

Slamon, D. J., Godolphin, W., Jones, L. A., Holt, J. A., Wong, S. G., Keith, D. E., Levin, W. J., Stuart, S. G., Udove, A., Ullrich, A. and Press, M. F. 1987. 'Human breast cancer: correlation of relapse and survival with amplification of the Her-2/neu Oncogene', *Science* 235: 177–82.

Smith, R. 2000. 'The failings of NICE', *British Medical Journal* 321: 1363–4.

Spear, B. B., Heath-Chiozzi, M. and Huff, J. 2001. 'Clinical applications of pharmacogenetics', *Trends in Molecular Medicine* 7(5): 201–4.

Speyer, J. 2002. 'Cardiac dysfunction in the Trastuzumab clinical experience', *Journal of Clinical Oncology* 20(5): 1156–7.

Stebbing, J., Copson, E. and O'Reilly, S. (2000) 'Herceptin (Trastuzumab) in advanced breast cancer', *Cancer Treatment Reviews* 26: 287–90.

Steimer, W. and Potter, J. M. 2002. 'Pharmacogenetic screening and therapeutic drugs', *Clinica Chimica Acta* 315: 137–55.

Sugarman, J., McCrory, D. C., Powell, D., Krasny, A., Adams, B., Ball, E. and Cassell, C. 1999. 'Empirical research on informed consent. An annotated bibliography', *Hastings Center Report* 29(1): S1–42.

Summers, W. K., Majovski, L. V., Marsh, G. M., Tachiki, K. and Kling, A. 1986. 'Oral tetrahydroaminoacridine in long-term treatment of senile dementia, Alzheimer type', *New England Journal of Medicine* 315(20): 1241–45.

Sun. 2002. 'Sun Says; Leading Article', *Sun*. 16 March, p. 8.

Sykes, R. 1999. 'Medical innovation and imperatives', *Getting Better: Developing Mechanisms to Ensure the Best Benefit for Patients from Medical Progress*, proceedings of conference, Brussels, 24 November, pp. 11–14.

Taylor, K. M. 1992. 'Integrating conflicting professional roles: physician participation in randomised clinical trials', *Social Science and Medicine* 35(2): 217–24.

Taylor, P. 1996. 'Anticholinesterase agents', in Goodman, and Gilman's *The Pharmacological Basis of Therapeutics*, ed. J. G. Hardman and L. E. Limbird. 9th edn. New York: McGraw-Hill, pp. 161–76.

Thomas, F. and de Ribains, G. 1998. *Pharmacogenomics*. London: Financial Times.

Thomas, S. 2001. 'Pharmacogenetics: the ethical context', *Pharmacogenomics Journal* 1: 239–42.

Thornton, J. 2002. 'Let this be last scandal', *Sun*, 16 March, p. 29.

Timmermans, S. and Berg, M. 2003. 'The practice of medical technology', *Sociology of Health and Illness* 25: 97–114.

Tiner, T. 2003. 'ABPI call for NICE guidance to be made mandatory', *Lancet Oncology* 4: 203–4.

Tollman, P., Guy, P., Altshuler, J., Flanagan, A. and Steiner, M. 2001. *A Revolution in R&D. How Genomics and Genetics are Transforming the Biopharmaceutical Industry*. Boston: Boston Consulting Group, http://www.bcg.com/publications/files/eng_genomicsgenetics_rep_11_01.pdf

Tozer, J. 2001. 'Postcode lottery has condemned me to death; Despair of the cancer victims hit by drug "rationing" ', *Daily Mail*, 15 August, p. 32.

Trojanowski, J. Q. 2002. 'Tauists, Baptists, Syners, Apostates, and new data', *Annals of Neurology* 52(3): 263–4.

Tsai, Y. J. and Hoyme, H. E. 2002. 'Pharmacogenomics: the future of drug therapy', *Clinical Genetics* 62: 257–64.

Tunstall, N. and Lovestone, S. 1999. 'Letter: UK Alzheimer's Disease Genetics Consortium', *International Journal of Geriatric Psychiatry* 14: 789–91.

Turney, J. 1998. 'Signs of life – taking genetic literacy seriously', in P. Glasner and H. Rothman (eds), *Genetic Imaginations – Ethical, Legal and Social Issues in Human Genome Research*. Aldershot: Ashgate, p. 131–40.

Van Gool, W. A. 1996. 'The use of apolipoprotein E genotyping as a diagnostic test in suspected Alzheimer's disease', *Annals of the New York Academy of Sciences* 802: 79–91.

Van Lente, H. and Rip, A. 1998. 'The rise of membrane technology: from rhetorics to social reality', *Social Studies of Science* 28(2): 221–54.

Varekamp, I., Krol, L. J. and Danse, J. A. C. 1998. 'Age rationing for renal transplantation? The role of age in decisions regarding scarce life extending medical resources', *Social Science and Medicine* 47(1): 113–20.

Vaszar, L. T., Cho, M. K. and Raffin, T. A. 2003. 'Privacy issues in personalized medicine', *Pharmacogenomics* 4(2): 107–12.

Vaszar, L. T., Rosen, G. D. and Raffin, T. A. 2002. 'Pharmacogenomics and the challenge to privacy', *Pharmacogenomics Journal* 2: 144–7.

Veenstra, D. L. and Higashi, M. K. 2000. 'Assessing the cost-effectiveness of pharmacogenomics', *AAPS Pharmsci* 2(3), article 29: 1–11.

Venter, C. 2000. 'Genomic impact on pharmaceutical development', in *From Genome to Therapy: Integrating Technologies with Drug Development*, Novartis Foundation Symposium 229. Chichester: John Wiley, pp. 14–18.

Vesell, E. 2000. 'Introduction', *Pharmacology* 61: 118–23.

Wachbroit, R. 1998. 'The question not asked: the challenge of pleiotropic genetic tests', *Kennedy Institute of Ethics Journal* 8(2): 131–44.

Waitzkin, H. 1991. *The Politics of Medical Encounters: how Patients and Doctors Deal with Social Problems*. New Haven: Yale University Press.

Walker, R. 2001. 'Letter: "Spinning" is not nice', *British Medical Journal* 322: 490.

Warren, V. 1999. *Genetic Tests and Future Need for Long-Term Care in the UK*. http://www.phgu.org.uk/info_database/policy/cccreport.html

Watkins, P. B., Zimmerman, H. J., Knapp, M. J., Gracon, S. I. and Lewis, K. W. 1994. 'Hepatotoxic effects of tacrine administration in patients with Alzheimer's disease', *Journal of the American Medical Association* 271: 992–8.

Weber, W. W. 2001. 'The legacy of pharmacogenetics and potential applications', *Mutation Research* 479: 1–18.

Wedlund, P. J. and de Leon, J. 2001. 'Pharmacogenomic testing: the cost factor', *Pharmacogenomics Journal* 1: 171–4.

Weinshilboum, R. 2002. 'The genomic revolution and medicine', *Mayo Clinic Proceedings* 77(8): 745–6.

Weiss, R. 2000. 'The promise of precision prescriptions; 'pharmacogenomics' also raises issues of race, privacy', *Washington Post*, 24 June, p. A01.

Welsh-Bohmer, K. A., Gearing, M., Saunders, A. M., Roses, A. D. and Mirra, S. 1997. 'Apolipoprotein E genotypes in a neuropathological series from the consortium to establish a registry for Alzheimer's disease', *Annals of Neurology* 42(3): 319–25.

Whitehouse, P. J. 1998. 'Therapeutic interventions in Alzheimer's disease: implications of genetic advances', in S. G. Post and P. J. Whitehouse (eds.), *Genetic Testing for Alzheimer's Disease: Ethical and Clinical Issues*. Baltimore: Johns Hopkins University Press, pp. 65–82.

Whitehouse, P. J. and Geldmacher, D. S. 1996. 'Reply', *New England Journal of Medicine* 335(26): 1997–8.

Wieczorek, S. J. and Tsongalis, G. J. 2001. 'Pharmacogenomics: will it change the field of medicine?', *Clinica Chimica Acta* 308: 1–8.

Wilcock, G. K., Lilienfeld, S. and Gaens, E. on behalf of the Galantamine International-1 Study Group. 2000. 'Efficacy and safety of galantamine in patients with mild to moderate Alzheimer's disease: multicentre randomised controlled trial', *British Medical Journal*, 9 December, 321: 1–7.

Wilcock, G. K., MacGowan, S. H., Scott, M. and Dawbarn, D. 1995. 'Apolipoprotein E genotype and response to tacrine in Alzheimer's disease', poster presented at the International Psychogeriatrics Association Conference, Apolipoprotein E et Maladie d'Alzheimer, 29 May, Paris.

Wiley, S. R. 1998. 'Genomics in the real world', *Current Pharmaceutical Design* 4: 417–22.

Williams, C. J. and Buchanan, R. B. 1987. *The Medical Management of Breast Cancer*. Tunbridge Wells: Castle House.

Winblad, B., Engedal, K., Soininen, H., Verhey, F., Waldemar, G., Wimo, A., Wetterholm, A. L., Zhang, R., Haglund, A. and Subbiah, P. 2001. 'A 1-year, randomized, placebo-controlled study of donepezil in patients with mild to moderate AD', *Neurology* 57: 489–95.

Wiseman, H. 1994. *Tamoxifen: Molecular Basis of Use in Cancer Treatment and Prevention.* Chichester: John Wiley.

Wolf, C. R., Smith, G. and Smith, R. L. 2000. 'Pharmacogenetics', *British Medical Journal* 320: 987–90.

Woodman, R. 2000. 'Storage of human organs prompts three inquiries', *British Medical Journal* 320 (8 January): 77.

Workman, P. 2001a. 'Changing times: developing cancer in genomeland', *Current Opinion in Investigational drugs* 2(8): 1128–35.

Workman, P. 2001b. 'Scoring a bull's-eye against cancer genome targets', *Current Opinion in Pharmacology* 1: 342–52.

World Medical Association 2000. *Declaration of Helsinki.* Geneva: World Medical Association.

Yaziji, H. and Gown, A. M. 2002. 'Testing for HER-2/*neu* in breast cancer: is fluorescence in situ hyridization superior in predicting outcome?', *Advances in Anatomic Pathology* 9(6): 338–44.

Young, R. and Surrusco, M. 2001. *Rx R&D Myths: the Case Against the Drug Industry's R&D 'Scare Card'.* Washington, DC: Public Citizen Congress Watch.

Yu, D. and Hung, M. 2000. 'Role of *erb*B2 in breast cancer chemosensitivity', *BioEssays* 22: 673–80.

Zussman, R. 1992. *Intensive Care: Medical Ethics and the Medical Profession.* Chicago: University of Chicago Press.

Zussman, R. 1997. 'Sociological perspectives on medical ethics and decision-making', *Annual Review of Sociology* 23: 171–89.

Index